To Sheila

from

Verinne Pascoe

STANDBY

STANDBY

Vivienne Pascoe

The Book Guild Ltd
Sussex, England

The Book Guild Ltd
25 High Street
Lewes, Sussex

First published 1997
© Vivienne Pascoe, 1997
Set in Times
Typesetting by Poole Typesetting (Wessex) Ltd, Bournemouth
Printed in Great Britain by
Antony Rowe Ltd, Chippenham, Wiltshire

A catalogue record for this book is available
from the British Library

ISBN 1 85776 200 2

To John

without whom none of this would have happened.

*To my sister Pat (Dame Patricia Evison DBE)
for her encouragement and help.*

And to all wives of airline pilots.

CONTENTS

FOREWORD

I feel very honoured that my sister has asked me to write the Foreword to her book, *Standby*.

Vivienne has been a wonderful sister to me and an outstanding role model – showing me how to successfully combine a career and a family. She has lived in many places and has always contributed so much to the communities in which she found herself. Vivienne and John and their three sons keep close family ties despite living in different countries.

On her eightieth birthday the family presented her with a ticket for a flight on Concorde from London to New York, to show their love and appreciation, and in recognition of her talent for encouraging us all to keep our feet on the ground but our heads in the air.

Long may she fly!

Dame Patricia Evison DBE

Places around the world flown to on *Standby*

1

The Surprise

The eggs, hard, yellow and shiny sitting on top of a layer of greasy bacon, glared at me from the purser's plate across the table. I felt sick – sick of the smell of bacon on a hot steamy morning in Lourenço Marques – sick with disappointment and utterly deflated that my surprise had gone wrong.

The purser, with sweat running down his face, munched at his breakfast. As he attempted to spear a piece of bloody kidney with his fork, he looked across at me and said sarcastically: 'I'm glad my wife doesn't spring surprises like this on me at six o'clock in the morning. You've given the Captain a real problem.'

I could have hit him. His remark was the last straw.

How on earth did I get myself into this ridiculous situation? Here I was, in 1945, married to John, a BOAC captain, marooned in a foreign country with Richard, a three month old baby – and on standby for a flying-boat service to Durban – which was already full.

Ever since we'd been married I had hoped for a flight in the Empire Flying Boats – those wonderful princesses of the air. During the war, military and diplomatic personnel had priority. The flying-boats only took 28 passengers and were nearly always full. It was difficult for a civilian to travel.

It had been an exciting thought – a three hour flight up the African coast to meet John on his homeward journey from Cairo. It was Ken, one of the other Captains who planted the idea. Mind you, he did have an ulterior motive behind his suggestion. He was to be married at the end of his next trip. He had ordered, from a firm in Lourenço Marques, a full-length grey Karakul fur coat as his wedding present to his wife. This was to be delivered to the Palmero Hotel in Lourenço Marques. But as the BOAC service didn't nightstop there, and he wouldn't have time to go and collect it, he was looking for a friendly female to bring it back to Durban in time for the wedding.

'Here's your chance, Vivienne,' he said. 'What about coming with me to Lourenço Marques next weekend when I go north. Imagine the look on John's face when he sees you and Richard on the wharf to meet him. I'll arrange everything – book you into the Palmero Hotel which is on the coast, and you'll have a wonderful holiday weekend. It'll be on a standby basis but as I'm captain, I'm sure I'll be able to fix something.'

I fell for it. The temptation was too great. I told Ken I would fly with him on the next service at the end of the week.

When Saturday came, I was thrilled and excited – but a bit apprehensive when I put Richard in his carrycot on top of the pile of nappies. This would be the first time I had travelled with a small baby. But Richard didn't seem to be worrying. He gurgled away and was full of smiles as the taxi drove us out to the flying-boat base at Congella.

The traffic officer met us and took charge of the luggage. 'The Captain told me to look out for you, Mrs Pascoe. It's OK. There is room so if you'll wait here until the other passengers have boarded we'll take you out to the aircraft.'

I looked through the window and saw the flying-boat gently floating on the water. She was *Cambria*, one of the C-class flying-boats. They all had names beginning with C. The pilots reckoned each plane had its own character and personality, and, like women, needed special handling and understanding.

'We're ready now, Mrs Pascoe,' the traffic officer said as he picked up the carrycot. 'Be careful of the steps going down to the launch. They're a bit slippery.'

The African boatman helped me into the launch, started the engine and we chugged out to the waiting flying-boat. As we drew alongside, Ken waved from the cockpit window. I climbed through the hatch door and was delighted with the spaciousness of the cabin. The purser showed me to a comfortable seat on the starboard side, put the carrycot on the table between the seats, and asked me to fasten my seat belt and hold Richard for take-off. Suddenly, I felt like a bottle of champagne ready to explode – all frothy and bubbly. I had finally made it! I was on board a flying-boat and ready for adventure.

I settled down in my seat and looked around. A stepladder led to the flight-deck where the captain, first officer and radio officer, operated the boat. In 1945 there were no pretty hostesses. A male purser looked after the passengers and did the paperwork.

It was a beautiful afternoon, clear blue skies and sparkling water. The four Pegasus engines started one by one. The cabin vibrated and the noise intensified. 'Let's go,' we heard the captain call, through his sliding windscreen as he eased the boat gently onto the flight-path. A launch pulled ahead to clear the path of all debris and small craft. Flying-boats' floats were easily damaged if they struck anything in the water.

The throttles opened. Gliding like a speedboat over the water it accelerated and bumped over the waves. Through the cabin window I saw the water outside build up into a huge wave. It came to the bottom of the window, then halfway up, and finally swished right across the glass. It was thrilling, breathtaking, like being in a submarine. Suddenly there was a change of tone – almost silence – as the bow wave fell away. Where there had been a wall of water only droplets glistened on the window-pane. Smoothly we rose from the water and began to climb.

Below us, the harbour was full of ships waiting to transport troops north to the Middle East, or south round the Cape back to England. I saw the top of the Edward Hotel on the Durban promenade, where the Zulu rickshaw boys in their colourful, full native regalia gave rides and posed for photographs. During the war letters were censored. No names of cities or countries were permitted. Families, however, seeing a photo of their loved one with a rickshaw boy, would know they had been in Durban.

The flying-boat reached its cruising height and glided along in the cloudless sky. Down below I saw the golden beaches of Natal. Away to the west, stretching for miles, the tall sugar-cane fields from this height, looked like a rippling green sea.

Nestling among the sugar-cane were small brown dots – the round thatched mud houses, or rondavels, of an African village. We flew over Zululand where the earth changed from green to brown. As we passed above the big game reserves, I looked down hoping to see some animals. But it was a hot afternoon and they were probably sleeping.

I put Richard back in his carrycot hoping that the constant hum of the engines would lull him to sleep. I wanted to relax and enjoy a drink and the first class meal. How different it was then – good food, excellent attention – peaceful and leisurely. Now passengers, packed like sardines, attack plastic food shoved at them by harassed hostesses manipulating unwieldy trolleys down narrow aisles.

I wondered if I'd been madder than usual coming on this flight. Travel, going places, seeing new things, adventure had always intrigued me. But with a small baby it was a challenge. Travel aids like disposable nappies and plastic bottle hadn't been invented. And there were no such things as folding pushchairs or kangaroo pouches. I would have to carry Richard wherever I went. Food wasn't a problem as I was still breast-feeding him. But in the heat he would need boiled water and the bottles sterilizing. Then there was the danger of malaria-carrying mosquitoes, dysentery and … Suddenly I felt panicky and wished I'd stayed quietly at home. Almost – but not quite!

Richard decided engines made an exciting noise and that sleep was a waste of time. He was wide awake and demanding attention. Perhaps it was that first journey when he was three months old that sparked off his passion for flying. Who knows?

The captain sent a message down that we had crossed the South African border into Mozambique. The country looked uninviting – brown, dry with no sign of life.

Suddenly my ears buzzed and blocked painfully. The purser, walking through the cabin noticed my distress and said: 'We've started our descent. Hold your nose and blow hard to release the pressure.' He watched me while I did what he told me but it gave no relief. 'Don't worry, your ears will clear as soon as we land.'

Richard began to scream and move his head from side to side. Poor mite! There was no way I could tell him to hold his nose and blow hard. I wished someone had told me to have a bottle of water or orange juice ready for him to suck when the aircraft was descending. Trying to comfort and console him I didn't notice the water coming nearer and nearer. There was a bump when the floats touched the water and we skidded along creating a bow wave that towered above the window. The speed decreased when the captain throttled back, and we taxied gently to the waiting launch. Richard stopped crying but I was still completely deaf. Everything seemed very far away … including Durban – 600 miles down the coast.

The passengers went ashore for refreshments while the boat was refuelled. As we climbed out of the launch onto the jetty I was surprised to see a ship nearby flying the German flag. Next to it a Japanese boat had a white and red flag fluttering limply against its mast. Strange, I thought, to see enemy ships here. I was forgetting that this was a neutral Portuguese port where ships of all nations came and went as they pleased.

The local BOAC traffic officer, Tony, stood on the wharf to greet us. Ken introduced me, asked him to look after us and explained that I wanted my arrival in Lourenço Marques to be a surprise for John when he landed on Monday morning. Tony agreed to play his part and picked up the carry cot. As we walked away Ken called out: 'Don't forget to bring back the coat.'

Tony hailed an ancient looking taxi and gave the Portuguese driver instructions to take us to the Palmero Hotel. We set off with a jerk and a screech of tyres and tore along the road towards the town. The driver gunned the engine and kept his hand on the horn as we navigated the untidy looking main street. I went into a state of suspended animation when we dashed through two red traffic-lights. It was a relief when we left the built-up area and sped along a country road lined with beautiful blue jacaranda trees. After a few miles we drove through an archway with a large sign saying 'Palmero Hotel'.

Although the buildings had a slightly faded appearance the hotel still retained a touch of the old colonial splendour. When we arrived, smiling staff rushed forward to help with the carrycot and luggage. The Portuguese love children and Richard was 'cooed' over as I signed the register. A porter took us to a little elevator with metal folding doors. With creaks and jerks we ascended to the third floor. Maria, a buxom maid in black with a pristine starched white apron and cap, greeted us. She unlocked the door of our room, turned on the ceiling fan above the huge double bed shrouded in a mosquito net, and with pride showed me the antiquated bathroom facilities and the balcony overlooking the sea. There wasn't a cot in the room so I tried, with great flourish of the hands, to make her understand that I needed somewhere for Richard to sleep – a cot with a mosquito net. '*Sim, Sim, Senhora,*' she said and disappeared, returning immediately with two other maids. They clustered around Richard shrieking with laughter and chattering away in their incomprehensible language, taking little notice of my frantic miming about bringing a cot.

Suddenly light dawned on one of their faces and giggling they went out of the room. I hovered uncertainly, wondering whether to start feeding Richard or wait. Minutes later there was a knock on the door, and the three girls struggled in pushing an enormous cot, obviously made for an oversized Portuguese baby. They put it beside the bed and demonstrated several times how one side slid down and clipped securely in place when it was pulled up. It all seemed simple enough. Finally they departed and I was left alone.

Although it was well past Richard's feed-time he had stayed remarkably undemanding. I climbed onto the bed and he nuzzled up contentedly. I found comfort in the physical contact. Mothers who choose not to breast-feed miss so much. I didn't have to worry about mixing milk powder with unboiled water or getting bottles sterilized. I cursed my wretched ears. They were still blocked and it had been a strain trying to listen and understand a foreign language. I was very glad of the peace and quiet.

Richard had a lovely splashy bath and smelt clean and 'Johnson's Baby Powderish' when I laid him in the cot. The maids had left the side down for me and I struggled to put it up. Every time I tried to click it into the right place, the side fell with a bang onto the floor. Obviously this cot had been made by a carpenter who had thought out ingenious ways of fooling unsuspecting mothers. I tried again. The same thing happened. Frustrated and getting angrier every minute I sat on the bed with tears streaming down my face. I pulled myself together and went back to the cot. Richard gave me a big smile. Gently I brought the side up and pressed it slightly inwards. I hardly dared take my hands away. Oh, the relief ... it stayed up! I tucked the net firmly around the cot and moved away. Richard changed his smile into a bellow of protest at being left. I escaped onto the balcony.

The hotel was perched on a cliff-face. It was a navy blue tropical night and far below, came the sound of the waves pounding against the rocks. The gentle breeze from the sea cooled and calmed me and I thought longingly of John. He would notice such a change in Richard after being away for five weeks. How wonderful it would be to see him again!

All was quiet when I went back into the room. Richard had accepted his new 'house' and as usual had turned over on his tummy with his legs curled under him. I felt it was safe to leave him and go and find something to eat.

I had been looking forward to this break from domesticity, but suddenly the idea of walking alone into a restaurant, and being faced with a menu in a foreign language was overwhelming. I debated whether I would have something sent up to the room. Curiosity – or hunger – got the better of me and I went downstairs to the dining room. The major-domo greeted me politely and seated me at a small table overlooking the terrace and swimming pool. He presented me with a large menu – in English – and I studied it carefully.

It was too hot for soup. Salads or any uncooked vegetables were a 'no-no' as they were one of the causes of the dreaded tummy-bug, dysentery. I thought '*fish à Portuguesa*' followed by chicken would be safest.

I gave my order to the waiter, sat back and amused myself by making up stories about the people in the dining-room. The men were of mixed nationalities. Two Japanese gentlemen at the next table were being entertained by a group of elegantly dressed Portuguese ladies. A Portuguese family was celebrating a birthday, and the little girl looking all pink in a fluffy organza dress, was trying to blow out the five candles on top of a beautifully iced cake.

I waited and waited. I thought the chef must have sent a boat out to catch the fish – it was so long in coming. By the time it arrived I'd exhausted my people-stories. I toyed with the fish and when the chicken eventually arrived it sat on a bed of soggy rice covered with an unappetizing pallid sauce.

The only dessert on the menu, apart from fresh fruit, was the inevitable crème caramel. As it was after eleven o'clock, I didn't wait for coffee but took an apple and banana back to the room. Richard was sleeping blissfully. I undressed quickly, fought my way through the yards of mosquito netting, and curled up on the big double bed with a thankful sigh. Only one more day and night to wait!

At quarter to six Richard demanded food and attention. There were never any half-measures with that young man. It was either sunshine or thunder. When he was happy there was nothing like his smile. It was fun having him with me.

In spite of the purser's assurance that my ears would clear, I was still very deaf. I had had this trouble once before when flying, and knew I would have to find a doctor to syringe them before I flew back to Durban. That might be difficult on a Sunday in Lourenço Marques. After breakfast in the room, I carried Richard downstairs to the lobby to make inquiries.

The receptionist, at the mention of a doctor shook her head and said, '*A manha, a manha.*' This was the most popular word in the Portuguese language. Everything would happen 'tomorrow'. Nothing was urgent and tomorrow was as good as today. The trouble was my ears needed syringing today and I wouldn't be here tomorrow. I stood my ground and grudgingly she went to the phone.

She returned to the desk saying, 'Doutor Pinto will see you at eleven o'clock – in town. I'll order a taxi for you at ten-thirty.' As I turned away she called, 'Oh Senhora Pascoe, a large parcel for you. *Está là.*' She went into the little room behind the desk and came out holding a very large brown-paper parcel.

The coat! I'd forgotten about the coat! I staggered into the lift with Richard and the parcel, closed the metal concertina doors and pressed the button. Up in my room I unwrapped the parcel. Well, there it was! The grey, Karakul fur coat! It was beautiful – soft and luxurious. I put it on and twirled around in front of the mirror feeling a million dollars. Now all I had to do was to get it safely back to Durban. And then a thought suddenly struck me. What about customs? Ken hadn't mentioned that! What was I to do – wear it, declare it or what? I decided to face that problem later.

We went downstairs to wait for the taxi. As I came out of the lift I heard my name being paged. 'There's a call for you Senhora.' The receptionist took Richard from me while I went to the telephone. I picked up the receiver.

'Hullo. Good Morning, Mrs Pascoe, this is Tony speaking. I'm afraid we've got a problem. A signal has just come in from your husband en route from Mombasa. It says: 'Aircraft full to Durban.' As it may be difficult to get you away tomorrow can I have your permission to send the captain a message to warn him that you're here. Sorry if this spoils your surprise. I'll let you know if I have any other news. The car will call for you at five-thirty tomorrow morning to take you to the port.'

The news was shattering. I could be sitting in Lourenço Marques for days while John was back home in Durban. So much for my surprise!

'Senhora, your taxi is here.' I was jolted back to the present, and taking Richard from the receptionist, I asked her to write a note in Portuguese for the doctor and give instructions to the taxi-driver. Lourenço Marques taxi-drivers act as if there might never be a '*manha.*' Mine drove like a maniac, swerving round corners and bouncing over the mosaic cobbled streets. We turned into a side-street and pulled up with a jerk in front of a depressing looking house. I was reassured when I saw a plate on the door saying 'Dohtor Mario Pinto'.

I rang the bell. Slow footsteps approached and the door was opened by an elderly grey haired man wearing a dirty shirt and grubby trousers. '*Bom dia,*' he said and I handed him the note. He took it and led the way into a small sparsely furnished room. He disappeared. I thought he had gone to find the doctor, but in a few minutes he was back, carrying a syringe and a kidney-shaped enamel bowl.

He pointed to a kitchen chair. As the table was the only other piece of furniture in the room I put Richard in the middle hoping he wouldn't fall off, and sat on the chair.

There were no preliminaries, like peering into my ear with a little light. Dr Pinto grabbed my ear and inserted the syringe. The force of the water made me dizzy. I tried not to pull my head away as the water swished into my ear. Four times he repeated the process

9

until all the water had gone. Then he poked the syringe into my ear and triumphantly pulled out a piece of wax about the length of my thumbnail, and scraped it into the bowl. He went out and returned with another full syringe. Indicating that I must turn round he grabbed hold of my other ear and pumped in the water. My head buzzed with the noise and my ears felt they would fall off.

I stood up shakily and rescued Richard from the table. The doctor handed me a piece of paper – presumably a bill. I opened my purse, gave him some escudos, and fled outside to the waiting taxi. As the car roared off I shook my head slowly to get rid of the excess water. Suddenly everything cleared and I could hear again. The horn blared more loudly than ever and Richard added to the noise by protesting at the treatment his mother had received.

I tried to contact Tony during the afternoon but there was no reply. It was six o'clock before I got through. 'Have you any news?' I asked anxiously.

'Yes but I'm afraid it's not good. The aircraft is full. I've told Captain Pascoe that you're here waiting to return to Durban with him.'

Poor John! So much for my big surprise! I fed Richard and tucked him into his cot. Then I slipped down to the swimming pool to cool off. It was too warm to be refreshing, but I floated on my back, watching the changing colours of a brilliant tropical sunset. On my way past the dining room I ordered a sandwich, coffee and fruit to be sent up to my room. At least I could eat that out on the balcony in peace.

Wishful thinking! With the darkness came the mosquitoes. They were hungry and found me a tasty morsel. I felt very disillusioned about hotel life in the tropics. The idea of having to spend a few days here on my own depressed me completely.

Richard was hot and very restless. I tried him with a bottle of water but he spat the teat out in disgust. Fed up, I crawled into bed, put the light out and lay in the darkness listening to the noise of the mosquitoes outside the net. When Richard started to cry again, I manoeuvred my way out through the net, turned him over and sang a lullaby until his thumb found its way into his mouth, and he fell asleep.

I wasn't so lucky. As soon as I got back onto the bed, a wretched mosquito started buzzing round my head. It must have got inside the net when I was attending to Richard. I swiped at it and buried my head under the sheet. But it was cunning and persistent. The more it buzzed, the more I thrashed about. Disgruntled I lay still, pretending to myself – and the mosquito – that I was asleep. Just as I began to relax, the irritating insect buzzed louder than ever, right inside my ear. I wished they were still blocked. The night seemed endless.

It was a relief when the alarm went off at 4 a.m. Not wanting to disturb Richard I crept around collecting all the paraphernalia. I packed as many nappies as possible at the bottom of the carrycot. There was not much room for Richard by the time I'd finished. I opened the wardrobe door to take out my clothes and there was THE FUR COAT. Somehow in the stress of Sunday's uncertainties I'd forgotten about it. But now there was no forgetting! I'd promised Ken and that fur coat HAD to go with me to Durban.

I was down in the foyer of the hotel with Richard, clean, well-fed and smiling, when the car arrived to take us to the wharf. As we neared the docks I heard the sound of the flying-boat overhead. It was a very still morning – not a breath of wind. The sea shimmered like glass and melted into the horizon – a hazardous condition for landing, Flying-boat accidents had been caused through trying to land on a glassy sea. We arrived at the wharf just in time to watch the boat come in over the town, skim above the water and make a perfect touchdown. John will be happy about that landing, I thought.

The launch fussed around the boat like a mother duck, waiting to take the passengers to the jetty where tables were laid for breakfast in a small wooden hut. The smell of fried bacon hovered around us.

I stood nervously on the edge of the wharf anxiously waiting for the first sight of John. He appeared at the hatchway in his BOAC uniform of khaki shorts and bush-jacket, his hat at a rakish angle, and the inevitable pipe in his mouth. He waved and jumped into the launch. On arrival at the wharf he bounded up the steps and gave Richard and me a real bear hug. I had been a bit apprehensive about greeting him in front of his passengers but there was no doubt about his joy at seeing us. He took Richard in his arms and said: 'Goodness, isn't he wonderful? He's grown so much.'

'Oh, Johnnie, I'm so sorry,' I said tearfully, 'I seem to have caused you no end of trouble coming here trying to give you a big surprise.'

He put his arms around me. 'Don't worry, darling. I'm sure we'll manage something. You go and have some breakfast while I talk to Tony.'

I walked into the restaurant, put Richard back in his carrycot and sat down at the crew table. I had met the first officer before but didn't know the purser. It needed only that snide remark from him about wives surprising their husbands to make me utterly miserable.

John came up to me with a smile on his face, 'It's all right, Viv, we're not going to leave you behind.'

'But how can you manage to take us if your plane is full?'

'Just relax. I'm going to have some breakfast now and chat to some of the passengers. The traffic officer will look after you and I'll see you on board.'

In a few minutes Tony came and picked up the carrycot. 'If you'd like to come now, Mrs Pascoe, I'll take you on board.' I grabbed the precious coat and hand baggage and followed him along the jetty to the waiting launch. It was like coming home to climb into the cabin of the boat and collapse into the safe comfortable seat. Tony put the carrycot on the table. Richard smiled at him. 'He's a dear little baby. Pity we couldn't keep the surprise but I'm glad everything turned out all right.'

'Thank you very much for all your help. I'm very grateful for everything you've done but very happy not to have to stay here.'

The flight to Durban was wonderful. After take-off, the purser came through and said: 'Mrs Pascoe, the captain would like to see you on the flight-deck if you'll come this way.' I followed him up the stairs to the cockpit. This was the first time I had seen John at the controls of an aircraft. He looked happy and at home surrounded by all those instruments. I stood behind him and enjoyed the wider view of the country below from the cockpit window.

'Everything all right, Viv?' he asked. 'We'll soon be home. Let the other passengers get off first . The traffic officer will come back for you and see you through customs.'

The mention of customs made me feel guilty. I hadn't had time to explain about the coat. I looked down on the buildings on the Durban promenade and we flew over the ships tied up at 'Maiden' wharf. The Australian troops stranded in Durban during the war, had a saying that the only virgin left in Durban was the 'maiden' at that wharf!

We glided down, the floats made contact with the water and we sped along the flight-path. The bow wave covered the window and obscured the view for a few seconds before we settled down on the water. As soon as the launch came alongside, a line from the boat was secured to the buoy. We were home!

My adventure was almost over. I gathered up my hand luggage, and flinging the coat nonchalantly over one arm, stood by the door until the traffic officer came back in the launch. The purser handed the carrycot down to him and we motored towards the steps near the customs shed.

'I'll take you straight through,' the traffic officer said, 'and the captain will see to your other luggage.'

We went into the customs shed. 'This is Mrs Pascoe, the captain's wife and son,' he told the official. 'They've just come from Lourenço Marques.' The coat over my arm weighed a ton.

'That's all right,' he said. 'Hope you enjoyed your flight.'

'Thank you, it was great. My first flight in a flying-boat – a real thrill – especially coming back with my husband.' Richard gave him an angelic smile. I walked out of the shed with an enormous feeling of relief. All was well and Ken's wife would have her wedding present. But I decided, there and then, that a future life of crime had no appeal.

That evening when Richard was safely tucked up in his own cot and we were having our coffee I turned to John and said: 'As a matter of interest, how did you find a seat for me on your fully booked flying-boat?'

'Well,' he replied with a grin, 'I managed to persuade one of the passengers that, instead of coming to Durban with us, he'd save time if he took the train direct from Lourenço Marques to Johannesburg. He was very grateful to me for pointing this out as it gave him an extra day in Jo'burg.'

13

'You crafty old thing! I wondered how you did it. Thank goodness for co-operative passengers.'

'And thank goodness for intrepid wives. But you must promise me never to surprise me again like that.'

'I promise,' I said, crossing my fingers behind my back and inwardly promising myself: Not until next time!

2

South Africa

The breakers pounded away on the golden sands at Isipingo Beach, south of Durban. I lay with my eyes closed, enjoying the warmth of the sun on my body and listening to the rhythmic ebb and flow of the water. John and Richard had been having fun in the water until an extra big wave bowled Richard over and he came up spluttering and crying. Now they were playing at the water's edge building sandcastles and digging moats around them.

How peaceful it was! John had just returned from a long trip and we'd been catching up with the things that had happened since he went away. We led a strange unsettled life. The ups and downs, highs and lows, certainly didn't make our marriage dull. The intense excitement I experienced when John was due home, sent me into a feverish spate of cleaning and tidying. John was a tidy person, couldn't stand the sight of nappies around the flat – unless they were neatly folded – abominated hair curlers, bedroom slippers or anything that suggested a suburban housewife. With an active child of 14 months, it was a struggle living up to his high standards. When he was away I relaxed as far as tidiness was concerned. And for five weeks I had the full responsibility of running the flat, paying bills, making decisions and looking after Richard – with the help of Katie, our Zulu maid. Then when he came home I would have to readjust suddenly, and learn to share responsibilities again.

It always took him a couple of days to wind down after a trip. While I was happy to relax on a beach and enjoy the sun and swimming, John disliked beach picnics and complained about sand in his sandwiches. After ten minutes sitting in the sun he would say: 'Come on, let's go for a walk,' and set off at a brisk pace. Richard, who had taken his first steps at ten months, would toddle manfully after his father for a little way, until John took pity on him and hoisted him up on his shoulders.

I looked across at John who was now lying on his back with his hat over his eyes. 'I hope he's asleep, and will stay that way for a while.'

My thoughts wandered to my family in New Zealand. I hadn't seen them for over five years and I was suddenly overcome by a wave of homesickness. What a lot had happened since I sailed away from Wellington in a little Dutch ship, the *Strait Malacca*, on September 11th, 1941. The details of my departure were so clear – Mother's lovely flowers in my cabin, Father's gift of two tins of special toheroa soup, and my dear little sister Pat's farewell present – a greenstone ring.

Years later, in an old diary of mine, I found a letter she had written on the day I sailed away from New Zealand.

Dear Diary of my sister Vivienne,

You are a true friend, because you listen and take everything in without disapproval or criticism, and as a true friend, you must know how your owner left us today to go to South Africa, and how we are going to miss her.

Dear Diary, it was such a rush. We got up early as the carrier was coming for the luggage at eight thirty. It was a glorious day – Wellington at its best. A low white early morning mist lay for a while on the sea, till the sun plucked up courage and shone forth.

Everything was packed and ready and Daddy, Viv and I had breakfast in the music room on the card table – without a tablecloth! This going-away business is dreadful. Every now and then my eyes would fill with tears at some thought of something we had done together, and though I tried to be very firm, the tears kept on coming. The two suitcases, whose locks broke last night when Daddy tried to close them, were taken to the locksmith and the rest of the luggage went to the ship.

We left home about nine. Viv looked lovely in her brown frock, hat and fur cape on which I'd pinned Betty's flowers – violets, primroses and boronia. She drove 'Billy' (the Morris car) for the last time. At the wharf, after seeing the customs men, Mother and I went on board while Daddy drove off to collect the two suitcases.

Ships are always fascinating. We inspected Viv's cabin which is very comfortable, put mother's flowers in the handbasin, and then went on deck to watch the airmen – 100 of them, come on board. I wish I were going with her. Talk about 100 men and a girl!

The time passed quickly. Daddy came back with the cases and they were put in the cabin. He had been to the bank and fixed up some money for her. Mother sat with friends in the lounge. At ten-thirty Daddy and I went ashore to arrange travel insurance. I wanted to buy her a greenstone ring as a parting gift, and Daddy bought two tins of toheroa soup.

When we returned to the boat the passengers had already disembarked, and we weren't allowed back on board. Daddy and I had to say goodbye to Viv at the top of the gangway (weeping too) in front of a policeman. We waited on the wharf looking up, gazing our fill of her for what may be a long time. I tried my best to be amusing and smile and keep Mother's spirits up by making jokes. The airforce boys lined the decks and all was cheerful with bright shouts from ship to shore. Then they began to sing 'Now is the Hour'. We all shed tears and bit them back. How hard it is not to cry or sob, when your heart is full almost to bursting.

The ship hooted and scared us back into laughter as she drew out. We stood at the end of the wharf. As the ship swung round, we could see Viv plainly, waving the magazine Daddy had given her. Gradually they drew out into the stream and we got into the car. We drove round to Oriental Bay point, and then to Breaker Bay hill. I stood on the summit and waved frantically when the ship came into sight just past the heads. We believed we saw Vivienne. I do hope she could see us. We watched until the ship was out of sight and then came home.

For dinner I began setting four places. I saw the serviette she'd used for breakfast, which she won't need any more.

Tonight I'm sitting in bed on the porch writing this. My letter from her is beside me and her dressing gown is round my shoulders – her legacy. That and the responsibility she has shouldered for the last few years. Oh God, may I be equal to it and not disappoint her, or Mother and Daddy. God keep her safe. Bless her and may she be very happy. Maybe we'll all be united once more – and may it not be too long in the future.'

Dear Pat! What a letter! And what a farewell! As the passengers included the first complete airforce squadron leaving New Zealand for Singapore, the Prime Minister, Peter Fraser, was on the wharf waving goodbye.

At midday when all the guests had gone ashore, the ship came to life, ropes creaked, bells clanged, and finally the gangway was drawn up. As the boat slowly pulled away, the passengers joined the boys in blue at the rails, and threw coloured streamers down to friends and relations on the wharf, where the airforce band struck up the Maori farewell song, 'Now is the Hour', and everyone joined in singing. Tears streamed down my face as I clung desperately to the red paper streamer – the last contact with my family. The propellers churned the water as we went astern, and one by one the paper ribbons strained, broke, and drifted down clinging limply to the boat's side. The ship hooted three times, and with the cheers from the crowds growing fainter, we gathered speed and headed past Oriental Bay and round Marsden Point. As we sailed past my home on Seatoun Heights, I wondered if the family had already returned and were watching, as we sailed out through the Heads into Cook Strait, setting course for Australia.

The die was cast. There was no going back. I was on my way to South Africa to take up a position as violinist in the Broadcasting Orchestra in Durban. It was the beginning of a long ten-week journey under wartime conditions. For four and a half days we bounced from wave to wave across the Tasman Sea. Not knowing whether it was day or night, because the porthole was painted black, I lay on my bunk, seasick, homesick and miserable. We stayed on the boat for eight days in Sydney, expecting to leave at any minute. During the war all shipping departures and arrivals were secret, and no one knew what was happening. At least it gave me, and many of the seasick airforce boys, a chance to recover from our uncomfortable journey. After a slow trip up the Australian coast we eventually arrived at Jakarta in what is now Indonesia but was then the Dutch East Indies, where I disembarked, and had a long anxious wait for another Dutch ship to take me across the Indian Ocean to South Africa.

What became of all those airforce boys who set off so confidently on their first overseas posting? The tragedy of Pearl Harbour happened soon after their arrival in Singapore. With Japan and America at war, many would be incarcerated in prison camps for the duration. I wonder what would have happened to me if I had been delayed in Jakarta when Singapore fell to the Japanese? I wouldn't be lying on the beach at Isipingo in South Africa with a husband and child by my side.

The memories of that journey were so vivid. A shiver went down my spine, and a thought flashed across my mind like a whirlwind. I looked across at John who was still lying asleep beside me.

'John darling, wake up.' I leant over and shook him.

He opened one eye. 'I wasn't asleep. What's the matter?'

I sat up and hugged my knees as I watched Richard playing in the sand. "I've just had an idea."

'Oh no, not another one! What is it this time?'

'Well,' I paused and took a big breath. 'How would it be if, instead of going back to England with you in the flying-boat, I took Richard to New Zealand to see his grandparents? After all he is the only grandson.'

'Goodness, that's a turnabout. You've been so keen for us all to fly to England together. Why this sudden urge to go to the other end of the earth?'

'I don't know,' I said stubbornly. 'I just have this gut feeling that I must go back to New Zealand and see my family before settling down in England.'

'That's a big decision to make and will need thinking about.' John sat up and put his arm around my shoulder. 'I guess if you feel strongly about it that's what you'll do. You're usually right when you get these sudden hunches. Let's go for a walk.' He pulled me to my feet. We collected Richard and set off along the beach. My knees felt wobbly. Why did I have to have this sudden impulse to return to New Zealand? It meant leaving John and losing the wonderful chance to fly with him to Cairo and on to England. Instead I would be going to the other side of the world on my own, with a small energetic boy to look after. It could be months before I saw John again. We walked and talked and thought about all the possibilities – and the difficulties, involved. But the more I thought about it, the more convinced I was that somehow I must take Richard to New Zealand.

John, who had been seconded to BOAC from the RAF, had operated flying-boats out of Durban for five years. Every six months or so, rumours flew round that the base was to be moved to another country. First it was Cairo, then Karachi, and even Augusta in Sicily was mentioned. We had lived with this uncertainty for so long that we no longer took any notice of the rumours. Then quite suddenly, BOAC announced that the Durban base was to be closed, and crews returned to England. Each captain was to fly a boat with crew and families, back to the new base at Poole Harbour, on the south coast of England. When this news hit us we were devastated. We loved South Africa and had made many friends. John and I were married in Durban in 1944, so it was a special place for us.

When I arrived in South Africa from New Zealand, the discrimination between the races – black and white – had shocked me. This was long before the word 'apartheid' came into vogue. As a schoolgirl in New Zealand, I had never been conscious of a colour bar between Maoris and Pakehas (white people). We were all New Zealanders.

So I was appalled when I saw notices 'Whites Only' or 'Blacks Only' on public toilets, buses and beaches. To me it was wrong and unjust, and I aired my views with little tolerance or understanding of the tremendous problems caused through living in a country with such a mixed population.

I had to learn – and to accept – many things. South Africa is a complex society – a melting pot of nationalities with different cultures and backgrounds. As well as the strong differences between the English, the Boers, and the Jews, each city has its own special racial problem – Indians in Natal, the Coloured people of the Cape, and a mixture of Bantu and other northern tribes in Johannesburg working in the gold mines. A special mine language, *Fanakalo*, was developed for safety reasons, and the miners had to learn the words for their tools, before going down into the mines.

Durban was a very English community when we were there. But I found a mixture of nationalities in the Broadcasting Orchestra. The Afrikaner players were excellent, hard-working musicians, but rigid in their views about the colour problem. Although generous to an extreme if they liked you, there was an inherent barrier and intolerance, which made it difficult to establish a real friendship.

Katie – our 'girl' – was a Zulu. The term 'girl' or 'boy' applied to any African worker, no matter what age. She was a devoted nanny, and Richard adored her. I would hear great chuckles of mirth coming from the nursery when she was dressing him to take him for a walk. Dear old Katie! What was she going to do when we left Durban? She had become part of the Pascoe household, and at the end of the war, jobs were not easy to find.

One day, when we were packing ready for our departure, Katie's brother came to see her. He told her their father had died and she must return to the village straight away. I knew that sometimes a family illness was used as an excuse to take someone away from their job, and I was a bit suspicious. I had learnt the hard way, that the African idea of time was different from ours. Before she left, I stressed that I needed her back as soon as possible, because there was so much to do. The days went by. There was no sign of Katie. I got more and more frustrated and harassed.

21

After ten days Katie arrived back looking quite unrepentant. I was annoyed and said: 'Well, Katie, this is a fine time to come back. It's ten days since your father died.'

'Yes Ma'm. But my father, he a little better now.'

' Better! What do you mean, better? Your brother came and told you he was dead.'

'Yes Ma'm, so he did, but he better now.' I gave up! It was useless trying to get an explanation.

Durban, being hot and humid in summer was a bad climate for chest complaints. The health authorities were making concentrated efforts to check the alarming growth of tuberculosis among the Africans. But it wasn't easy! An African would willingly go to hospital for a minor complaint to get some *mutti* or medicine, but if he felt really sick he would limp back to his village – or *kraal*. If he was suffering from TB his family and friends would run the risk of becoming infected. The doctors tried hard, but could do little to stop the spread of the disease.

One day Katie complained that her leg hurt. She said she'd fallen against a stick. It was difficult to tell how inflamed it was because the skin was so black. I put a poultice on it and sent her home. When she didn't arrive for work the next day, I put Richard in the car and drove out to her village, some miles from Durban. It wasn't easy to find her rondavel, as they all looked alike. When I did find her, she was lying on a bed in a tiny hut, surrounded by female relations. The leg looked worse and obviously needed medical attention.

I knew very few words of Zulu so it was difficult to communicate with the sisters and aunts who clustered around. I told Katie firmly that she must get up and come with me. The ladies moaned and groaned and tried to stop her getting into the car, but I won the day and we drove away to the hospital. We waited over an hour in a crowded, stuffy waiting room. The doctor said the leg required lancing as it was badly infected, and she must stay in hospital. Katie sobbed and refused to stay because she said there was no one to look after her *piccanin*.

I calmed her down, promising to bring her *piccanin* to see her the next day. This meant another visit to the *kraal* and an even greater confrontation with the aunts when I picked up a small girl, about four years old who looked like Katie. They were most suspicious when I took her away and I prayed I'd got the right child. I'd never seen Rose before – anything less like a rose I couldn't imagine – but the absolute joy on Katie's face when I appeared with her small daughter was worth all the effort.

The following day Katie arrived back at the flat, large as life, saying her leg was quite better. I'm sure she was supposed to have remained in hospital but I couldn't persuade her to go back.

Food was not rationed in South Africa during the war, as it was in England, but there were always shortages. When there was a severe drought and the mealie crop failed, thousands of Africans were at starvation level, because *mealiepap*, a white sticky porridge, was the staple diet. The Africans like sweet things and in a household, sugar, jam and tea disappeared at an alarming rate, unless rationed by the housewife.

There was a strange law in force because of a shortage of white imported flour. No bread, cake, or food made from flour could be served in a restaurant after three o'clock in the afternoon. Anyone found sifting the bran out of the poor, brownish local flour, was fined £200. Catering for functions, like weddings, was very difficult. Promptly, at three o'clock, the waiters would descend and remove all sandwiches and goodies made with flour. When we were married, the reception had to be timed so we cut the wedding cake and handed it round before three o'clock. It made me feel like Cinderella with her time limit at the ball.

We had had a wonderful time in Africa. We loved it. The sunshine, the rich colourful flowers and shrubs, and the friendliness of the people, both black and white, had made our lives full of fun and interest. We were happy and secure in our little flat on the Berea, a hill suburb in Durban, and loathe to leave it.

But we had no choice when the letter came from BOAC saying that the base in Durban was to close. That was final, and now I had complicated matters by wanting to return to New Zealand. There were no flights from South Africa to Australia, so it meant trying to find space on a ship. But the ships were full of troops returning home after being overseas. Sailings were erratic and the shipping companies we visited held little hope of a passage to Australia.

Just before Christmas, I heard that the *S.S. Nestor*, a Blue Funnel line ship made regular trips to Sydney. When we went to the office to inquire about sailings the receptionist was not very encouraging. 'Yes,' she said, 'the *Nestor* leaves for Australia sometime in January but it is fully booked.' I asked if my name could be put down on the standby list.

'There's not much chance, I'm afraid, but leave me your name, address and telephone number, and I'll contact you if there's a cancellation.'

Now I was on standby – not for an aeroplane – but a ship. At least I knew that if the New Zealand trip fell through, John would take us to England in his flying-boat.

He was due back from Cairo on December 24th. He had been away last year so this would be our first Christmas together. Richard was old enough to enjoy looking in his stocking and tearing the wrapping paper off parcels. We wanted to watch him together and be a real family.

Amazingly, John got back on schedule, and we made the most of our last Christmas in South Africa. Several of the flying-boats had already left. Because of the uncertainty of my trip to New Zealand, John had volunteered to operate the last service to Cairo, and do a month's flying there before returning to England. That would not be a great hardship, as he enjoyed staying on the BOAC houseboat anchored on the Nile River at Rod al Faraq. He would be well-fed and pampered by Hakim, the Egyptian chef who was in charge of the boat.

New Year dawned! – 1948! We wondered where we'd celebrate next New Year's Day.

I inquired constantly at the shipping office for a standby space. Helen, the receptionist, was patient and long suffering. She assured me she would let me know immediately if there was a cancellation.

Because of the winding down of the base, normal flying schedules were suspended. We enjoyed taking Richard to the beach in the afternoon. The war was over, but there was a feeling of unrest and uncertainty in South Africa and we wondered if we would ever return.

Driving home from the beach one afternoon I said to John: 'Please stop at the Blue Funnel office. I won't be a minute.'

Helen saw me as soon as I went in and rushed over. 'I've been trying to get hold of you all afternoon. A tiny cabin on B-deck of the *Nestor* has suddenly become available. You'll have to decide right away if you want it.'

I didn't hesitate. As always on standby you have to grab every opportunity. 'Yes please. I'll take anything. When do we sail?'

'On January twelfth. That only gives you five days. I'll confirm your booking now and if you bring a cheque tomorrow I'll have the tickets ready.'

There was no need for John to ask questions when I jumped into the car. The smile on my face, told him all he needed to know.

We cabled my family. Father, who in his heyday, had played cricket for New Zealand, replied that he'd meet me in Melbourne. The New Zealand Broadcasting Company had offered him a job as cricket commentator for the first test match since the war, between Australia and New Zealand. This was to be played on the famous Melbourne cricket ground. Father, since his retirement from the Methodist ministry, had been writing and commentating on cricket. Such exciting news! I couldn't believe it. Only five days before sailing. It was a mad rush. There was no time to dwell on the thought of leaving John and saying goodbye to South Africa.

Courage nearly failed me when it was time to board the *S.S. Nestor*. It was such a little ship with a very high blue funnel that made it look top heavy. We went down to inspect the cabin. It was very small and I hoped my cabin-mate liked children. We would be sharing this tiny cabin for several weeks. I noticed she had already settled her things on the lower bunk. That meant I'd be climbing up and down the little steps every time Richard needed me. First come, first choice, I suppose! A small canvas cot was rigged up on the far side of the cabin, hardly secure enough for an active climber like Richard.

All visitors ashore, the siren sounded. I clung to John trying to keep back the tears. He carried Richard to the top of the gangway. With a last kiss and a hurried hug he put Richard in my arms.

'*Totsiens*', he said. 'As the South Africans say, *Alles van die beste*. Take care of yourself and our son. Have fun!'

He turned quickly and marched down the gangway.

I felt utterly desolated. Richard was excited and full of energy. He was fascinated by the little ladder leading to the top-bunk. He could climb up but not down, so every few moments there would be a cry: 'Down, Mummy, down, Mummy.'

Having a 'bibby' cabin meant that the porthole opened onto a tiny passage away from the bunks. At least it wasn't painted black, as it had been on my journey to South Africa. My cabin-mate had already stowed her belongings in the only free space available.

The engines began to throb and the cabin vibrate. I picked Richard up and rushed to the stairway leading onto the deck. I gazed longingly down at the wharf but couldn't see John among figures standing below. Perhaps it was just as well. It was too heart-rending.

Richard tugged my hand and we did a turn round the deck. It was a blustery afternoon and as soon as we passed the heads, the ship began to roll in an uncomfortable manner. I began to have that uncertain feeling.

Oh damn, I said to myself, surely I'm not going to be seasick on top of everything else. Who will look after Richard?

A bell rang for the children's tea. The dining-room was several decks below, and the motion of the ship got worse and worse as we went down the stairs. The tables were already full of children, much older than Richard. The steward found Richard a seat, but it was too low. He needed a highchair. I sat down and took him on my knee. A large plate of scrambled eggs was put in front of us. I took one look at it and felt my tummy heave. With grim determination I spooned the egg towards Richard, who reluctantly opened his mouth several times and then turned his head away and refused to eat any more. From a bowl of fruit in the centre of the table, I took a banana and mashed it up with some sugar. This was one of Richard's favourite dishes but after one mouthful he shut his mouth firmly and shook his head.

I got up from the table and tried to find my way back to the cabin. A motherly looking stewardess was standing near a stairway.

'Can you tell me where Cabin Fourteen-C is, please?'

Taking one look at my green face she gathered Richard in her arms and said: 'Follow me.' As we passed a door marked Bathroom and Toilet I dashed inside. I only just made it.

Seasickness is utterly demoralizing. Personally I think the world is divided into two lots of people – those who have never been seasick – and those who have! While I was on deck in the fresh air I was fine, but the minute I went below, the peculiar shipboard smell upset me.

I felt ghastly! My head ached, my tummy didn't belong anywhere and on top of everything I had the 'curse'! I was absolutely and utterly miserable.

Mary, the stewardess, was wonderful. 'You get into bed,' she said, 'and I'll look after this young man.' Unsteadily I climbed the ladder, cursing my cabin-mate for taking the bottom-bunk. Lying still with my head down and my eyes shut, I told Mary where to find Richard's nappies and pyjamas.

Chatting cheerfully Mary undressed Richard, changed him, and tucked him up in the canvas cot. She handed me a glass of soda water. I took a sip and then retched my heart out into the horrible little paper cuspidor hooked on the side of the bunk. I felt awful and very, very sorry for myself. How was I going to cope with an energetic 15 month-old boy who demanded constant attention.

I raised my head from the hard pillow and looked down at Richard. He'd turned over on his tummy and was fast asleep. The effort of raising my head made me sick again. Mary appeared with a fresh cuspidor.

'Ring the bell if you need me,' she said. 'Your cabin-mate is just coming along the corridor.'

'Please ask her if she'll try not to wake the baby when she comes to bed.' Mary disappeared and I tried to control the seesawing of my stomach.

There was a shuffling noise outside the cabin. The door opened. Framed in the doorway was the largest lady I had ever seen. She was a female colossus. In order to squeeze through the narrow door, she had to turn sideways. I lay very, very still with my eyes shut. I'd had ideas about asking her to swap bunks so I could get to Richard more quickly during the night. But there was no way that great bulk could make it up the frail little ladder. She switched on the little light at the head of her bunk instead of the main one, and I silently blessed her for that. There was so much thumping and heaving, that I wondered anxiously what would happen if the ship gave a sudden roll and she crashed down on the flimsy cot. Richard would be squashed flat! It was a great relief when I felt the whole structure of the bunks shake and shiver and knew the lady was safely in bed.

With difficulty I peeped over the side to make sure. It was comforting to know that Richard was sound asleep after such a harrowing day. Gradually the rhythm of the ship and the constant throb of the engines reassured and relaxed me, and I drifted into oblivion.

The rattle of teacups woke me in the morning. Mary came in looking fresh and cheerful.

'How are you this morning?' she chirped.

'Better, I hope.' I raised my head and took the cup of tea. But one sip was enough. Nothing would stay down.

'Don't worry,' she said, 'just lie still. I'll be back in a minute as soon as I've finished the tea-round. I'll dress Richard and take him down to breakfast.'

I had to climb down the ladder, find something for Richard to wear, and stagger along to the bathroom. Richard was shaking his cot vigorously when I returned. The canvas cot was so unstable. I lifted him out and put him on the potty while I hunted for a dry nappy. The potty was a good, solid white enamel one with a flat bottom. As it slid easily across the floor, Richard used it as a means of transport. He propelled himself around to the small chest of drawers. Before I could stop him, he had pulled open the bottom drawer and started to climb. Fortunately Mary returned and took him with her to have his breakfast.

I climbed thankfully back onto my bunk and lay feeling annoyed with myself for being so feeble.

'My name's Harriet', a deep voice informed me from the bottom bunk.

'Mine's Vivienne. I'm sorry if I was sick and disturbed you during the night.'

'Nothing disturbs me,' the voice went on, 'I'm over twenty stone and I'm never seasick.'

Bully for you, I thought bitterly to myself.

'I'm a nurse,' she continued. 'What you need is a slice of ham and some good yellow pickles. That'll put you right. I'll get up and go and see what I can find.'

I clutched my stomach and shut my mouth suddenly. The vision of yellow pickles floated in front of me – that bilious looking cauliflower and sickly pale-yellow cucumber. Ugh!

Harriet rumbled on.' I'll get up now. This cabin's so small there's hardly room to move.' I agreed with Harriet that indeed the cabin was so small that two of us couldn't stand. Part of the problem was her enormous bulk took up half the space. I watched her as she heaved herself around and unwound yards of cotton-wool from her breasts. They were monumental. I was fascinated. She finally left the cabin and I snuggled down in bed not wanting to be disturbed or make any effort to get dressed.

Presently the door banged and Harriet manoeuvred through, balancing a plate in her hand.

'Now sit up, and eat this. I've gone to a great deal of trouble to get it for you so don't make a fuss. GET IT DOWN.'

Reluctantly I raised myself into a sitting position. Oh what a sight! Ham and pickles! Not even a nice dry cracker biscuit.

'Oh no, Harriet,' I said tearfully as my tummy did another flip, 'I just can't face that.'

'Rubbish. Don't know what you can do until you try. It'll do you the world of good.' She stood like the Rock of Gibraltar hanging onto the bunk and I tentatively picked up a small piece of ham. My mouth was so dry, but somehow I got it down.

'Now the pickles –'

I shut my eyes and shoved the cauliflower into my mouth, and then the piece of onion and cucumber.

'That's the stuff. Good girl. Now, up you get and into the fresh air. I'm off.' And she wiggled her bosom through the narrow door and lumbered away.

I felt sure that as soon as she had gone, all her good works would return and be deposited in the cuspidor. But somehow I managed to climb down and get dressed without losing even one small piece of pickle.

I'll never know whether the ham or pickle cured my seasickness, or whether I was too intimidated by Harriet. But it worked! On that voyage I never suffered again from the ignominy of being seasick.

3

Sea Journey

The days settled into a pattern of shipboard life. The outside world, struggling to regain its sanity after years of conflict, hardly caused a ripple on the surface of the daily routine of the ship. A news bulletin was posted on the notice board each morning, but as the days went by, people hardly bothered to read it.

The sea was calm and the skies blue. Looking after Richard was a full time job. Being the youngest on board, and with his fair curly hair and engaging smile, he soon became the darling of the ship. For me, the open rails at the edge of the deck were a constant source of anxiety. It was too easy for a child to climb through and fall overboard. At first I left Richard in the cabin with the door shut when I went to have my shower in the morning. But it wasn't long before he learned how to open the door.

One morning when I came back from the bathroom, the cabin door was open and he had disappeared. I rushed down the corridor calling: 'Richard, Richard.' I knocked on all the cabin doors along the corridor, getting more and more frantic. Then Mary appeared dragging a reluctant little boy behind her. She'd found him climbing the stairs leading to the top deck! Mary, bless her, was a tower of strength.

The *Nestor* had been a troop ship during the war, and little had been done to refit her and make her into a comfortable passenger ship. Amenities were basic and we were very crowded. The third day of the voyage the cabin water supply was cut off, and we were told that it was unlikely to be put right until we reached Perth. There were queues for baths and showers and I was always dashing along to the bathroom to rinse nappies before sending them to the ship's laundry.

Because there were so many children on board, the purser set aside a room for a nursery, and the parents organized a roster for an hour every morning and afternoon. It was absolute bliss to have that free time and I enjoyed slipping away to play deck tennis on the top deck.

The passengers were a mixed bag. One of the most interesting was Lord Nuffield, formerly William Morris, the inventor of the famous Morris car. He was over 70 but very fit. There wasn't an ounce of surplus fat on him. He was a very modest man with a thin face, and keen, piercing blue eyes hidden behind a pair of old-fashioned steel-rimmed spectacles. It was a challenge playing deck-tennis against him, because he was so shrewd. Although he hardly seemed to move about, he managed to throw the quoit just out of reach. He was difficult to beat. The top-deck was out of bounds to children. After a hard game we would be invited to his suite for a drink of cold fruit juice. It seemed strange that he should choose to travel on this rather scruffy little ship, when he could have the very best accommodation on any ship. But he had done several trips to Australia during the war on the *Nestor*, and there was a private suite available for him whenever he wanted it.

During the voyage we had the usual organized entertainment – housie-housie or bingo, a concert and a fancy-dress ball. Bridge went on all the time, morning, noon and night, but I refused to get involved. The highlight of the trip was the children's sports event which took place on a grey, blustery day as we neared Perth.

The first race was for the youngest ones – under three. I explained to Richard that when the man said 'Go' he had to run as fast as he could to the rope at the other end of the deck. But when the starter said 'Go' and the other children set off, Richard stood still, looking very puzzled. I took his hand and we both ran to the other end – coming in last! Then the next race was lined up – under five. On hearing the word 'Go' Richard, seeing the other children running, decided to join in and toddled away towards the rope – finishing the course – last. He was greatly taken with the idea of running along the deck, and after that, no matter what the age

31

group, he joined in, getting a great cheer when he completed the course – always last.

At the finish of the races Lord Nuffield presented the prizes to the winners. But a special prize was awarded to Richard – for coming last in every race. Lord Nuffield gave him a car – a toy green convertible about 8 inches long. I decided we'd better take great care of this. Who knows! Perhaps we could swap it for a real Morris when we arrived in England. The car became Richard's favourite toy. It went everywhere with him – even to bed. He still slept on his tummy, and when I turned him over, I'd find the car underneath him.

Alas, the car never made it to England. The day before we arrived in Melbourne, Richard and another little boy were playing with the car on the deck. They got a bit violent with it, making it charge along the deck at great speed. It ran into the scuppers, bounced, and before I could rescue it, flew overboard. I watched it falling, falling down into the sea.

Oh dear, I thought, there goes Richard's chance of a trade-in for a new Morris. I felt movement by my legs and grabbed at young Richard who was trying to climb through the rails after his beloved car. There was a howl of despair when I picked him up. When Richard made a noise, he made a real noise and the whole ship soon knew that he'd lost his car – and I'd nearly lost him.

I had my last game of deck-tennis with Lord Nuffield who said he was sorry to hear that Richard's car had gone into the sea. He knew how much cars meant to people. I felt he might suggest replacing it – but no such luck.

During the voyage I hadn't seen much of Harriet. Once she was dressed and had manoeuvred herself upstairs, she stayed put in her special chair in the lounge, playing bridge most of the day. She had been kind and I had forgiven her for forcing me to eat her beastly yellow pickles, especially as they seemed to have cured my sea-sickness.

Most of the passengers were going on to Sydney. I hadn't had any news from Father since we left Durban, and wondered what I would do if he wasn't on the wharf to meet me. I felt vulnerable and unhappy at the thought of leaving the security of the ship and saying goodbye to the friends I had made during the three-week voyage. As we steamed through the narrow heads into Port Phillip Bay, I thought about my grandfather, who arrived in Melbourne nearly 100 years ago. He had left England in a small sailing ship. It took 93 days to make the voyage to Australia. His diary, a fascinating document, tells of the hardships of the journey and his arrival in Melbourne in the rain, with mud everywhere. He describes the dirty, yellow looking Yarra River. And how, as he had only half-a-crown left, he left his luggage on board, until he got some money from a bank to pay for the carriage of his suitcase to Melbourne.

At least the day we arrived was fine and sunny. I stood on deck as we drew alongside the wharf. Bells clanged, ropes were thrown down and secured to the bollards as we edged into the berth. Anxiously I peered down at the sea of faces, hunting for that familiar face. Then, joy of joys, I saw him, his bald head shining in the sun, as he waved his hat vigorously. I knew he had seen me when he blew me a kiss. I rushed down to the cabin to collect the hand luggage and say goodbye to Mary. Impatiently, with my arms full of Richard, handbag and violin, I waited at the top of the gangway until it was made secure. I was first off and almost tumbled as I ran down. There, waiting for us at the bottom was Father, with his arms outstretched.

'Darling, darling, Daddy. Oh, it's so good to see you! Here's your grandson, Richard John Pascoe'.

We got all muddled up together; Father, Richard, me and the violin. It was a very special moment of reunion. When I stepped ashore the ground was going up and down as if I was still on the ship. I felt weak and feeble. It was such a relief to know there was someone to take care of me.

As we walked over to the customs shed Father said: 'If you give me a list of your luggage I'll find it, and we'll get through customs as quickly as possible. We're staying in the Methodist manse out at Footscray. The Rev Duffield and his family are away on holiday and they have kindly lent me their house and car.'

I felt a bit disappointed as I had hoped we would be in an hotel where I would not have to do any cooking. But this was typical of my dear father. Our childhood holidays were always spent camping, or in borrowed houses. There was never enough money

33

for hotels. It was part of a Methodist parson's tradition to borrow or exchange houses for holidays.

'How long will we be staying in Melbourne?'

'Four days. The cricket test between Australia and New Zealand started on Tuesday and they've already played for two days. I'll have to leave you at the house as soon as we've unloaded the luggage. I must get back to my job at the Melbourne cricket ground. I may be a bit late back as I'll have to do the broadcast to New Zealand as soon as the day's play is finished.'

We wound our way through the suburbs of Melbourne. Richard was bouncing up and down on the seat, delighted to be in a car again. He got really excited as we pulled up beside a tram – something he had never seen before. 'Bus,' he said, 'bus.'

'No, Richard,' said Father, 'that's not a bus. It's a tram. There are lots of them in this city. You'll be able to have a ride in one tomorrow.'

Father drew up at a dreary looking wooden house that could have done with a coat of paint. 'Here we are. Out you get, young man.'

Richard needed no second bidding. He was out of the car like a shot, running round the garden, tumbling on the green grass which needed cutting. He loved the feel of grass under his feet, after walking on the ship's wooden decks.

We carried the baggage up the steps and into the hall and Father opened a door to one of the bedrooms. 'You'd better sleep in this room as it's got two beds. There are eggs, butter and bread in the cupboard in the kitchen, but I haven't had time to get any milk. There's a small dairy about three blocks away. Here's an Australian pound. Now I must go. Hope you'll be all right.' And off he went cheerfully to his cricket match.

I looked around the house. The long corridor with rooms either side led down to the kitchen which had a sink, table and two chairs, gas stove and large cupboard. The lounge drawing-room parlour, whatever you liked to call it, was a mixture of colours and ill-matching furniture, obviously given by parishioners wanting to get rid of their odd bits and bobs. In pre-war days any old thing would do for the manse, where the parson and his family lived. Maybe parsons were supposed to have their thoughts on higher things, but the parson's wife was hard pressed at times to be charitable towards those responsible for the furnishing and comfort of the manse. My mother, who had a wonderful sense of colour, had suffered over the years as we moved from manse to manse and she struggled to create harmony out of discord.

I felt lost and depressed. 'I'd better make a cup of tea before I do anything about unpacking.' I filled the kettle but couldn't see any matches to light the stove. It's hopeless trying to find things in someone else's kitchen. I opened cupboards and pulled out drawers but there were no matches to be seen. Oh, for Mary, and the clatter of the teacup by my bunk!

'Well, there's nothing for it. We'll have to go and find the dairy,' I grumbled aloud to myself.

I called Richard, who was still enjoying himself in the garden. Father hadn't told me the direction of the dairy and there was no one in sight to ask. We went out the gate and turned right, but we crossed three intersections without any sign of a shop. A boy came by on his bicycle and I called him to ask where the dairy was. 'You're going in the wrong direction,' he said. 'It's at the other end of the road.'

Turning round I retraced my steps. Richard decided he'd walked far enough and demanded to be carried, so I picked him up. He was heavy. I was light headed and the six blocks before I saw the sign 'Dairy' seemed endless. The man behind the counter looked up from his paper. 'G'day, what d'yu want?'

'A box of matches and a pint of milk, please. ' I struggled to think what else I needed. 'Oh, and a jelly and two bananas.' With no idea how much it would cost I handed him the pound. 'Will this be enough?'

'OK, mate, 'er's yu change.'

We struggled back to the house with Richard protesting at having to walk some of the way. It was hot and humid and I hadn't had time to find him clean clothes. When I got inside, I grabbed the matchbox and lit the gas burner under the kettle. Then I went into the bathroom to turn on the water to give Richard a hot bath. After the salt baths on the ship when the water stung his eyes, a fresh-water bath would be a treat, and he could play in it while I had my cup of tea. The taps didn't say 'hot' or 'cold', so I turned them both on and kept testing them. They stayed cold! Stymied again! Father hadn't thought to mention how one got hot water.

I unpacked a few things and found something cooler for Richard. A pile of nappies needed washing. Gathering them up, I went to look for the wash-house. That was the last straw! A concrete tub with a cold tap and an old-fashioned copper with a pile of wood beside it. I hadn't lit a fire for over five years and had certainly never tried washing nappies in a copper. Living in Africa, Katie had washed all the nappies. Suddenly I realized how spoilt I had been all that time. I sighed heavily and set to with dread and determination to get the fire lit under the copper.

The next morning Father was up bright and early and Richard trotted out to see him. When I joined them in the kitchen, Richard was sitting on his knee and Father was trying to teach him to say 'Bumpa'. This was the name my niece, Jayne, had given her grandfather when she started talking, and it had stuck. The trouble was that Richard got hold of the first part and was shrieking, 'Bum, Bum.'

'You'll have to get him to add the last bit, Vivienne. I don't think "Bum" is a suitable title for a grandfather who is a Methodist minister.'

'I will try, but Richard can be quite obstinate about words, and you may find you're stuck with "Bum, Bum" for a while.'

Father put on his black New Zealand blazer with the fern-leaf pocket, and took his cap and binoculars. 'I'll have to get away now. I've reserved a seat in the stand for you this afternoon. You can get a tram to the cricket ground after lunch. If you give me a piece of paper I'll write down the number of the tram.'

'Please give me full instructions, Bumpa. I don't want to get lost like I did yesterday. Richard's too heavy to carry any distance.'

Father was an Australian. He was born in Warrnambool, Victoria. Cricket was his passion. He had a fantastic memory and could quote the number of runs made in cricket games played before the First World War. We could never be sure which came first in his life – being a minister – or a cricketer. As children we always went with him on Saturdays to watch him play, while Mother provided tea for the players. When he strode out to the wicket we watched each ball with bated breath. He was a tremendous hitter and swung the bat with confidence. To see a ball flying over the heads of the fieldsmen and out over the boundary fence for six, was the thrill of the afternoon. If he should be bowled for a duck we felt as if the world stood still, and were there to greet him when he returned to the pavilion.

I wished he was out in the field that afternoon, when Richard and I finally found our way to the seats in the stand. It would have been wonderful for Richard to see his grandfather play. Instead, he was in the press box gazing intently at every ball bowled. In between the overs he waved to us and at the tea-break came over and took us to meet some of the other commentators. Richard was fascinated by the men in white running about the field. But I kept a firm grip on him, in case he thought he was back on the ship running races. I didn't think Bumpa would be very happy to have play stopped because his small grandson was running onto the field.

After the first grim arrival day, the time passed quickly. I don't think Father had any idea what agonies I had gone through. The abrupt transition from being pampered on the ship where everything was provided, to a house without normal conveniences had been drastic. Once the test match was finished he was full of good humour and help. I loved to watch him taking Richard for a walk, – this big tall man and a little blonde boy holding his hand, trotting beside him.

Before we left South Africa, John had written to his aunt and uncle who lived in the fruit-growing district of Shepparton, some 150 miles north of Melbourne, telling them that we were coming to Victoria. When Bumpa arrived from New Zealand, he phoned them, and arranged a time to visit before we travelled onto Sydney and New Zealand.

4

Australia

Although he was only seven at the time, John remembers vividly the wedding of his Auntie Nona to a local farmer, Harry Preston. It caused a sensation in the conservative Cotswold farming community when Harry decided to emigrate to Australia, with his new bride. Applying to the Australian Embassy in London for an assisted passage for his wife and himself, he was promised a grant of farmland when he arrived in Victoria.

They were married in the Methodist chapel in Chipping Norton in 1924 and immediately after the ceremony were driven to Charlbury station, where they took a train to Southampton and boarded a ship for Australia. None of the family had seen them since that day.

On arrival, they were told that they had been allotted 80 acres of irrigated, but undeveloped, land near Shepparton in the fruit-growing Goulburn valley. Their house, originally erected on a gold-mining site, had been transported to the farm and re-erected. It was neither comfortable – nor beautiful. Auntie Nona, the youngest of six children, had led a sheltered life on a Cotswold farm. Her mother had died when she was a baby and she had been brought up by two domineering sisters. A cook and housemaid came daily from the village to Blaythorne Farm, so she had never had to do any housework. She was totally unprepared for the harsh life in a strange country, and without the protection of her family, and the comfort of her lovely old Cotswold stone home, she must have wept many times, as she struggled to produce meals on the black range that burnt wood and coal.

Life was tough in those pioneering days in Australia. The land had to be broken in – fruit trees planted – but there would be no income from them for several years. Then, when the fruit was ready for marketing, the growers were at the mercy of the local canning factory which had a monopoly, and could condemn, or accept, as much of the fruit as they liked.

It was high summer when Bumpa, Richard and I arrived in the Goulburn Valley. The trees were heavy with fruit; pink-cheeked peaches, luscious golden apricots, and huge green pears just beginning to ripen. As we had been married in South Africa, I hadn't met any of John's family and I was looking forward to chatting to Auntie Nona about the farm and family in England. But she was reluctant to talk about her childhood or her family. She had cut herself off completely from her old life. Perhaps it was the only way she could survive. Being proud and independent, she didn't want the family to know about her hardships. Even after all those years, she was still cooking on the same old black kitchen range, the bathroom facilities were primitive, and the lavatory was down the garden path – 'the little privy'– as it was called. I remembered a book I read, with amusement, about privies, called *The Specialist*, which gave lurid descriptions of the various sized 'holes' provided for privies. With the thought of snakes coiled up in unexpected places and poisonous spiders lurking in dark corners, I was reluctant to take a trip down that garden path.

And the flies! They were everywhere. The stickiest, most persistent creatures God ever made. He must have created them on one of his off-days – or were they meant as a punishment to Eve for eating the forbidden fruit? The first morning at the farm I washed my hair and sat outside enjoying the sunshine. I lasted about two minutes. The flies zoomed in around my eyes, up my nose, buzzed round my head and in my ears. I lashed at them with my towel. It was impossible to sit still. However did Auntie Nona cope in those early days, without any wire-screening on doors and windows? Now, at least, all the windows were screened. But it was still necessary to cover the jug and sugar basin with little net circles weighed down with beads, and the smell of meat acted like a magnet. Without electricity, there was no gleaming white refrigerator in this 'un-modern' kitchen. Auntie had made do all these years with a small, ancient kerosene fridge.

Auntie Nona said she would rather I didn't tell the family much about their life. 'It's much easier now, but I've never written to my sisters about the difficult times we've had, or the primitive way we still live. They've never moved away from their sheltered environment, and they just wouldn't understand. They'd be horrified.'

' Wouldn't you like to go back and see them all now the war is over?'

'No, I don't think so. I wouldn't have anything in common with them now. My sisters were always critical of everything I did, and they didn't approve of my marrying Harry and coming out to Australia. I don't think we'll ever go back, even for a visit.'

The morning we left the farm I picked a bagful of the largest, juiciest apricots I'd ever seen. Richard loved all kinds of fruit and after the limited amount of fruit on the ship, he thought it was wonderful to eat fruit picked from the trees, still warm from the golden sunshine.

I was full of admiration for John's aunt, but felt sad that family ties had been broken. I wondered how I would get on with her two sisters, John's mother, Winn, and maiden Aunt Maye, when I met them in England. They sounded rather formidable.

We went by train from Shepparton to Melbourne, where we waited several hours before catching the express train to Albury, the border town between Victoria and New South Wales. When the hundreds of miles of railway lines were being laid across Australia, there was great rivalry and division between the states. They couldn't agree on the width of the track. Victoria wanted the wide gauge, but New South Wales decided that, in their state, they would use the standard distance of 4 feet 8½ inches between the rails. This meant passengers had to change trains when travelling from one state to another – most inconvenient.

I didn't know anything about this until we pulled into Albury station at midnight. Richard was asleep, curled up on the seat beside me, and I was dozing. The train stopped suddenly and Father said: 'Wake up. We have to change here. I'll go and check the luggage in the van, but hurry, we haven't much time.'

I woke Richard, bundled things into the bags, and struggled onto the platform. The Sydney train was some distance away. I looked for a porter to help us. What a stupid arrangement having to change trains in the middle of the night!

Father came along pushing a large trolley. 'Better be quick. Our train was ten minutes late and we've only a few minutes before the Sydney one leaves. Here, Richard, up you get.'

Richard, now wide awake, enjoyed the ride on top of the luggage as we rushed along the platform.

'You stay here while I find our reserved seats.' Father went ahead and then beckoned furiously when he found the carriage. There was no time to find the luggage-van so, between us, we heaved the heavy cases up the steep steps into the carriage.

'All aboard.' The guard was shouting as we climbed on. He blew his whistle, and the train started with a jerk.

When we did find the seats, I collapsed with a sigh. 'Whew,' I exclaimed, 'if they must make you change trains in the middle of the night, surely they could have some porters to help. That was a ridiculous rush. What time are we due in at Sydney?'

'The train should arrive at eight a.m. and we'll take a taxi to the YWCA where you're booked for a night. I'll be at the YMCA which is some distance away. But we've a busy day ahead. As I've earned money in Australia through my broadcasting, I need a tax clearance before I can leave the country, and you need an export form signed. We'll have to go to the tax office.' It sounded complicated. I was tired. The train settled down to a rhythmic clackety clack and lulled me into a fitful slumber.

I wasn't sorry when the train pulled into Sydney Station. Once again we disgorged ourselves and our luggage onto the platform. All was bustle and hurry … quite bewildering. I held Richard's hand very tightly. It would be the last straw if he made a dash for it and got lost in the crowds. Father found a willing porter who put us in a taxi. At the YWCA Father carried Richard into the foyer, and made sure that our room was booked.

'Now you stay here and have a rest. I'll be back later when I've found the address of the tax office.'

I was tired and all I wanted to do was lie down on a comfortable bed and sleep. Richard had other ideas. He wanted to play and bounced on the bed and jumped on my tummy. 'Come on then.

41

Let's go for a walk and find a milk bar.' After weeks of the ship's powdered milk I enjoyed the clean taste of a glass of cold 'proper' milk. Richard loved drinking a frothy, pink milk shake.

It was going to be a hot day. The room was stifling when we returned and I opened all the windows. The morning wore on without any news of Father. All we had to eat were the lovely apricots from the farm. They were delicious and thirst-quenching. Richard and I played games with the ever increasing pile of kernels. We made roads for his Dinky cars and fortifications with the stones. We kept two of the largest apricots for Father. He looked hot and bothered when he finally arrived about half-past two and was glad to sit still and enjoy the fruit.

'I've found the address of the tax office, so let's go. The sooner we get this clearance the better.'

No taxi this time! Father believed in using public transport whenever possible. Richard was excited when we got on the top of a red bus, but insisted, as Bumpa had taught him in Melbourne, that it was a tram.

The tax office was crowded and airless. We were herded into a waiting area. Although I'd armed myself with a couple of books to keep Richard amused, I knew this wouldn't occupy him for long. As I hadn't earned money during my brief stay in Australia, I couldn't understand why it was necessary for me to have a clearance certificate, but Father assured me that I could not leave the country without it.

We waited and waited. The queue hardly moved. I thought there should be some preference for women and children, but no one took any notice of us. Richard was getting more and more obstreperous and difficult to control. Although I held him firmly on my knee he wriggled like a worm, squirming all over the place trying to get free. Suddenly I had an idea. In my handbag was a travelling sewing-kit. Opening the bag, I drew out a needle from the kit and – without thinking too much – I gave Richard a sharp jab. He let out an almighty howl of protest. He went on creating a noise that was difficult to ignore. It was too much for the office staff and a young man suddenly appeared and beckoned to me.

'Would you come this way, please, and fill in these forms?' I followed him without any guilt-feelings about jumping the queue by foul or fair means. Father came, looking slightly surprised. He handed in his completed forms and we left hurriedly. Once outside Richard stopped crying.

'How did you manage that?' My father looked at me suspiciously.

'Oh, just personal charm.'

'Baloney! What did you do to make Richard cry like that?'

'I'll tell you about it sometime. But now, let's get away from this wretched place and find somewhere to eat. I'm starving.'

We found a pleasant café nearby and ordered a delicious Australian salad with cold meat. Over a good hot cup of tea I confessed my sin. Bumpa laughed heartily. 'Well, it did the trick, but don't make a habit of it. Poor little chap!'

He told me we would have another early-morning start. 'I've checked with the airline, and we have to report at the flying-boat base in Rose Bay at six o'clock. We'll go back to the YWCA now so you can get some rest. I'll call for you at half-past five in the morning.'

I set the alarm, and woke refreshed and excited at the thought of crossing the Tasman Sea in a flying-boat. It made me feel closer to John. I wondered how he was getting on – if he was still in Cairo or back in England with his family.

The last lap of the journey went smoothly. I was packed, ready and waiting when Father arrived in a taxi and we were soon speeding along the marine drive to Rose Bay. The water glinted in the early morning sun. The purser met us and took Richard with him out to the boat in the crew launch. After the necessary formalities, Father and I followed and settled in our seats, ready for take-off. I'll never tire of the thrilling sight of the wall of water growing higher and higher, splashing against the window as the flying-boat picks up speed and rises like a bird, shaking the drops of water from its feathers.

I was going home! After the adventures of the last five years I would soon be back with my family in my own homeland. What a wonderful thought!

5

New Zealand

HOME! What a wonderful word! After five years of hazards with uncertain travelling during the war, it gave me a great feeling of safety and security to be with my parents again in Seatoun, Wellington. Here nothing seemed to have changed – except a few more grey hairs on Mother's head, and a few less hairs around Father's bald pate. It was such a relief to be able to talk to them about my experiences and adventures, instead of trying to explain things in letters. I loved them dearly. They were patient and understanding. I missed my younger sister, Pat, who had sailed for England a few months before. But we would have a joyful reunion with her, when Richard and I arrived in England.

The morning sun came streaming in through the windows of the porch where I slept. I enjoyed looking out on the blue-green waters of Wellington Harbour. With clouds scurrying along, casting shadows over the distant hills, it was an ever-changing scene. Staying with my parents in such a beautiful place, I should have been happy, but as the weeks went by, I longed to see Johnnie. It was nearly three months since I'd said goodbye to him. As I gazed out of the window watching the waves breaking over the sail-boats anchored in Worser Bay, I wondered where he was and what he was doing.

Richard's cry from his cot in the room next door, disturbed my reverie. He made sure I hadn't time to sit around and mope. I sighed and went in to see him before he woke Mother. As I bent over his cot to lift him, I heard a whistle – at least I thought I heard a whistle – a very special whistle. John and I had used the first four notes of

Beethoven's Fifth Symphony – the victory call – as our recognition signal – ever since we were married. It was handy for finding one another in a crowd.

As I picked Richard out of his cot, I thought I heard it again. Don't be so stupid, I said firmly to myself. You're still dreaming! John's in England, thirteen thousand miles away. Stop imagining things.

But again I heard it, nearer and louder. With Richard still in his pyjamas I went to the front door and opened it, and there – walking down the path – was John. I gasped! I just couldn't believe it! I thought I was not only hearing, but seeing things. I couldn't move. John ran down the last few steps and Richard and I got tangled up in his arms. Tears ran down my cheeks with shock, surprise, and happiness.

'Oh, John, Johnnie, what are you doing here? How did you get here? Why on earth didn't you let us know you were coming?' The questions tumbled out as I tried to believe this was real. It was wonderful, wonderful, to see him again.

Father had been in the dining room enjoying his favourite breakfast of meat paste on toast with raw tomatoes. When he heard the shrieks from the front door he came out to see what was going on. He looked a bit surprised to find me in the arms of a strange young man.

'Daddy, this is John! He's flown all the way from England. I don't know how, and I can't believe it, but isn't it terrific?'

Father greeted John warmly – as if it was a normal thing to find a son-in-law he'd never met, on the doorstep at eight o'clock in the morning. 'Come in, come in, John. Welcome to our home.' He picked up John's only piece of luggage – a blue canvas parachute bag John and I had made together in South Africa – and we followed him through the lounge into the dining room.

'Let's have some breakfast. You sit this side, John, and then you can see our wonderful view.'

When Mother came out of her room to see what all the noise was about, she was quite overwhelmed to find her new son-in-law sitting, with Richard on his knee, at the table calmly eating breakfast, as if he'd been there for days.

'So this is John! How wonderful to meet you at last.' He got up to greet her and gave her a big hug. 'But what a surprise. It's quite taken my breath away and I'm sure Vivienne is speechless – for once.' She twinkled at me and joined us at the breakfast table.

'Well,' said John, 'I've never known Viv at a loss for words, but yes, she certainly was surprised.'

'Here's a good hot cup of tea, Mother. I think you'll need that. It's not every day you have a son-in-law drop in unexpectedly.'

She sat down at the table. 'And what do you think of this young man? We're very proud of him. You love to come into Minga's "pozzy" in bed for a story and a cuddle, don't you darling?' She stroked Richard's fair curls affectionately. Again it was Betty's daughter, Jayne, who had christened Mother, 'Minga' because she couldn't say 'grandmother'.

'He's just great, and grown so much. The New Zealand air must agree with him.'

I had so many questions I wanted to ask and said impatiently: 'Come on, let's go and sit in the porch. I'm dying to know how you managed to get here when you're supposed to be in England on a flying course.'

'Oh, I hitch-hiked,' John said nonchalantly.

'Oh, don't be so infuriating. You just don't "hitch hike" on aeroplanes.'

John gave my hand a squeeze. 'Well, it seemed a long time since I'd seen you and I thought it was a good idea to come over and meet your parents.'

'It's a marvellous idea. But what about your flying, and your conversion course? Haven't you started that yet?'

He explained that, when he arrived back in England after a month in Cairo, he had been granted leave as the course was postponed.

'I managed to wangle a flight as Supernumerary Crew on a flying-boat going east. It was great fun. I spent a night in Augusta in Sicily, another in Alexandria, and then one at the old rest-house in Karachi, where the staff gave me a big welcome. We spent a night in Rangoon before going on to Singapore. I wasn't sure how I was going to get a flight down to Australia...'

I could see Bumpa was intrigued with the matter-of-fact way John talked about his adventures and the uncertainties of his journey.

46

'Luck was with me in Singapore,' John continued. 'I heard that Qantas had an ex-bomber Lancastrian flying to Sydney. I talked the manager into letting me have a seat. It wasn't exactly a comfortable flight – but here I am.'

'Just like that,' I said. Flying in a converted bomber would be very different from the comfortable armchair seats of the flying-boat. I thought of the long hours flying from Singapore to Sydney and the noise of the Lancastrian as it lumbered along. John never seemed to notice aircraft noise. During the war, flying Wellington bombers, he had become immune to it. But he would have enjoyed the trip more if he had been piloting instead of a passenger.

On arrival at Kingsford Smith Airport he put his name down as 'standby' for the TEAL flying-boat, leaving Rose Bay the following morning. This was John's first trip 'down under', but later he flew regularly to Australia and New Zealand. He felt more at home on the S.30 flying-boat flying across the Tasman Sea. Looking down on that fearsome ocean he remembered Sir Francis Chichester, that intrepid flyer-sailor, who navigated and flew a Moth aircraft, fitted with floats, on an historic flight across the Tasman to Norfolk Island, and on to Sydney.

Landing at Mechanics Bay in Auckland, John then had to find the best way to get to Wellington. He thought about phoning us, but decided it would be more fun to spring a surprise.

'And what a surprise!' I said. 'What would you have done if we'd been away?'

'Oh, I felt sure someone would be home, so I didn't bother.'

We laughed when John described the train journey from Auckland on the Limited Express. I don't know how this particular train got its name. Perhaps because it had 'limited' facilities or possibly 'limited' stops. It certainly wasn't an 'express', as it took all night to do the 400-mile journey from Auckland to Wellington. In England the trains have small compartments for six or eight people. The Limited Express had no sleeping compartments and the Pullman cars were long carriages with hard upright seats.

Shortly after the train left Auckland, John went to look for a restaurant car. He walked the length of the train, but found nothing. Before he sat down again, he decided he had better find the toilet. The door was not locked and he was surprised to find a man inside tipping a large bottle of beer down his throat. He felt embarrassed and could not understand why the man should choose such an unlikely place for his refreshment. John knew nothing about the liquor laws in New Zealand which, at that time, restricted the time and place for consuming anything alcoholic.

'Come in, come in, and shut the door,' the man said quickly. John was a bit suspicious, but he squeezed in through the door and was handed the beer bottle. 'Ere you are, mate. Have a bloody good swig.'

John took the bottle from his 'mate' and had a good swallow. He was glad when the man took it back and went out with the bottle hidden under his jacket. This left the coast clear for John to make use of the toilet. When he got back to his seat, he found that his companion was none other than his drinking mate. He wondered what kind of a night it was going to be, and how many more bottles were hidden in the luggage on the overhead rack.

'Wot's yer name, mate? Mine's George,' he said and he stuck out a large hand. 'Where'd yer come from?'

George chatted away non-stop, telling John stories about life on a New Zealand farm. John had flown with many New Zealanders during the war and had great admiration for their courage and resourcefulness. He also knew that their language was colourful and the word 'bloody' was not considered a swear word.

As they pulled into their first stop at Frankton Junction, George said, 'Now mate, you be ready to hop out bloody smartly as soon as the train stops and find the pillow guy. See you get two pillows because they're usually in bloody short supply. I'll dash along and get us some tucker.'

John followed instructions and paid 2 shillings to hire the pillows for the journey. When he got back in his seat his mate arrived, balancing plates full of hefty ham sandwiches and solid sausage rolls, on top of the thick cups. 'Ere yu'are, mate, careful of the tea. It's bloody hot.'

As John took the cup, the train started with a malicious jerk and the tea slopped into the saucer. George had already got stuck into his sandwich. 'Bloody good tucker, eh?'

'It was too,' John told us, 'but there was no mustard on the ham. Pity – it was such good ham.' He was a stickler for certain English culinary traditions like mustard with ham, mint sauce with lamb, and horseradish sauce with roast beef. Even on a picnic he would insist that these things be provided, and he was a trial to the catering staff on his aircraft.

As the night wore on George made frequent visits to the toilet. John was amused because no one could mistake the bulge under his coat. Finally George slumped down in his seat and fell asleep. John tried to adjust his pillow into a comfortable position and ignore the loud snores that came from his mate. The regular rackety-rack of the train as it sped along was soothing, but he wished it had been a daylight journey so he could see something of the beautiful country he had heard me talk about.

Whenever the train stopped at a station, everyone made a dash for the railway café. John soon learnt that if you wanted a cup of tea and something to eat, you had to be quick and determined, or the hefty New Zealanders would get in first.

He was glad to see the sun rise and think that his long journey was nearly at an end. The hills were blue and the sea glistening as the train approached Wellington. Strangers to a city, wanting to find a house in the suburbs, would take a taxi. But not John! For him taking a taxi was a confession of weakness. He much preferred to walk. Inquiring how to get to Seatoun, he was told it was too far to walk. But he could take a tram. The tram took him through the city, and over the hills, right out to the Seatoun terminus. There he asked a paper-boy where Beerehaven Steps was – the address of my parents' home – and set off cheerfully to climb the hill on the last part of his 'hitch-hike'.

Before I went to South Africa, I was given a present of an oil painting by a well known New Zealand artist. It was of the view from our Seatoun home, and when I was feeling particularly homesick, I would gaze at this painting and remember the blue-green sea and scudding fleecy clouds over the water. When John topped the hill he recognized the view from the picture, and saw the other landmark I'd told him about – the garage on stilts which stood so high above the house. John knew he'd come to the right place, and had no hesitation in whistling our whistle as he strode down the path. Time seemed to stand still as we sat and chatted. I kept looking across at him. It was quite unbelievable that he was really here with me. Knowing that he must be tired, I suggested that he had a sleep.

'No, fear, I've done enough sitting and sleeping the last few days. I want to take Richard for a walk and go exploring.'

'I'm sorry, darling, but Richard can't walk very much now.'

'What do you mean, can't walk! He was running all over the place before you left Durban, so of course he can go for a walk.'

'Didn't you get my letter explaining about taking Richard to a bone specialist, and that he now has to wear callipers?'

'No, I certainly did not. What's this all about?'

I told John that my parents were worried about Richard's bandy legs, and suggested I took him to a specialist to see if anything could be done to straighten them. Richard had walked at an early age and slept on his tummy with his legs curled under him.

'I don't know why I should be blessed with a husband who is terribly knock-kneed and a child with bow legs,' I said rather pointedly.

I had made the appointment to see the consultant, Mr Anderson quite cheerfully, but I wasn't prepared for the advice he gave. He said that while I was in New Zealand, Richard should wear steel callipers during the day, and special padded splints when he went to bed, to try and teach him to sleep on his back with his legs straight out. I agreed to try it but it was cruel.

Richard, who toddled, climbed and ran everywhere like a bit of quicksilver, was suddenly manacled. Those beastly steel contraptions were so heavy and the poor little chap had to learn to walk all over again. My heart used to break when he fell over the slightest uneven surface. He was too young to understand what it was all about. It needed great patience on my part. Every time he used the potty the callipers had to be unstrapped. I don't think John would ever have agreed to this severe treatment – or thought it necessary. But because the doctor assured me it was worthwhile, I persevered. He recommended that the sleeping splints be used for some time after we left New Zealand.

John and Bumpa quickly became good friends, and they would escape the household chores and go for long walks around the hills. I trembled a bit when I heard the conversation turn to Father's favourite subject – cricket. I wasn't sure that John knew much about the game. But then I remembered his cunning and resourcefulness when he wrote to 'Bumpa' to ask if he could marry his daughter. He had written it in cricketing terms. I still have a copy of the letter tucked away somewhere and I'm sure that, even if Bumpa hadn't approved of a son-in-law he had never met, he would have been attracted to a man who referred to his wife as a 'batting partner'.

I was booked – yes, actually booked – to sail on the S.S.*Rangitata*, via the Panama Canal about the middle of May. As John only had three weeks' leave we had to make the most of our time together in New Zealand. John didn't get much peace as all our friends and relations wanted to meet him. We went to stay with Betty, my sister, who lived on a farm outside Feilding, about 120 miles from Wellington. John was a farmer's son and he was very happy walking over the green fields with my brother-in-law, Don. He found it strange that a sheep farm in New Zealand could be run by one man. It was so different in England. There was plenty of labour and the men employed on his father's farm, had worked there for most of their lives.

In 1947, the world was still suffering from shortages caused through the war. Transport was difficult and petrol was in short supply. We were very thrilled when Betty and Don said they had saved enough fuel to drive us to Auckland and show John something of the North Island. Mother and Father agreed to look after Richard – providing he didn't have to wear his day-callipers.

The four of us drove away from the farm in high spirits. It was a real break for Betty and Don as they had been tied to the farm for a long time.

New Zealand had never looked as beautiful to me as in those few days when I saw it through John's eyes. We drove along the Desert Road with the snow-clad peaks of Mount Ruapehu and Tongariro towering above us. At Jellicoe Point by the waters of Lake Taupo we picnicked – hot soup, cold farm lamb, and salad. John gave Betty full marks because she spread a tablecloth over the picnic table. We walked along the shore and picked up some pumice stones to take back to England. The water was shiny and blue but there was quite a wind blowing. A few picturesque yachts sped along close to the shore. We drove 40 miles along the lakeside to Taupo, and on to Wairakei to show John the geothermal site there. It's an awesome sight to watch the steam belching forth from the huge grey pipes running along the ground, and frightening to realize the power generated so near the surface of the earth.

'Ugh! What's that peculiar smell?' John asked as we came near Rotorua, the thermal wonder of New Zealand.

'Don't worry. You'll soon get used to it.' I told him, 'It's the smell from the sulphur gasses escaping from the hot pools.'

It was many years since I had been to Rotorua. John was fascinated to see steam coming out of the bush and scrub by the side of the road. It had been a long day and was dark by the time we found the Central Hotel in Rotorua's main street. There was only one double room vacant. Betty very kindly said we could stay there, and they would find another hotel nearby.

'Let's go to the Blue Baths and have a hot bath after dinner,' I said. John had never had a sulphur bath.

'Why can't we go and have it now?' said John. 'And then we'll enjoy our dinner.'

I explained that hotel meal-times in New Zealand were very rigid, and if we weren't in the dining-room before 6.30 p.m. we would miss out altogether.

'Seems a silly idea to have to eat so early.'

'Well, that's the way it is here because hotels can't get staff to stay any later.'

Betty and Don joined us for dinner. The hotel they found wasn't up to Betty's standards, and I felt very guilty. But I hardened my heart, and made up my mind to enjoy the comfort of our room, as it was our last night together in New Zealand.

It was raining hard and quite cool when we walked down the road to the baths in the botanical gardens. But when we got into the hot water we all relaxed. John – always energetic – thought he'd swim several lengths, but he soon gave up and came and joined us. The warmth seeped through into our very bones, and we spent half an hour just sitting around in the water, chatting, until we all felt deliciously sleepy, and decided that bed was the best place.

Maybe that was the night that Number-Two Son came into being. I could never be quite sure, but as I lay in John's arms I was very, very happy, and grateful to have this unexpected time with him.

The next morning it was a different story. I never got used to these farewells. The life of a pilot's wife is an all or nothing existence. One minute you have a husband by your side sharing all the responsibilities and the next moment...whisht...away he flies, and you are left, literally, holding the baby.

The drive to Auckland passed in a kind of dream. We drove straight to the flying-boat base and there she was – the graceful lady sitting in the water ready for her flight across the Tasman Sea. John turns into a different person at the sight of an aeroplane. He immediately identifies himself with the plane, and his eyes sparkle at the thought of taking to the air again. Sure he loves me, but it's a schizophrenic existence.

He boarded the launch which took the passengers out to the floating flying-boat. I stood disconsolately on the little wharf with Betty and Don. We watched the hatch-door close and heard the engines start up one by one. Then she moved forward and gathered speed along the flight-path, flinging the water from side to side. Away she flew, climbing smoothly over Rangitoto Island, and turned her nose northwards up the coast, to cross the Tasman Sea, on her way to Australia. We watched until the tiny dot disappeared in the clouds.

I turned away sadly, gulped a bit, and got back in the car. How long would it be before I heard that whistle again?

6

Journey to England

Memory is like strands of wool – some brightly coloured and easy to see, and others, grey, hazy and impossible to unravel. The memory of my departure from New Zealand, is like the latter: grey and tangled. I remember I was devastated saying goodbye, once again, to my parents. Mother had grown so fond of Richard. It was a terrible wrench for her to kiss her grandson goodbye, without knowing when she would see him again. And Father would miss the little boy who sat on his knee to play the game of 'the watch'. Father was so proud of his gold fob watch that hung across his ample middle. This had been presented to him when he was captain of the Otago Cricket Team, after they had won the Plunket Shield for the first time. Father would hold his watch and tell Richard to blow. The watch would miraculously spring open, and Richard would shriek with delight. That picture will always remain one of those bright, vivid strands of memory.

We were booked to sail from Auckland on the *Rangitata*, a New Zealand shipping company vessel. Mother hated farewells so Father took us to the Wellington station, a large imposing red-brick building, to catch John's famous overnight Limited Express train. As we walked along the platform Father looked at me and with a twinkle said: 'You know, Vivienne, you're a born traveller. Your eyes light up at the thought of "going places and seeing things". You may feel miserable at this moment, but there's a big adventure ahead of you. I'm quite sure you'll make the most of every opportunity.'

The train pulled out of the station, and skirted the harbour with the lights of Lower Hutt twinkling in the distance. Richard was exhausted and cuddled down against me as I read him one of his favourite Tank Engine stories. The train chugged on and the monotonous rhythmic sound made me feel sleepy. I thought about my father's words. I've always wanted to travel but could travel become a bug? Once it entered the system it could develop into an incurable disease, speeding through the blood and throbbing through the veins crying 'On, ever on.' Would I be able to get rid of this bug and be content to settle down in England, as a shy everyday housewife? Time would tell!

I was very glad to see my cousin, Geoff, and his wife Meg on the platform to meet us when we arrived in Auckland early next morning. They drove us through some lovely New Zealand bush to their home in the Waitakere Hills where we rested and had lunch. Later that afternoon, Geoff drove us back to Auckland to the pier where the *Rangatata* was berthed. He took care of all the luggage and saw us safely on board. I don't remember anything about the actual departure. I was too busy unpacking and settling in for the five weeks at sea.

The ship had been built in the early 30s to accommodate 250 passengers. During the war it had done great service as a troop ship. It was still under war-time conditions and we had 800 souls on board. Richard and I shared a cabin with three ladies. The two-berth cabin now had five bunks in it – two one side and three the other. When Richard lay in the bottom bunk it was difficult to change his nappy without bumping my head.

Before leaving Wellington I had taken Richard back to the doctor who had put him 'in irons'. The doctor said his legs were straighter, but he advised me to keep him in the padded plaster mould at night. At least this would keep him from climbing off the bunk and getting into mischief. I talked to the stewardess, and said I was worried about leaving him in the cabin alone when I went to have dinner. She found a tennis quoit net, and we rigged it so it hung down the side of the bunk and tied Richard in. The only trouble was that it had to be untied, when I lifted him out to 'pot' him at ten o'clock every night. Before the invention of disposable nappies, this was part of the routine child-training, to save wet beds.

I hadn't been feeling very well those last few weeks at home. When I went to see our doctor, he smiled, and told me that once again, I was 'a lady in waiting'. No doubt a result of John's unexpected visit to New Zealand! John would be delighted. But I was not sure it was the best way to start off on a five-week sea voyage. The combination of the ship's movements as we ploughed out into the Pacific Ocean and the physical upheavals taking place inside me resulted in the usual ghastly seasickness. Food was the last thing I could face, and I didn't even have my colossus, Harriet, to force ham and pickles down my throat. I can think of nothing more nerve-wracking when you are not feeling well, than trying to look after a small child on board ship. Richard had to be watched every minute, in case he slipped between the rails, which were the only protection from the sea. One of the officers assured me that more children were hurt falling out of bunks than falling into the sea. A child may have an innate sense of danger, but I doubt if any mother could sit back calmly in a deckchair, and relax.

I became even more distraught and miserable when Richard developed tummy trouble. He had developed gastroenteritis as a baby and I was always nervous about any tummy troubles. The only thing he seemed to be able to eat was jelly. I got tired of the wobbly stuff that came in such bilious colours: red, orange, green and yellow.

It is a long way across the Pacific Ocean to the Panama Canal – just water, water everywhere.

The only excitement came one moonlit night when we were called on deck to look at the blurred outline of Pitcairn Island. This remote island is about 5,000 miles east of Australia. It is famous as the home of the mutineers of Captain Bligh's sailing ship *The Bounty*. In 1790 nine men from that ship landed on the island, with six men and twelve women – natives from Tahiti. After several years of fighting over the women, all the men were dead except for the Englishman, John Adams. No one knows how they died, but John Adams lived to rule the island peacefully, and being the only male, did a good job increasing the population.

The present Pitcairn Islanders live in wooden homes in Adamstown, the only village on the island. They farm the land,

and sell their goods to the passenger ships that call. Huge breakers dash against the steep rocky cliffs and there is no safe harbour for ships to enter. Smal boats and canoes, expertly handled by the Islanders, come out to the waiting vessels with fresh fruit and handicraft for sale.

The passengers lined the rails to watch the small boats battle with the huge waves and paddle out to the ship. A mixture of fair and dark-skinned men, descendants of John Adams, clambered on board with their full baskets. There was good-humoured bargaining between the Pitcairn Islanders and passengers. I bought a gaily coloured basket with a lid for Richard's Dinky toys which were always scattered about – and a small carved figure of a woman.

The gentle movement of the ship in the swell, the moonlight on the water, and the peace without the throb of the engines, was a welcome change. Then the ship's horn gave three blasts to tell the Islanders it was time for them to leave. There was some hurried last-minute haggling, the Islanders disappeared over the side into their boats, and waved us goodbye as the engines started again, and we steamed away. We had a gentle stroll round the deck in the moonlight before going below.

I wrote a long letter to John to be posted when we arrived at the next port of call, Panama. It was a miserable letter, full of complaints about the awful journey, the cramped conditions, and how sick I felt. I had written to him before leaving New Zealand about my 'condition', and I hoped he would understand some of the reasons for my distress.

But things improved! The canal was fascinating. I remembered my first trip through it in 1935 when my sister, Betty, and I were on our way to England to study at the Royal College of Music in London. Then our ship, the *Jervis Bay* had tied up at the Port of Balboa to refuel, and we had gone ashore with some of our friends to have a wonderful, carefree day visiting the city of Panama. But this time, on entering the canal zone, the notice on the board informed us that we would not be allowed ashore, until we had passed through the canal and reached the city of Colón on the Atlantic Ocean. It was disappointing, as we had all looked forward to getting our feet on dry land again. Getting through the locks was regulated by the amount of shipping waiting at either end of the canal.

It was an exciting day going through; fascinating to watch the water being pumped into the locks and feel the ship slowly rising. We passed through the two locks at the Pacific end, and into the Gaillard Cut. Here, in places, the canal is only 150 metres wide. You can almost touch the cliffs that tower above on either side. I'd been reading a library book, about the building of the canal. For centuries sailors and navigators had dreamed about finding a passage between these two great oceans – the Pacific and the Atlantic. But it wasn't until war broke out on the other side of the world, August 1914, that the first ship, *S.S.Ancon*, sailed through. Because of giant landslides in the Gaillard Cut, and political difficulties, the official opening of the canal didn't take place until July 12th 1920. Thousands of labourers worked, using steam shovels and dredges in jungles, hills and swamps. But the greatest obstacle in the building of the canal was disease – the dreadful loss of human life through tropical diseases – yellow fever, malaria and bubonic plague.

Now we sailed through it effortlessly, out into the wide Gatun Lake. It was a beautiful clear day. We sat on deck and basked in the sunshine happy that we could see LAND on all sides.

At Cristóbal, the port of Colón on the Atlantic side of the canal, we were given 12 hours to go ashore and explore. I felt I couldn't do much sightseeing with Richard, but a young man, Peter, and his two friends took me under their wing and we had a blissful day – just being tourists. After nearly three weeks at sea it was great to walk on firm ground again, although the earth seemed unstable and kept coming up to meet me. The boys hired a taxi and we cruised around and stopped at a Spanish-style restaurant for a late leisurely lunch – lots of rice with beans and meat. Richard enjoyed the tortillas smearing the spicy sauce over his face. I hoped his tummy wouldn't object.

After leaving Colón that evening, and dropping the pilot, who had been with us all the way through the canal, we sailed out into the Atlantic Ocean for another ten days or so at sea. Things definitely improved. Peter, who had left a wife, and a son the same age as Richard, in New Zealand, offered to take over bath duties. I found bending over the large bathtub very sick-making. Peter and his two friends worked out a roster to help me. Jim volunteered to take Richard to lunch, and entertain him while I had a rest and Bill played games with him in the morning. I found it an excellent arrangement. At night, if there wasn't any other entertainment, the four of us played bridge. It is the only time in my life that I have been persuaded to play this game. It filled the evenings very pleasantly and I enjoyed being so well-looked-after. I think my cabin-mates felt it was hardly fair that I should have the attentions of three young men, when men were in short supply. The sun shone and the Atlantic rolled on without too much movement or drama. Under these new arrangements, I found shipboard life very pleasant, leisurely and secure.

We were due to arrive in England early in July, but instead of coming into Southampton as scheduled, the captain told us, at our farewell dinner, we would be berthing at Tilbury Docks in the port of London.

I felt sure John would find out about this change, and hoped he had managed to organize things so he was not out on a trip. I didn't have too much faith in the airline co-operating over such things as the arrival of a wife from the other end of the globe.

England looked cold, grey and uninviting, as we steamed up the Channel and entered the Thames Estuary. Although mid-summer, it felt more like an autumn day. I stood at the rails with Richard, Peter, Jim and Bill, watching as we tied up to the wharf and the gangway was lowered into position. We seemed so far above all the people crowded together on the wharf. I searched and searched for John, wondering again what I would do if he was not there to meet me. It was hopeless! I could not find him in that crowd. And then, behind me, I heard the whistle and turned to see him hurrying along the deck. Oh, what a joyous relief. He seemed a bit taken back, after receiving my unhappy letter from Panama, to meet a particularly healthy wife with four males in attendance. I felt quite sad saying goodbye to my kind escorts after five weeks of companionable life on board. John took Richard in his arms and I followed them down the gangway and stepped onto English soil, to face the responsibilities of a new life in a new country.

England was recovering very slowly from the shortages caused by the world war and the winter of 1947 had been one of the worst in history. People could not keep warm because of electricity cuts.

Fuel and food were rationed, and it was almost impossible to buy a new car.

John had managed to hire a jeep to meet us at Tilbury and drive us to Southampton.

'When did you find out that we weren't coming into Southampton?' I asked him.

'At about six o'clock last night when I rang the New Zealand shipping company. It was lucky the garage hadn't closed. I was to have picked the jeep up this morning.'

We left the docks behind, but as we drove through the East End of London, and through the City, I was saddened to see the gaps and the rubble left from the bombing. Building was going on, but it would be many years before the scars would be completely healed. I was heartened to see St Paul's standing mighty and firm, and said a prayer of thankfulness that this wonderful Wren church, had been spared.

'Now, tell me about the house. Is it ready yet?' There were so many questions I wanted to ask. Before we left Durban we had decided to build a house in Southampton. John's parents had found a suitable piece of land in Bassett, a suburb about two miles from the centre of the city. An uncle of John's had a building firm in Southampton and he had sent us various house plans before we left South Africa. The size of a house was restricted to 1,100 square feet and it was difficult to get building permission. Dick had promised to do everything he could to get the plans passed, and build it for us.

John sent glowing letters to New Zealand, full of enthusiasm about the site, house, and garden. I was excited at the thought of our first real home, and was quite sure, from his letters, that as soon as I arrived, we would be able to move in.

As we drove south, I chattered away about the house and the plans I had made. John was very quiet. He couldn't get a word in edgeways. Then, ignoring all my enthusiastic plans, he started to tell me about our friends who had recently arrived from Durban. I tried again.

'Darling, it's wonderful to be with you after this long time and hear all this but I want to know about the house. I'm dying to know when we'll be able to move in.'

'Well,' said John reluctantly, 'there were all kinds of hold-ups over the planning permission. Then, because of the delay, Dick was called away to do another job. Don't worry too much. I've done a lot of work on our room and put a partition up so Richard won't ...'

'Room!' I exploded, 'I don't understand. What do you mean, "room"? You mean to say we are going to live in one room – not even a flat?'

'I'm sorry, darling, I know this must be a big disappointment for you. Southampton was so badly bombed during the war, and parts of it completely flattened. Flats are scarce. I really have tried. I was fortunate to find this big room in a large house where some of the other pilots stay. They'll keep an eye on you when I'm out on a trip. Our furniture is still in store, but I've managed to buy all the essentials. I've even found a lovely three-sided mirror for you.'

I just stopped myself from saying that in my present condition, and for the next few months, a three-sided mirror was the last thing I wanted. I certainly didn't want to look at the 'bulge' from all angles.

'And how do I cook in this wonderful room?'

'Oh, I've managed to find a double gas ring.'

'You mean I don't even have an oven?'

'Now, darling, I'm sure you'll manage to produce all kinds of good things on that little stove. It's hard to accept the delays, but try to make the best of it. After all it's only temporary.'

'Yes, but how temporary? How far have they got with the house?'

John hesitated. 'There was another hold-up because of the shortage of cement. The foundations weren't laid until a couple of weeks ago. Dick says the builders will be free to start work in a few days. The house should be ready in about two months.' Poor John! He hated to tell me this after the glowing reports he had sent to me.

'What about your parents? Can't we go up and stay with them for a while? I'm sure they're longing to see their grandson – to say nothing of meeting their new daughter-in-law. I hope I'm not too much of a shock for them.'

'I didn't tell you in the last letter, but they've sold the house in Aston Rowant and moved into some rented accommodation until they decide where they want to live. At present they don't have a spare room for us. The house in the Chilterns wasn't a success. They found it terribly cold and weren't used to being so far away from their family and friends.'

We had known, before we left South Africa, that John's father had been ill, and the family farm had been sold. This was just before the end of the war. His parents retired, and bought a house in the village of Aston Rowant.

As we drove through the beautiful English countryside, I tried to relax and enjoy seeing the quaint thatched houses with their colourful gardens. I knew John had tried hard to make our arrival special, but I needed time to adjust to the thought of living in a single room. Richard, who had fallen asleep almost as soon as we left London, was demanding a drink.

When I saw a sign, Southampton, I said, 'How near are we to where we're going to live – Bassett Heath Avenue isn't it? Let's drive down and see how the house is getting on?'

'No, I don't think that's a good idea. It's been a long exciting day for you and Richard needs something to drink. I've got some lovely strawberries for you. We'll go and see the house tomorrow, after you've had a good night's sleep.'

We drove down the avenue, past tents where German prisoners were still living while they waited to be repatriated. We passed a big park on the right and then turned left into Winn Road. John stopped the car outside one of the big, old-fashioned houses.

He bent over and kissed me. 'This is it. Welcome back, my darling. It's not what we planned and hoped for, but together we can make it home.'

7

Southampton

The house in Winn Road was large and rambling with the bath-room and loo halfway up the stairs. Our room was big, but, with a double bed, the partitioned part for Richard's cot, a table, chairs, and the small gas stove in the kitchen department, it was crowded. The big sash windows rattled in the slightest breeze, and the door had an annoying habit of opening, even though it had been shut firmly. John said that, although this house hadn't actually been bombed, it had suffered damage, because of a blast in a nearby street. Now nothing fitted properly.

The building of our own house, which we had decided to call 'Anakiwa', made slow progress. Sometimes when John was away on a trip, and it was fine, I made a picnic lunch, and pushed Richard in the pram to Bassett Heath Avenue, to watch the men at work. Richard loved to tear around the unmade garden and find bits of wood the builders had discarded, to build his own house. The section was steep and the house below road level. They had dug a narrow path between two high clay banks down to the house, but it wasn't wide enough to take a pram. A lot more excavation would have to be done before we could drive to our front door.

Even though the war had been over for two years there were still many restrictions. Coupons were needed to buy meat, eggs, milk, sweets and furniture. These had to be collected every month from a central depot. Each new household was given enough coupons to buy two suites of furniture. So you couldn't have a lounge, dining-room, AND bedroom suite. As we had sent over beds from South Africa we decided to use the coupons for the lounge and dining room suites. That 'utility' furniture, as it was named, was basic, but well-made. Not much choice but very serviceable.

Curtain material also needed coupons. John said he had packed the curtains from our Durban flat. So when we did get our cases, I thought I could make those fit some of the windows of the new house. In later years, as we moved from house to house around the world, I developed a thing about the remaking of curtains. My dream was that one day I would go into a shop, choose the material, give an order for the curtains to be made and hung by a professional. It hasn't happened yet – but some day!

Southampton's shopping centre had been badly bombed. The furniture shop we dealt with, Plummer Rodis, was being rebuilt and in the meantime its various departments had moved to different suburbs. Curtain fabrics were in a shop in The Avenue, but the flooring department had moved into a makeshift warehouse near the docks.

For me, those first few months in England were grim. I tried hard to hide my misery from John. He had looked forward to returning to his homeland. He loved his job with BOAC. It was up to me to adjust to the difficulties in England and accept the responsibilities of being the wife of a pilot. But it was all so strange after our life in Africa. Because we didn't have a car, I couldn't even have the joy of meeting the flying-boat when John returned after the long five-week trips. The rumours, before we left Durban, had been that the operational flying-boat base would be in Southampton. That was the reason we had chosen to build a house here. But the rumours turned out to be only 'rumours', and the base was still at Poole Harbour, near Bournemouth. Until we managed to buy a car it was impossible for me to get over there.

Then a wonderful thing happened. An act of friendship from an unexpected source lifted me out of my depression and made life worthwhile.

It happened on the day John was due home after a long trip, and I was feeling particularly fed up that I couldn't go and meet him. When Richard and I returned to the house in Winn Road from a walk in the park, we found a note on the hall table. It said quite briefly: 'I'm bringing my car around at two o'clock so you can have it for the afternoon. There will be enough petrol in it for you to go over to Poole and meet your husband.' It was signed 'Margery'.

Margery Minns! I hardly knew her. Because meat was rationed you had to be registered with a butcher. One of the pilots, Ally, who was Richard's godfather, had taken me to a butcher's shop nearby, and introduced me to a tall lady in a white coat who ran the business. She knew a number of the flying boat captains and one of them rented a room in her flat. She accepted my coupons and said she'd do her best to keep me supplied with meat. She was rather reserved and somewhat forbidding, as she eyed Richard making a sawdust castle on the floor of the butcher's shop. She asked if there was anything else she could do for me. I must have said something about the difficulty in not having a car. But I didn't realize what a fairy godmother she would turn out to be.

I could not believe my luck when I found Margery's note that morning. Promptly at two o'clock I heard the car pull up and rushed down to thank her. But typically, she had left the keys on the hall table, and disappeared.

I was so excited and exhilarated to be behind the wheel of a car again. I drove slowly through Southampton and out onto the open road into the New Forest. It was a perfect summer day with the sun peeping through the thick green foliage of the trees. Trees, and more trees in all their summer glory. Driving in the country and breathing good clean air. Bliss! I stopped the car when I saw some brown, silky New Forest ponies by the side of the road, and watched them as they munched away contentedly at the grass. I wanted Richard to see them, but, as usual, he had reacted to the motion of the car and was curled up on the back seat, fast asleep. I was left on my own to enjoy the countryside. Bournemouth's a confusing city and I got lost trying to find the way to Poole Harbour. But it didn't matter as I was in plenty of time. I parked the car alongside the water and waited until I heard that welcome sound overhead. Richard woke and we got out of the car and watched the flying-boat come glinting out of the sky like a great big seagull. It glided gracefully onto the water with hardly a splash.

Well done, John, I thought. That was a peach of a landing. Hope you did it and not the first officer.

It seemed an eternity before John finally got through the formalities and came out ready to get into the crew car to take him to Southampton. His face lit up when he saw me.

'Good gracious Viv, what a surprise! How on earth did you get here?'

He gathered us into his arms oblivious of all his crew members watching. John is very 'English' at any display of emotion in front of people. But this time, he had really been taken by surprise and couldn't help showing his delight and affection .

'It was Margery's idea,' I explained. 'She knew how disappointed I was not to be able to come and meet you, and lent me her car. I think it was a wonderful thing to do. Fancy lending a car full of petrol to a comparative stranger. I'll never forget her kindness.'

'You drive,' John said as we got into the little Ford. After a long trip he was very content to let me take over the wheel. He liked to light his pipe, unwind, sit back and enjoy the countryside. As we drove along we passed several wayside stalls selling strawberries.

'Let's be extravagant and have strawberries for supper,' I said.

I stopped the car and John got out and bought two punnets of the luscious big berries. Richard decided that he couldn't wait until supper so his father indulged him and picked out a particularly big juicy one.

'Watch out!' I cried. 'The juice will be all over the place.'

Too late! The juice oozed down Richard's chin and onto John's uniform trousers.

'Ugh! What a mess!' said his father, taking out his handkerchief and wiping Richard's face – and his trousers.

I grinned to myself in spite of the trouble I knew I would have trying to get the strawberry stain out of the white handkerchief. It was always the same. John hated messes, especially sticky messes. But then, when a father has been away for weeks, he is apt to be indulgent one minute and upset the next – especially when the child gets fruit or ice cream over his clothes.

We enjoyed the strawberries for supper but then, alas, I went on enjoying them all night. I found that 'Opus 2' strongly objected to strawberries and kicked out against them. I tried several times during the next few weeks while the strawberries were so plentiful.

The result was always the same; uncomfortable wind rumbling around inside trying to find an exit! I decided that the pain inflicted wasn't worth the pleasure.

The day after John came home, a long awaited letter came from BOAC. It said that our car was ready to be collected from London. It was almost impossible to order a car through normal channels. All motor firms had a long waiting list of people wanting new cars. When the crews returned from Africa, they were given the chance to order a car through the airline. John had hoped he would have ours by the time Richard and I arrived in England but nothing had happened. BOAC had ordered the cars from the Vauxhall works but everyone had to wait their turn.

This was wonderful news. John said he would look after Richard while I went to London by train to collect the car. Our joy was somewhat dashed when we listened to the news that evening. The Government regretted that it was necessary to bring petrol-rationing back. Coupons would be issued immediately. I cheered up a bit when I heard there would be an allowance made for pregnant women. Good to know there were some advantages in being pregnant! This would give us a few more gallons. But oh, the joy – the wonderful thought of having a car again!

My sister, Pat, was in London doing a stage production course at the Old Vic Theatre. She was very busy and hadn't been able to get down to Southampton to see us. I phoned her that night, and we arranged to meet for lunch at the Royal School of Music, just behind the Albert Hall, where I had spent four years before the war, studying violin and singing. I was longing to go back and see if any of my old friends were still around.

It was a wonderful day. I bubbled over. I walked up Prince Edward Road to the college. A cacophony of sounds greeted me as I climbed the steps into the entrance hall. It all looked much the same although the tennis court at the back, where Betty and I used to play tennis, had been built on. I looked into the hall where I once played the solo violin in the *Symphonie Espagnole* concerto by Lalo with the first orchestra under the baton of – the now Sir – Malcolm Sargent. Sargent was a 'glamour' conductor, a dynamic personality who made an orchestra sparkle. He was not always kind to soloists, especially student soloists. I remember at the final rehearsal, he started the last movement faster than I could play it. He glared at me when I stopped, and asked him to take it slower. I don't remember much about the concert. I was so nervous.

I sat down at the back of the hall and listened to a string quartet rehearsing. Memories, memories! There was no one I knew in the office. I went down to the restaurant to wait for Pat. The menu hadn't changed much; still baked beans and Scotch eggs. Because it was the cheapest dish, Betty and I usually ordered baked beans on toast.

It was seven years since I had seen Pat. My little sister! I wondered how much she had changed and if I would recognize her. But when she walked in, there was no mistaking that 'Blamires' look. It was an emotional greeting. We had so much to talk about. She was very enthusiastic about her work at the Old Vic. It was the first course in production to be held since the war. She had had quite a fight to get accepted.

'I had to use a letter of introduction from the New Zealand High Commissioner in London, Bill Jordon, to get an interview with Dame Sybil Thorndyke,' Pat told me. 'She was most encouraging and we had a delightful talk. She had a warm spot for all New Zealanders as she had enjoyed her visits there. A few days after the interview, I had a phone call from the Old Vic Theatre to say I was accepted for the production course, so she must have done something to help.'

' Aren't you disappointed not to be in the acting course?' I asked her. Pat was very gifted and had many talents but her heart had been set on becoming an actress.

' There wasn't a hope of getting on that course. It was booked months ahead. I'm working under wonderful producers. There's so much to learn and it's a terrific challenge.'

She asked if we were in the house yet. She said she was dying to come down and see it, and could she bring a friend.

'Male or female?' I asked rather jokingly.

'A rather interesting male, Roger Evison – quite special.'

'We'll be delighted to meet your friend. Come any time. Is it serious this time? You haven't met John or your small nephew yet, and he's very special. It's great to feel I've got some of my own family in England. I've been a bit overwhelmed meeting all John's relations It's a most complicated family.'

I was dying to hear more about this 'friend' but I had to collect the car at two thirty. Pat came with me to the garage where we found our beautiful, new, shiny, blue car already for the road. I proudly signed all the papers and handed over the cheque.

I drove Pat to the nearest Underground station, gave her a big hug and drove away – the proud owner of a Vauxhall Velox motor car.

8

Bill's Arrival

The months went by. I got bigger – if not better. I was seldom on my own because, when John was away, the other pilots living in the house would take turns in 'Richard sitting'. They had a habit of appearing at meal times. I became an expert at making a little go a long way – adding this to that. It's wonderful what can be produced on two gas rings, without even a refrigerator.

Our special New Zealand pilot friend, Ally, and I would sometimes wander down to the local pub, the Cowherds which was at the bottom of Winn Road. If it was fine we would sit outside, enjoy a beer and sandwich, and then take Richard to the pond in the park, where he could sail his boat. Ally, a confirmed bachelor – as we thought – had just become engaged to Mary. Ally was full of plans for their wedding in a few weeks' time, and was looking forward to having a home of his own.

Tragically, he was later killed in one of the very few flying-boat accidents. This happened on Ally's first trip away after their honeymoon. The boat was on its way back to England, and came to grief at Bahrain when trying to land on a glassy mirror-like sea. The captain survived, but Ally, who was the captain under supervision, died. Ally was one of the 12 pilots who had been seconded to British Overseas Airways from the Royal Airforce, and sent to South Africa to learn to fly flying-boats. When demobbed, most of them signed contracts with BOAC.

Mary, Ally's wife and I had become good friends. I was devastated when the BOAC manager in Poole, phoned me immediately after the news of the accident came through, and

70

asked if I would go and tell Mary. It was a heart-breaking job. Poor Mary! She was in her flat at Hythe, and had everything prepared for her husband's return. An absolute tragedy. It was impossible to believe. They had been so happy and looking forward to settling down and having a family. I brought her back to Southampton to stay with her mother. After a few days, Mary called and asked me to go to her flat and clean out the fridge. She felt she couldn't face doing this herself. She wanted me to use whatever food I could find. I brought a cooked chicken back with me – a delicacy in those days – and served it for dinner. Somehow we couldn't bring ourselves to eat it.

John hated not having his carpentry tools around him. He was like a caged lion in that one room. One morning when he had arrived back from a trip to Australia, he was very quiet at breakfast. Suddenly he said to me: 'Look, Viv, I've been thinking. I know you're utterly fed up living in this room. If I can get the firm to lay the carpet and the linoleum this week, how about moving into the house, even though it isn't quite finished? I could do so much more work there if I was on the spot. The builders might get a move on too, if we are there to annoy them.'

'What about painting and decorating? In my present state I can't do much of that.'

'We have to leave the plaster inside to dry, before we can paint or paper, so we can't do any decorating yet. I'll phone the warehouse and see when they can deliver our crates from South Africa. I'd like to see you settled in the house before I go away again. What do you think?'

Think! All I wanted to do was get out of this room and have some space to move. I had come back to England with such enthusiasm, looking forward to moving into our own home. These few months had been dreary with nothing but delays – delays with the builders – delays over materials – delays over anything we ordered. It was already October and the days were getting shorter.

'OK. Johnnie. Let's try and move out of here on Saturday – even if we have to camp in the house.'

The day we piled our suitcases in the car and drove to our new home, was wintry, cold and damp. The house with three bedrooms – or rather – two bedrooms and a tiny boxroom upstairs, seemed palatial after Winn Road. There was still only a steep path down to the front door, and John slaved away all the time he was home, widening the path to make a drive, and carting wheelbarrows of earth and clay to the back of the section.

He heard it was possible to employ German prisoners from the rehabilitation camp in the evening. They would do gardening and odd jobs in exchange for a meal. The first POW, Heinz, was a big chap, over 6 feet. He would cycle from the camp on Southampton Common and work in the garden until it was too dark to see. He helped John build the garage. John didn't know how he was going to get the cement up from the mixing floor to form the flat roof. It was no trouble for Heinz. He stood on the ground, and with the greatest of ease threw shovelfuls onto the roof.

Waiting such a long time to be repatriated was hard on these prisoners. Karl, the second prisoner who helped us, had a son a few years older than Richard. He liked having Richard working beside him using his little red wheelbarrow. They would come inside and sit beside one another at the table to have supper. Richard was a friendly little chap and talked away quite happily to Karl. Sometimes I would go into the dining room to set the table and find them both sitting on the floor mending a Dinky toy. Richard's toys always seemed in need of repair. Karl was an industrial chemist from Dresden. When he returned to what was then East Germany, I sent him parcels of clothes, orange juice and codliver oil for his young son. Every year since then, no matter where we have been in the world, Karl has sent us a Christmas card, giving us news of his family.

Sometimes when John was away, I would shut the lounge door, open my violin case, take out my fiddle, and try and get my fingers working again. Richard was not very co-operative and would keep banging on the door. He didn't like being shut away from me and I think he felt that the violin was a threat. For months I had been his security as we travelled around the world in ships and aeroplanes, living in different houses and meeting new people. I wondered how he was going to react when another little Pascoe arrived.

Somehow I got through my first Christmas in England. John was sent out unexpectedly – he'd been on standby – and Margery, once again played fairy godmother. She cooked a full Christmas dinner – chicken with all the trimmings and plum pudding. We had a Christmas tree and presents and then Richard sat on a little stool and entertained us with his loud rendering of his favourite carols, Twinkle, Twinkle, Little Star and Away in a Manger. Once he got started it was difficult to stop him.

Margery had a great way of gathering 'strays' into her home. The young flying bachelors frequently appeared around about meal-time, bearing gifts of goodies from abroad. If Margery wasn't at home, they called at the little house in Bassett Heath Avenue.

It was hardly a restful place. There were too many jobs to be done. If any of the boys came, they were soon given jobs, while I provided food at frequent intervals. I suppose because food was rationed and difficult to get, they appreciated home cooking. I enjoyed their company, especially when they brought news of John from somewhere along the route. Richard acquired a bevy of 'uncles' standing in for his daddy.

I never really believed the saying that you developed strange longings for a particular food when pregnant. But suddenly, I found my mouth watering and a great desire to suck a piece of fresh pineapple. It became an obsession! Very little fresh fruit was available and tinned fruit was a luxury. One of the captains, Bill, hunted around the shops and managed to find a tin of pineapple. I was very grateful, but it didn't satisfy my longing. The taste was completely different – nothing like that peculiar tang of fresh pineapple. I would wake up in the night and wonder how I could satisfy this craving.

The days dragged by, and I knew what it meant to be 'heavy with child'. I hated to feel restricted. It was irksome to be so cumbersome and not able to spring out of a chair. When the baby was several days overdue, I began to worry because John was still away. I didn't know whether to be glad or sorry that 'he' or 'she' was delaying the arrival.

John was due home sometime in the afternoon of January 7th. It was a wet, windy winter's day and I thought, 'It'll be just my luck if he's delayed because of the weather.'

At about eleven o'clock in the morning I began to feel a bit peculiar – nothing very definite – just 'off'. When the phone went

I rushed to it – as much as I could rush anywhere – thinking it would be news of John's arrival. But it was the Welsh pilot, Taffy Barrow.

'Hullo,' he said, 'still there! How are you?'

'Oh, I'm fine.' (Was I or wasn't I?)

'I saw John a couple of days ago in Karachi and he told me to standby in case you needed a ride to the nursing home. I'm coming up now. I've got a present for you.'

' Taffy, will you check with operations before you come and find out when John is due, or if he has been delayed.'

'OK. I'll be up for lunch.'

I put the phone down. Blast, I thought, I don't feel like cooking anything for anybody. I went into the kitchen and wondered what I could provide in the way of lunch. I guessed it would have to be sausages and mash, but the thought of food made me feel queasy.

'Maybe it's not my tummy objecting, but this young blighter at last deciding it's time to come out and look at the world.'

There were squeals of delight from Richard when he saw Taffy coming down the path. I went slowly to the door. There was a definite pain now and I wondered what kind of standby young Taffy would be. About the only thing he knew about childbirth was the short paragraph in the operations manual giving the captain instructions what to do in case of a birth on board. John had certainly never had to deal with such a situation and I doubted if Taffy had read the instructions carefully.

I opened the door and there stood Taffy holding a beautiful golden, yellow pineapple with a lovely green, frilly top. 'This is for you,' he said.

'Oh, how wonderful!' I gave him a big hug and clasped the pineapple to my prominent middle. All the juices in my mouth were working in anticipation. I rushed to the kitchen and attacked the pineapple as if my life depended on it. I thought I would sit down and eat the lot. But in the strange way with so many cravings, as soon as I had smelt and tasted the pungent fruit, I found I couldn't eat more than one piece. I carefully put the rest of it in the fridge. I wasn't sharing this treasure with anyone.

Taffy and I sat and chatted, but every now and then a twinge of pain would overcome me. Taffy looked at me nervously.

'Are you all right, Vivienne? Don't you think it would be better if I took you into the nursing home now?'

'I'm not sure, Taffy. I really would like to wait for John. Would you phone the office again? There must be some news of his arrival by now.'

Taffy went out into the hall. 'The ETA is four o'clock,' he said when he came back into the lounge, 'then it'll take him at least an hour to clear customs and drive over from Poole. Do you think you can wait that long?'

'I hope so. But I think I'll go and lie down for a while. Lunch is almost ready. Can you cope with Richard and give him something to eat?'

I left them to it and went upstairs. I felt so miserable and alone. It must be wonderful to have one's mother nearby at times like this, I thought tearfully. Mother was 13,000 miles away – at the other end of the earth. She had never discussed childbirth with me. Strange that nowadays, when every child has sex education at school, to remember how ignorant we were. I had never even seen a lamb being born, and I still knew precious little about the process of birth, even though I had produced one baby.

I thought of ringing Margery. But Margery was a spinster and childbirth had not been one of her experiences.

I thought back on Richard's birth in Durban. I had read and dreamed about the wonderful experience of giving birth. How beautiful and fulfilled the mother looked when she held her child in her arms, after she had recovered from her labours. My experience was nothing like that! I went into the Berea nursing home in Durban, on the afternoon of September 6th 1945, with pains coming and going. Most of that night I spent on a hard bed in the labour ward, alone, wondering what on earth was going to happen next. The uncertainty, ignorance and aloneness are the feelings that remain uppermost in my mind. It had taken over 24 hours for Richard – a 9 pound 5 ounce baby, to force his way into the world. During the last hectic moments the anaesthetist managed to spill some ether in my left eye. Beautiful and fulfilled! I looked red, puffy and bleary-eyed. So much for childbirth being a 'natural' process!

I dragged myself downstairs. Taffy was fussing around like an old hen, dying to take me to the nursing home and hand over his responsibility. I made a cup of tea and we sat at the table with the lights switched on. The wind whistled around the house and at times I could hardly breathe. I knew I was supposed to be noting the time between contractions. I could see Taffy surreptitiously looking at his watch every time he saw me flinch.

I went to the toilet for the umpteenth time that afternoon and found a show of blood. The departure couldn't be put off any longer.

'OK, let's go,' I said to Taffy who was still hovering uncertainly. I felt quite cheerful and in command. It's always like this, I thought. I'm hopeless when things are indefinite or uncertain, but the thought of action, any action puts me on my mettle.

Taffy put on Richard's coat and picked up my small suitcase. As we walked to the door I heard the sound of a car coming down the street. It was nearly half past five. The crew car stopped and John jumped out.

'And where do you think you're going?' He hugged me tight and then looked down at the bulge. 'Oh no. Surely it's not time yet is it?'

He sounded surprised – as if he'd forgotten about the baby. 'Do you think you can wait a few minutes while I get out of this uniform?'

'No,' said Taffy firmly. 'You just get going straight away. I've been here all day. Viv's been determined to wait until you arrived, but now there is no sense in any more delay. Here are the keys. Off you go. I'll look after Richard.'

John helped me into Taffy's car and we sped up to the main Southampton road. There were lots of questions I wanted to ask about his trip, but it was only a couple of miles to the rather dreary looking nursing home, and nothing seemed important except getting me there quickly.

'I'm glad I got back in time, darling. You'll be all right.' He bundled me out of the car and helped me up the steps to the entrance hall. Taffy had phoned the nursing home as soon as we left. They were expecting me. The nurse took one look and hurried me to the stairs.

'I'll see you in the morning, sweetheart, have a nice time.' John called out as he bounded down the steps – and he was gone.

I was furious. Have a nice time indeed! What a stupid thing to say. Did he think I was coming here for a picnic? I thought husbands were supposed to give loving support to their wives on occasions like this.

'Oh, hell,' I muttered savagely. 'Who'd be a pilot's wife? You go through agony waiting for him to come home, get all excited and worked up at the thought of seeing him again, and then he is either late or too tired to think straight and says the wrong thing at the wrong time.'

It was a blurry experience. I was given a bath, shaved with a very blunt razor which hurt, prodded and peered at by a man in a white coat. The pains came and went – people came and went. I was just a body, wracked with pain and effort to get rid of something inside, that seemed to be showing great reluctance to come out.

'Push,' said a voice. 'Don't push. Push! Relax! When the contractions come put your thumb over this gas bottle. Relax – push – breathe deeply. Steady, take it easy. That's right. Push again.' It went on and on. Have a nice time indeed. What absolute rot! 'Now steady. No, don't push, the baby's coming. That's it. Hang on.'

There was an explosion at the other end. I had no control left. My hands grabbed the iron rods of the bedhead behind me. My whole being seemed to empty out. Then I heard a cry, an unmistakable cry of protest.

I opened my eyes as the doctor bent over me. 'You've a fine healthy baby boy Mrs Pascoe. Well done.'

'Can I see him?'

'In a minute. He's just being cleaned up and weighed.'

I could hear through the wall more furious cries. 'There doesn't seem to be anything wrong with his lungs,' I said feebly as the nurse came and handed me a swathed bundle. He was all red and wrinkled with eyes puckered up and mouth open.

I peered down at him. He had such a funny old-fashioned look. 'He's not exactly beautiful is he?'

'Newborn babies seldom are,' said the nurse comfortingly. 'Now that's enough, you'll see him in the morning. We'll phone your husband and tell him he has a son.'

'What's the time?'

'The baby was born at eleven forty-five p.m. He's nine pounds six ounces, a big baby and very strong.'

I sighed. 'At least there's an end product, after all that effort. I thought of John: 'I bet he's asleep – having a nice time.'

And he was! The nurse tried off and on during the night to give him the good news. He finally heard the phone about eight o'clock.

'For unto us a son is born!' He had sang lustily to Richard when he woke him. They both came to visit me at ten o'clock, bringing me a wonderful bouquet of red roses. Richard gazed rather uncertainly at his new brother and took hold of the tiny hand. Gathering the baby in his arms, John said proudly with a twinkle in his eye: 'Look what we've got from our night out in Rotorua.'

We called him William Blamires Pascoe – a mouthful – but he was always known as 'Bill.'

9

Next Move

Bill quickly established himself as part of the family. He was a sunny contented baby taking everything in his stride. There was only one exception – FOOD! As soon as he was put in his high-chair for breakfast, he opened his lungs and let fly. There was no quietening him until I had his Farex ready, and could stop his mouth with gooey porridge. I learnt that it was much easier on everyone's ears – and nerves – to have breakfast ready before I put him in his chair. He was so different from Richard who had been a finicky eater; played and dreamed at meal-times, and had an annoying habit of turning his head away, just as a spoon was on its way to his mouth – result – nasty mess – that his father did not appreciate if he was feeding him!

Richard had accepted the arrival of a baby in the household but I had to watch him. One day I had a fright when I came into the sitting-room. Richard was lying on top of the baby in his pram bouncing up and down. I suppose he wanted to have someone to play with, but the pram was rocking dangerously and Bill was being squashed. There were screams of protest when I lifted Richard out of the pram. Fortunately Bill survived.

It was a relief when Richard started kindergarten. He was very proud of his uniform: a grey blazer with green braiding, and a grey peaked cap trimmed with green. Every morning we walked up the road to the little school. The house was beginning to feel like home and the garden was a constant joy. We planted new shrubs and made a rose walk at the side of the house.

With Richard away for the morning I started practising again while Bill slept in his pram out in the garden. I had an interview with the Southampton Educational Authority, and arranged to do some school recitals. I was happy to be playing and I found a good pianist, Jean, who was an excellent accompanist. As we didn't have a piano, I went to her home to rehearse. She was keen to play sonatas and we started to practise the G Minor Grieg Sonata together. It is a challenging piece for both violin and piano but easy listening for school children.

Margery still played a big part in our lives and found me a 'treasure' in the form of 'Mrs Bone'. She came to help two mornings a week, while I went to Jean's house to practise. Mrs Bone was clever with her hands and loved to trim hats. She bought hats at a jumble sale, and with some ribbon or a flower, transformed them into the latest model. She was always appearing in a new creation.

One morning she arrived at the house looking very sad and sorry for herself. 'I'm afraid I'll not be able to come and help you any more Mrs Pascoe. I've just been to the doctor and he told me that I've a cataract in one eye and will need an operation as soon as possible. I mustn't bend down, so I won't be able to clean floors.'

This was a blow. She was so good with the boys. Bill was easy to manage, but Richard led her a dance whenever he could. It was a good thing he went to school and left Mrs Bone adoring the baby. She had fallen out with her own family and was a lonely soul who needed something to do.

'Don't worry about the floors, Mrs Bone, I'll do those myself. You come as usual and look after the boys so I can carry on with my music.'

I needed someone reliable in the house if I was going to play my violin. It worked well, but sometimes when I arrived home after a rehearsal, and was greeted at the door by a very smartly dressed Mrs Bone, I felt she was the lady of the house, and I was the visiting charlady.

We were all settling down and getting used to life in England. It was good to be playing and earning again so I could pay Mrs Bone. Since our return to England, we had had very little money as all our spare cash was swallowed up trying to pay off the house mortgage. We were managing, but there was nothing left for extras like going out for a meal, or buying new dresses. Before leaving South Africa, I had two very smart, slim-fitting dresses made, and sent to England. Because I was pregnant on arrival, and bulging in the wrong places, I couldn't get into them. One was black with tiered fringes – quite the latest design – and they were both short – above the knee. Suddenly overnight, the fashions changed, and the so-called 'new look' came in. It was a drastic change. Now skirts were worn well below the knee – at calf level. My beautiful South African models were quite out of fashion and hung unworn, in the wardrobe.

John had spent months studying for his First Navigation Certificate. The flying-boat base moved from Poole to Berth 50 in Southampton, which made departures and arrivals easier for us. Then came the sad news that BOAC had decided to withdraw the flying-boats from service, as the bases around the world were costly to maintain. Land planes, the British Handley Page Hermes aircraft were to replace them. They took 56 passengers – almost double the number of passengers on a flying-boat. Rumours floated round, and the flying-boat crews were very unsettled. When the pilots came to visit John, there were lots of arguments about the new planes, and discussions regarding conversion courses and postings abroad. But that was flyers' talk, and I didn't take much notice.

We had a great life in South Africa, but now we were making a home in England and thinking about where the boys would go to school. So many schools had been bombed or evacuated during the war and there were not many suitable ones nearby. Richard was only five, and it seemed strange to me, as a New Zealander, that plans had to be made so far ahead for the education of one's son.

Pat had been to visit us several times, but she was very busy in London. We were absolutely delighted when she brought Roger down to Southampton. It was a great day when they announced their engagement and told us they were going to be married on August 28th at the Marylebone Presbyterian church in London. Pat asked me to be Matron of Honour and it was exciting to be planning a wedding. John and I looked forward to visiting London together, and we asked Mrs Bone if she would look after the boys while we were away. A few days before the wedding John, who was on standby, got called out for a flight to India. It was bitterly disappointing, especially for me. I don't know that these things ever worried John. He was perfectly happy flying his aeroplanes. I set off alone to drive to London.

Pat had written and told me that her wedding dress was being designed and made by one of the New Zealand students on the design course at the Old Vic, Ralph Dyer. She had chosen cream, moiré silk taffeta material. The bridesmaids' dresses were white taffeta with a sweetpea floral design.

When I arrived at her flat in London, Pat hugged me excitedly and said: 'Come and see my lovely dress. It's just arrived. Isn't it gorgeous?' It was hanging up on the outside of a makeshift wardrobe.

'Oh, it's beautiful, darling. I love the plaited material around the neck and the sleeves. Let's see the back because that's the most important part of a wedding dress.' The front skirt was straight but the back was full and gathered into a train.

She took the dress off the hanger and put it carefully on the bed. 'See all these wonderful little loops down the back?'

'Yes' I looked carefully at the dress. 'But how do you do it up? Where are the buttons?'

'Here they are.' Triumphantly she unearthed a large envelope among the mess on the table and handed it to me. 'This is the job I've left for you. Ralph didn't have time to sew on the buttons and I've been too busy these last few days. Anyway you're much better at sewing than I am. Here's the needle and thread.'

'What about a thimble? I'll never sew all these buttons on without a thimble.'

Pat rummaged around in her sewing box and finally produced a battered thimble. 'This will have to do. I never use one.'

The telephone rang and Pat went to answer it.

I settled myself down on the bed, draped the lovely dress over my knees, threaded my needle and prepared myself to fiddle with those 57 – or was it 58 – slithery little buttons. As always when I have a repetitive job to do, my mind goes into orbit. The thought of a wedding took me back to the first time I met John.

When I went to Durban to play with the orchestra the only people I knew there were an Australian pilot, Jack Slatter, and his wife

'Bertie'. I met them when I spent a wonderful weekend at Victoria Falls in Rhodesia (now Zimbabwe). Jack was one of the airforce pilots seconded to the BOAC flying-boats and Bertie and I often did things together when he was away on the route.

One morning, in August 1942, after the broadcasting session I went round to her small flat. It had been a particularly difficult programme with the orchestra and I was feeling very frazzled. I remember I was proudly wearing my lilac suit that Mother had made – lilac blouse, shoes, hat and handbag – everything to match. (Years later I found that John hated the colour lilac.) When I walked into the room I was surprised to see a young man in uniform sitting on the bed looking very much at home.

'This is Johnnie Pascoe,' Bertie said. 'Known as "Farmer Pascoe". And he's just brought me a letter from Jack. Forgive me if I go and read it.'

I flung my hat on the bed and took my shoes off. I looked at this young airman. He was not exactly tall but certainly dark and handsome in his uniform with a wicked twinkle in his eye and a roguish smile. He spoke with a strange burr and at first I took him for a Canadian.

'Would you like to go and have lunch at the Mayfair?' he asked. Bit sudden and down to earth, I thought. But I was in the mood for anything. I can't remember what else he said but that was the beginning of a stormy two year friendship. We really were poles apart. John was a farmer at heart and had never had anything to do with anyone in the artistic world. Feelings – love? – grew strong on both sides, but he didn't want to be committed and I didn't want to interrupt my career. And yet – I sighed as I struggled to thread my needle again and count the last ten buttons – here I am, madly in love with a husband, proud mother of two sons, and sewing buttons on my young sister's wedding dress.

The evening sped by. Friends popped in, we drank numerous cups of coffee, and at about nine o'clock Pat made some sandwiches. I was hungry as I had left Southampton just after lunch.

August 28th was a clear beautiful day – just the day for a wedding. Pat looked regal as she walked down the aisle on the arm of Bill Jordon, the New Zealand High Commissioner in London.

I had made sure that all those fifty-seven buttons were securely fastened and the dress and train fanned out behind her. I know that Pat was wishing, as I had, when we were married in South Africa, that 'Bumpa' could have been there to give her away. It was sad for our parents that two of their daughters were married away from home. I was proud to act as hostess, as well as Matron of Honour, but felt a bit emotional when a toast was made to 'absent family and friends'.

Our lives in Southampton had fallen into a pleasant pattern, and we were being accepted around the neighbourhood – something that takes time in a conservative suburb in England. We didn't have much money, but we had our two sons, John had his flying, I had my music, and we all had Mrs Bone. What more could we want?

I was busy writing a letter to my parents one morning when the phone rang. 'You answer it, John, I'm busy.'

I heard him say, 'Hullo, Steve,' but I didn't listen anymore. When he came back into the room he said: 'That was Steve.'

'Oh, yes and what did he want?' I went on writing. Steve and John had been friends for many years. When they were seconded from the RAF and sent to Durban, they had shared a flat. Steve was the Best Man at our wedding. In John's eyes Steve could do no wrong. I don't think Steve approved of me. I found him a pretty ruthless character and very ambitious. I felt he used John for his own ends. Perhaps I was jealous of the friendship.

' He wants me to join him in Asmara,' John continued.

'Mmmm,' I murmured not taking much notice. 'I thought he was abroad somewhere. What's he doing back here?' I said thinking that the place John had mentioned was somewhere in Wales.

'He's come back to recruit some pilots for Aden Airways. Crews will be seconded from BOAC and live in Asmara. He's just asked me if I'd like to join him.'

'Asmara! Where on earth's that? I've never heard of it'.

'It's in Eritrea.'

'And where's Eritrea?'

'Really, Viv, your geography is hopeless. Where's the atlas?'

While John was hunting in the bookshelf for our rather outdated atlas, I vaguely remembered talking to a BOAC engineer who'd been stationed in Asmara during the war. He said it was an odd place, where eggs took a long time to boil. I couldn't think why this piece of useless information had stuck in my mind. Or why boiling eggs there, should be any different from boiling them in other places.

'Here it is.' John found the page in the atlas. 'You see it's in East Africa, on the opposite side of the Red Sea from Aden.'

'Is it on the coast then?'

'No, it's some way inland, about eighty miles from the sea.'

'But surely all that part of Africa is desert? It must be terribly hot.'

'No, Steve says it has a splendid climate.'

He would say that, I thought, if he wants you to do something.

John brought the atlas over to me. 'Look, it's right in the mountains. The town of Asmara is nearly eight thousand feet. above sea level. That's why it takes such a long time to boil eggs.'

'Why does it take such a long time?' I demanded. 'It seems to be the only thing that anyone remembers about Asmara. One must do something else there besides boil eggs.'

'Oh, Viv, didn't you take physics at school? You can't boil an egg properly unless the water is boiling. Water boils at a lower temperature at a high altitude and it takes longer to get to that temperature.'

'I never put eggs in boiling water anyway.' John and I could not agree over boiling eggs at the best of times. I used the cold water method, he used boiling water and they had to be timed exactly – four minutes.

'Oh, forget about the eggs. Steve has been appointed Operations Manager of Aden Airways and is looking for pilots.'

'If it's called "Aden Airways", won't the crews be based in Aden?' Years ago I had sailed through the Red Sea and spent 48 hours in Aden and I wasn't impressed with what I'd seen. I couldn't imagine living in that barren rocky place.

'No, Steve says that the crews will live in Asmara, because it has such a good climate. According to him, it's an ideal place to live.'

'But you've just done all this study and converted to flying Hermes aircraft. What kind of plane would you be flying out there?'

'Aden Airways has DC3s. It's a small plane but the routes take us all over the Middle East. Besides Steve says…'

'Steve says, Steve says! What do YOU say?'

'I say that if the allowances are good, it'll give us a chance to save a bit which we haven't managed to do while living in England. What do you think?'

At that moment I thought a lot. I couldn't see us gathering up our bits and pieces, to say nothing of two small boys, and going off to a strange country to live in a place I had never heard of. John seemed happy flying his planes to the Far East and Australia. We had been through the difficult stage of readjustment. and our house was beginning to feel like a real home. I looked at John perched on the arm of the sofa. There was a light in his eye, and I could feel that this offer presented a challenge to him that he was longing to accept.

'Are you serious about this?'

'Well, it sounds interesting. Steve, –' he broke off, ' I think we could have some fun.'

'Fun!' I exploded. 'And what about all this? We've got our house, our car. Richard is happy at school and I'm playing my fiddle again. It would mean a complete upheaval. And what about accommodation? Do the company provide us with a house? And furniture? Do we have to take furniture out with us?'

'Well!' Just for a minute John sounded doubtful. 'At present Steve says all the crews live in a block of flats, Palazzo Valetta. It's right in the centre of town.'

'Oh no,' I exclaimed. 'Not another flat. You know you hate being in a flat without your workshop and a garden.'

'But Steve says,' (Steve says a lot I thought.) John went on, 'Steve says, that if I'd like to look for a house he's sure something could be arranged. At present there's some slight trouble in Asmara and it's better for all the families to be together in town.'

'What do you mean by "slight trouble"?' I tried not to sound cynical.

'He didn't give me any details, but said there had been some unrest among the local population and with the "Shifta"- bandits who live in the hills. But now two British battalions are stationed there things are getting under control.'

The more I heard, the less I liked the sound of this mountain city. 'And when would we go?'

'That's the snag.' My dear husband had the grace to look slightly guilty. 'Steve wants me out there straight away, so I have to make up my mind pretty quickly. Some new aircraft are being delivered and he's short of pilots. You and the boys mightn't be able to come for some weeks. It would be better for me to go out first anyway, and get everything ready for you.'

I nearly said 'Like having us live in one room when we arrived in England', but stopped in time.

'And this house? What do we do about our home?'

'Oh, we shouldn't have any trouble in letting this for two years.'

' Two years! Won't we be back in England on leave during that time?'

'Well, no. Apparently we get two months' overseas leave every two years and local leave each year.'

There were dozens of questions I wanted to ask. It seemed a crazy thing to be doing and I doubted the advisability of such a move.

'Come on, you know you'll enjoy it once you get there. You'll be able to have servants to look after the boys and a cook. I'll be able to show you many of the places we used to visit when we were flying from Durban. You know you've always wanted to see them. It will be such an adventure.'

It was no use. I could see John had made up his mind, and as A.A. Milne said, 'And that,' said John, 'was that!'

10

Departure

A few hectic weeks dashed by. John did what he could to organize and arrange some of the necessary details for letting the house, storing furniture, and selling the car. He sorted his papers and flying manuals and decided what tools to take with him.

'Don't you think you're rather overdoing the tools?' I asked him. 'Won't you have a weight restriction if you're flying as a passenger? Surely if you're going to be away from England for two years you'll need clothes for all kinds of weather?'

'Oh, we'll be issued with Aden Airways uniform. Most of the time we'll wear bush shirts and shorts. I can always have clothes made in Aden.'

I gave up. Clothes were not important to John. He was addicted to buying tools and collected them wherever he went. His suitcase often had more tools in it than clothes.

Before he left he wrote out a long list of instructions and pinned it up on the board in the kitchen.

Then he was off – leaving behind a very bewildered wife and two small boys. I studied the list but didn't know where to start. In fact I decided I could not start anywhere, until I heard from John and had some idea how long it would be before we could join him. There was no sense in trying to find a tenant for the house until I knew when it would be available for renting.

Margery was a great comfort, and when things got too much for me I would dash down to her flat and unburden myself. Not that Margery ever said very much, but she was a wonderful listener. The BOAC boys who came to the flat affectionately called her

'Minnie'. During the day she managed the butcher's shop, but in the evening and at weekends there was a welcome to all who called, and a full coffee pot on the stove. It was good coffee too, not just hot water poured over some inferior grains, but freshly ground and percolated.

Letters came from John written from the Chao Hotel in Asmara where he was staying. He said we could not come out until there was a flat available. There were more instructions! When I read them I got hopping mad.

'What does he think I am? As if I haven't enough to do looking after Richard and Bill without having to see to all these other things,' I grumbled to Margery.

One day a letter arrived from him marked 'Important' on the envelope. I opened it wondering what had happened. It said: 'Dear Viv, please ring the BOAC Medical Centre immediately, and make an appointment for you and the boys to have a full medical, including X-rays. This is necessary before you are allowed to travel out to this area.'

The letter said other things like what a good time he was having and how he was enjoying being in a small airline and flying around the Middle East. It sent his special love to me – and the boys – and at the end he said: 'I know you'll be worried about this medical, but I'm sure it will be all right. You are coping wonderfully with all the things that have to be done and we'll soon be together again.'

A medical! Don't worry! I remembered with horror the fuss there had been the last time I had a medical. This was in Durban when John was demobbed and signed a contract with BOAC. For insurance purposes it was necessary for wives to have a full medical examination. I was not worried because I had always been a remarkably healthy individual and had had few of the usual childhood diseases. Blood tests and X-rays were taken and I was surprised when the office phoned to say the doctor wanted to see us. We had gone along quite cheerfully. 'I'm sure it's only a formality,' John said, 'There'll probably be some papers to sign.'

When we went into his surgery, the doctor was studying X-rays. John and he were good friends and they chatted for a few minutes. Then he turned to me and started to ask me all kinds of questions. 'Did I have a persistent cough? Did I ever cough up phlegm? Had

I had pneumonia as a child? Did Richard have a cough? Did I tire very easily?'

It went on and on and I began to feel very uneasy. I answered 'no' to all the questions.

'What's this all about, Doctor? I fee: very well. I don't have any throat trouble and seldom get a cold or cough.'

The doctor held up the X-ray. 'The X-ray of your chest shows a definite dark shadow on your left lung, and this will have to be investigated before we can accept you for full medical insurance. I've made an appointment for you to visit the chest hospital on the Berea, next Monday. It's necessary for you to have tests as there is always the possibility that although you may not suffer yourself from tuberculosis, you could be a carrier.'

I went out of his surgery feeling unclean and upset. As far as I knew there was no history of TB in our family. I panicked and had visions of being isolated for months in a sanatorium – unable to have any contact with my little son, or have any more children.

The chest hospital I visited every month was full to overflowing. I hated going there. I was a very reluctant 'spitter' and couldn't produce any satisfactory phlegm. After six months I went back to see the BOAC doctor.

'I've got your latest chest X-rays here, Mrs Pascoe. There's still a dark shadow on the lung but it hasn't changed. All the other tests are perfectly normal, so I think we can say that there is no danger of you passing on the disease. Just in case, I suggest you take these X-rays and this report with you when you leave Africa. Always try and keep fit and don't get overtired. I would advise you to wait for a while before having another child.'

I thanked him and walked out of his surgery with a light step. It was such a wonderful relief to be given an all clear.

That all happened two years ago. When I took the two boys down to the X-ray department of the huge Southampton hospital, all the fears and thoughts came tumbling back. Bill gave no trouble and stood perfectly still, as requested, when the X-ray was taken. But for some unaccountable reason, Richard took one look at the nurse's white coat and all the equipment and went rigid with terror. He was usually fascinated by machines and I thought he would be interested in all the gadgets and cameras. But not a bit of it! He screamed and wriggled when the nurse tried to get him to hold still while she took a picture.

'Perhaps, Mrs Pascoe, it might be better if we do your chest X-ray first. Then Richard can watch and see what's happening.'

So I stood still against the plates of the X-ray machine and tried to talk to Richard and calm him down. But by this time he was too upset to listen. A doctor came in to see what all the noise was about and picked Richard up while I was getting dressed. But he struggled and fought. Finally after a very frustrating quarter of an hour, which was absolutely exhausting as far as I was concerned, they managed to get some kind of a picture. I wished the doctor luck when he came to examine the negative.

I had an appointment to see the BOAC doctor a few days later and left the boys with Mrs Bone. So much depended on the results of these tests and I didn't want any more scenes with Richard. Poor little chap! I wish I knew what had frightened him so much.

The doctor looked a bit solemn when I went into the surgery.

'Good afternoon, Mrs Pascoe. Do sit down. I understand that you are wanting to go out to Asmara to join your husband who is flying for Aden Airways.'

'Yes that's right. We'd like to go as soon as possible because John has already been out there for six weeks. If we have to wait much longer the boys won't recognize him.'

'I've had the results of the tests and X-rays. The children are fine, but –' he paused. (A lot you could see from Richard's X-rays, I thought to myself.) ' – but now as far as you are concerned -' he paused again, and then the questions started. Did I have a persistent cough? Did I catch cold easily? When was the last time I had a sore throat? Had I ever been hospitalized with any lung trouble?

I could see our posting abroad getting further and further away. I told him that I had never had any trouble with my lungs and if it hadn't been for the medical in Durban when we joined BOAC, I would never have known there was a shadow on my lung.

'You see,' the doctor explained, 'if you became ill in Asmara we would have to bring you and the children back home. The company is responsible for the welfare of the whole family. This,' he said tapping the X-ray, 'shows a decided dark spot on the left lung. I don't know that the climate in Asmara would be good for you.'

'But I'm told that Asmara is eight thousand feet above sea level. People with tuberculosis are always being sent to the mountains in Switzerland to be cured. Surely living at such an altitude as Asmara would be ideal.'

Suddenly my old fighting spirit came back. I was determined to convince that doctor I was perfectly healthy and that nothing was going to stop me joining John in Eritrea. I remembered that somewhere, I still had the X-rays taken in South Africa.

' If I bring you the X-rays taken in Durban two years ago, and there is no change, surely my condition, whatever it is, is stable, and not likely to cause me, or anyone else any trouble. You said the boys were perfectly clear so that must prove I've passed nothing on to them.'

'Well,' said the doctor, 'you seem healthy enough in every other way. If you bring me those Durban X-rays and let me compare them with these recent ones, I don't see any reason why you can't go out to Asmara.'

I went home and rummaged around in the old packing case where we had left a lot of our papers and letters. I couldn't remember seeing the X-rays since we arrived in England. John had done the final packing when leaving South Africa, so goodness knows where he had put them. Getting more and more desperate, I took everything out of the tea chest and there, right at the bottom was the large brown envelope. Leaving all the mess I bundled the children into the car and drove down to the doctor's consulting-rooms.

The receptionist took the packet and said, 'The doctor will call you when he has had time to look at these.'

I went home and spent an agonizing few hours waiting for the doctor's decision. At six o'clock when I had given up all hope of hearing, the phone rang. It was Doctor Sybald.

'Mrs Pascoe? Thank you for bringing in the X-rays. I've good news for you. There's been no change at all in this shadow so I feel I can give you a clean bill of health. Come and see me again when you're home on leave. Give my greetings to your husband and have a happy time abroad.'

If he had been in the room, I would have hugged him. All of a sudden things seemed to be falling into place. I was excited at the thought of going to Africa again. Different from South Africa, no doubt, but I would smell again that very distinct African smell.

The next day there was a letter from John saying he had moved into an Aden Airways flat. If all was well with the medical, I was to phone the office and get our names put down on standby for the flying-boat service to Khartoum, in two weeks' time.

'Only standby,' I fumed. 'You'd think that for once, as it's a BOAC posting, we would have a firm booking. I guess wives and children don't rate very highly on the priority list.'

I advertised the house for rent. I advertised the car for sale. Between deciding what had to be packed to be sent out to Asmara and what left behind, I answered inquiries and showed people over the house. I had no time to pine over leaving our first real home. There was too much to be done. As John was too far away to be consulted, I had to go ahead and make all the decisions.

The boys began to sense something was going on. Richard had a way of delving into the case where I had packed his toys and bringing them out again. He loved his Dinky toys and knew instantly when one was missing.

John had written – in one of his many letters – that our main luggage would take some time to arrive in Asmara. He advised me to bring as much as possible with me. But being limited, weightwise, things like books and music had to be left behind.

I thought if I knew the captain who would be flying us out of Southampton, I would try and persuade him to allow Richard's small two wheeler bike and Bill's tricycle to be put on board. Margery said she would look after the bikes if the captain wouldn't take them.

Dear Minnie! What a tower of strength she was! The night before we were due to leave, she collected us and all our luggage from the house in Bassett Heath Avenue, and took us to her flat. The service departed early in the morning, so it meant leaving the flat by five-thirty. I was exhausted but the boys were bubbling over with excitement. When they started to chase each other around the flat, I took them down into the garden to run off some of their surplus energy. I was being fussy about keeping them clean. I didn't want to have any more dirty clothes than necessary. They were tumbling over each other on the lawn when Bill suddenly announced in a loud voice, 'Wee-wee.' I ran to him, and tucking him under my arm, rushed to the stairs that led to the second floor where Minnie had her flat. The last thing I wanted was wet pants.

In my hurry to get up the stairs, my sandal caught on the edge of the concrete step. Trying to save myself from falling, I dropped Bill who fell face downward with a great thump. When I picked him up there was blood everywhere, and he screamed with fear and hurt. Minnie came dashing out to see what was wrong. I carried Bill into the flat and laid him on the bed while Minnie filled a basin with warm water and Dettol. As I washed away the blood, I saw there was a nasty gash on his chin near the mouth.

'I think I'd better take him to the doctor in case this needs stitching. Would you phone the surgery please, Minnie?'

His mouth was beginning to swell, but as far as I could see there were no teeth missing. I felt terrible, that just because I had tried to save the washing, I had let Bill fall. Such a stupid thing to happen. I suppose most accidents are caused through carelessness. It all happens in seconds.

I carried him to the car and Minnie drove us to the surgery. Our friendly family doctor was surprised to see me as I had already said goodbye. He dressed the cut and assured me that it didn't need stitching.

'There's no real damage but the mouth will swell and he'll have difficulty in eating. Before you travel it would be a good idea to get some drinking straws. They won't hurt his mouth as much as a cup or glass. He'll need plenty of fluid on a long flight to stop him getting dehydrated. I'll give you a prescription for a tranquilliser and something to help him to sleep on the aircraft. I'm afraid he's going to have a very sore mouth for a few days.'

We tried to find a shop that sold drinking-straws. It was too late. All the shops were closed. We found a chemist and had the prescription made up but there were no straws. The boys were getting tired and niggly so we went back to the flat. Bill didn't want anything to eat or drink – most unusual! Richard had a boiled egg – a real farm egg with brown bread fingers to dip into it. Eggs were still rationed and I had been using dried eggs for cooking.

One fresh egg a week per person meant we seldom had boiled eggs. This was a special treat from Minnie, who sometimes managed to get a few fresh eggs from a poultry farm where she bought chickens for the shop.

Minnie, whose orderly household had been thoroughly disrupted by the influx of unruly young Pascoes, hunted through her cupboards and found a packet of straws that had been there since before the war.

Bill had never seen a straw before and it was a bit like taking a horse to water and trying to make him drink. He chewed the straw, blew into it, making lovely bubbly noises, but could not get the idea of sucking and pulling.

I called to Richard: 'Have you finished your egg? Come here and help me. See if you can show Bill how to drink through a straw.' Richard had been upset over Bill's fall – almost as upset as Bill. He was very protective of his young brother and hated to see him crying. He hadn't tried drinking through a straw before, but he soon got the hang of it and sucked at a raspberry milk shake that Minnie had made for Bill.

'Hey! Don't drink it all. That's for Bill.' He put the straw in Bill's mouth and pursed his own lips and made a sucking sound. 'Come on, Billie, you can do it. Take a big breath through your mouth.' When he thought Bill was doing the right thing he put the straw in the glass and held it. Bill was highly delighted when he got some of the milk in his mouth and the glass was soon empty.

When they were both in bed I gave them a dose of the medicine. Richard went to sleep immediately, but Bill took a long time to settle. I made sure everything was ready for the morning before I went to bed. I tossed and turned. My mind wouldn't settle and through all the wandering thoughts was the fear we would get down to Berth 50 in the morning and find there were no seats for us on the flying-boat. John told me in his last letter that this would be the last flying-boat service to Khartoum as they were all being taken off the routes. If we missed this one I didn't know how or when we would be able to get to Asmara.

I was almost glad when the alarm went off and it was time for action. And there was plenty of action in getting the boys dressed and the last minute things packed away. Richard had his precious cars in a little suitcase but no matter how many times I shut it, as soon as my back was turned, it would be opened again and Richard would be 'brum-bruming' along the floor with a car.

Minnie stood by patiently, but gave a great sigh of relief when we finally got into the car. As we drove down to the wharf, my 'butterflies' started. It all depended on the airline – 'to go or not to go;' that was the question. When my inside was churning over and over, it was hard to appear calm and collected, speak gently to the boys and remember where I had put all the important documents. I felt sick. When we walked into the small passenger lounge there were far too many people milling around for my liking. I looked at them angrily. What right had they to be there? Why should they be wanting to travel today taking up all the seats?

The traffic officer recognized me and came across to greet me. 'Good morning, Mrs Pascoe. Is this all your luggage?' I wondered if he was being sarcastic as he looked at Bill clutching his koala bear, Richard hugging his suitcase, the bike, the tricycle, three suitcases, the parachute bag and me – holding tightly to my most treasured possession – my violin. 'Can I have your tickets and passports please? I'll go and see what the seat availability is like. We'll certainly do our best to get you on. I think you know the captain on this first leg. It's Captain Glover.'

I searched in my handbag for the documents and handed them to the traffic officer. 'Thank you. You're very kind. Yes, Captain Glover is an old friend from Durban.' I heaved a sigh of relief because I felt sure that 'Uncle Glover', as he was nicknamed, would not leave us behind if he could help it. He was a bachelor with a soft spot for children and I felt he would try to find space in the aircraft for the boys' bikes.

The purser came forward and showed us to a table. He brought Minnie and me a cup of coffee and gave the boys a glass of milk and some biscuits. Bill sat on my knee and tried to drink through the straw, but his mouth was very swollen and it obviously hurt him. Richard had undone the toy suitcase again and was playing with the cars under the table.

'Minnie, would you look after Bill for a minute? I'll have to try and find a piece of string and tie up this darned suitcase until we get on board … if we get on board,' I corrected myself. A piece of string is a very simple thing, but it is amazing how difficult it is to find when you want it. No one had anything that could be used. Then I remembered a pair of Richard's gym shoes in the bag. I found them, took the laces out, tied them together and put them round the suitcase. Richard let out a howl of protest when he zoomed back to the table and wanted another car. I was losing my cool and said 'No' very firmly. I was at the end of my tether and the waiting was agonizing! Some of the passengers were standing outside ready to go down the steps onto the Solent Flying Boat moored up at the jetty. I tried to count them. There still looked too many for a boat which took 40 passengers.

'Do you think you can put up with us for a bit longer if we don't get away, Minnie. I'm sorry we've been so much trouble.'

Minnie smiled. 'Don't worry, Vivienne, there's a bed at the flat and a welcome for you whatever happens. I hope for your sake that you get away today.'

As the crew boarded the aircraft, Uncle Glover turned and waved to me – but he didn't give any indication whether we were on or not.

'They surely must know soon,' I said to Minnie, 'because they're due to take off in half an hour's time.' I couldn't bear the suspense any longer and got up from my seat to look for the traffic officer. He came hurrying up the steps.

'It's all right, Mrs Pascoe. Come along quickly now and we'll soon have you settled. There are only two seats left which means that you'll have to hold this young man for take-off.' He took Bill from me and held Richard's hand. I gathered up my fiddle and hugged Minnie, fighting back the tears that suddenly overwhelmed me.

'Thank you, thank you, Minnie, for all you've done. I don't know how we'd have managed without you.' Minnie never showed her feelings and looked embarrassed at my emotional embrace.

'Hurry up now,' she said, 'they're waiting for you. Give my love to John.' She stood at the top of the steps waving as we walked across the small gangway into the flying boat. Everyone else was already comfortably settled. The purser came forward, showed us our seats and helped strap us in. Richard sat by the window and was quite at home but poor Bill looked bewildered by it all. This was a new experience. The fall had shaken him and his mouth was sore.

The door was shut. Upstairs on the flight deck the captain opened his side window and blew the Morse code C for castoff on his silver whistle. The radio officer went into the forward hatch to pull in and secure the mooring rope, and the first officer, from his seat, released the switch for the aft rope. The captain started the engines and the large seaplane began to move slowly away from the jetty.

There was quite a breeze blowing and Southampton water looked choppy. I gazed anxiously out of the window as we gathered speed and bounced across the water. Richard was fascinated as the wall of water outside grew bigger and bigger, the slap of the waves against the hull got harder and harder and the engines louder and louder. Bill hid his head on my shoulder and hung on tightly.

Then suddenly, all was quiet, the water disappeared from the window and we began to climb and set course across the Channel. I let out a huge sigh of relief. Wonderful! We were away!

11

Journey to Eritrea

Keeping small children amused in a confined space on a long journey is a challenge for any mother. I thought that with the excitement and the medicine I gave Bill, he would nod off as soon as the engines settled into their rhymic purr. Far from it! When he'd got over his surprise and apprehension during take-off, he became very lively. All I wanted to do was to sit back, relax, and sleep.

The purser had put us in the forward cabin and the seats – two either side of the table – were luxurious armchairs upholstered in pastel colours. How different from the cramped economy-class seats of a modern aircraft, where there is hardly room to move your elbow without annoying your fellow passengers. On a pristine white starched tablecloth, the table was set with sterling-silver cutlery, a silver cruet and BOAC blue and white company china. Fresh pink carnations with maidenhair fern were arranged in an elegant silver vase. A small table lamp was fixed to the side of the aircraft just below the window. It was luxury and I wanted to enjoy every minute of it.

One of the men sitting opposite me had already hidden himself behind *The Times* newspaper. Must be an Englishman, I thought. He was very correctly dressed – everything matched. The pale blue tie was the exact colour of the handkerchief folded carefully in his left pocket. Although I couldn't see his socks I was sure they must be pale grey – or blue. His slightly wavy dark hair was parted on the left side and a small well-trimmed moustache sat on his upper lip. I decided he must be an army officer. On take-off he had eyed the boys disapprovingly, annoyed no doubt, to find that at the last minute someone was sitting opposite him.

The other man sitting next to the window had silvery grey hair and a kindly expression. He had a grandfatherly look and when he saw Bill clutch me as we sat down, smiled sympathetically. When we were airborne, Richard tried to undo the shoelace around his little case and when unsuccessful – as I had tied it very firmly – beamed hopefully at the elderly gentleman. Before I could stop him, he pushed his little case across the table and said: 'Please would you untie this?' When it was undone, Richard disappeared under the table to unpack his goodies. Then he drove the Dinky cars over the polished shoes of the army-man, and out into the aisle. Bill watched for a few minutes and then scrambled off my lap and joined him. The purser, very different from the purser on my first flying-boat journey to Lourenço Marques, didn't seem to mind two small boys under his feet. In fact he was happy to enter into their games when he wasn't attending to his passengers.

As soon as we were well over the Channel and settled into a flying pattern, Captain Glover left the flight-deck and came down into the cabin. It was a tradition with the Imperial Airways commanders and the BOAC captains, to walk through the cabins and chat to the passengers. It gave them a chance to check the aircraft and it reassured the passengers that all was well on the flight-deck.

In the huge bus-like aircraft of today, the captain is a voice on the PA system, pointing out interesting places or waking you up with weather news and time of arrival.

Captain Glover stopped at our table. The military character looked up from his newspaper when the captain said: 'Good morning, Colonel Morris. I hope you are comfortable?' I felt smug that I had put him in the right category. I love watching people, making up stories about them and what they do. I could just hear this man barking orders to his officers. I wondered if he would tell the captain he wasn't satisfied with his seating arrangement and insist on being moved. But he did not get a chance.

Uncle Glover turned to me. 'Well, Vivienne, I'm sorry you had such an anxious departure. Is everything all right now?'

'Fine, just fine. Thank you very much for getting us on the aircraft,' I said gratefully, 'and especially for letting the bikes come on board. It'll make such a difference for the boys to have them to ride when we get to Asmara. If they had to go by sea we could wait months for them.'

'I'm glad there was room. You were lucky. Two people cancelled at the last minute. This is the last flying-boat service to Khartoum and also my last trip on flying-boats. I'll be starting a conversion course on the Hermes aircraft when I get back.'

'It's so sad the flying-boats have to be taken off. Everyone enjoys flying in them. They're so comfortable. Do you really think it's necessary? I thought the wonderful 'Princess' boats being built on the Isle of Wight were to be the ultimate luxury in air travel.'

'The company say it's too expensive to maintain the flying-boat bases around the world. Engineers are needed at each stop to service the boats and spares must be readily available. There have to be crews to man the launches, and it's a costly business keeping the various crew rest houses up to standard. But I agree with you. I've loved flying these old boats and nothing will ever be quite the same again.' As he turned to continue his walk through the cabins he said: 'Bring the boys up on the flight-deck later when we get near the French Alps. If it clears a little we should have a magnificent view.'

The morning wore on very pleasantly and the boys were well-occupied. Bill's mouth was still swollen, but it didn't seem to be troubling him too much. He liked drinking through the stripy coloured straw the purser found.

He didn't want to eat anything – which was unusual for Bill. We affectionately called him 'Our Dustbin', as he was always willing to finish anything Richard left on his plate.

The air outside was crystal clear and there wasn't a cloud in the deep blue sky. I could see in the distance the snow-peaked mountains of the Alps. The purser came to the table. 'The captain says you can come up to the flight-deck in a few minutes. You should have a great view of the mountains.'

I wasn't game to carry Bill up the steep ladder leading to the cockpit. He clambered up himself. Richard was after him in a flash, but I held his hand firmly once we were on the flight-deck. It was a breathtaking sight. We looked down on mountain tops where the snow dazzled us with its whiteness. It was as smooth as the icing on a cake. Away to the left the huge peaks of Mount Blanc stood out majestically. The flying-boat seemed a fragile, insignificant craft compared to the towering peaks around us.

Richard was more interested in all the instruments and the 'driving wheel'. He wanted to hold the joy-stick and climbed onto the first officer's knee. We stayed there for a while enjoying the uninterrupted view of the glorious mountains, but I didn't want to disturb the crew and took the boys back to our seats.

Soon below us the coast of the French Riviera came into view. The sea sparkled in the sunlight. It looked very inviting and my mind flashed back to a visit to Monte Carlo which Pat and I, and another friend, made just before Pat's wedding. We were on a very strict budget. Just after the war in Great Britain, there was a currency limit of £30 sterling per annum, for anyone travelling abroad.

It was late when we arrived in Monte Carlo, and we had difficulty in finding somewhere to stay. We were tired and finally, in desperation, we booked into a place high on the hill. It was far too expensive – probably a brothel – although we didn't realize it at the time. I have a vivid recollection of that room. It was very dark with heavy, red velvet curtains drawn over the windows. Gold tassels dangled from the pelmets and mirrors in gold frames adorned the walls. In the centre of the room was an enormous four-poster bed draped with red satin trimmed with gold braiding.

After we washed and tidied ourselves, we walked down the hill to find the casino. We were very innocent and nervous about such an adventure. As a Methodist minister, Father had strict ideas about gambling. Pat and I wondered what he would say if he could see his two daughters entering the famous casino at Monte Carlo. We didn't know if we would be allowed in or what we were supposed to do. But it was very simple. We bought a very limited number of chips from the bank at the entrance. They didn't last too long. No fortunes were made for us that night at Monte Carlo. With fascination we watched the concentration of the interesting characters sitting round the gambling table. One elderly lady, wearing a shabby, old-fashioned evening dress and down-at-heel satin shoes, was losing badly. She sat with her head bowed and then suddenly, got up from the table and walked towards the door. But she didn't go through it. Something pulled her back and soon she was sitting at another table trying her luck again.

It was fun weaving fantasies about the gamblers. We stood behind a very beautiful girl, elegantly dressed with jewels flashing round her neck and in her ears. She was on her own and seemed desperate to win, but all the time the chips were being pushed away from her. When we were walking up the hill after midnight to our – whatever it was – she roared past us in an open sports car. We wondered if her luck had changed and if she would be back at the casino the following night. We decided to 'top-and-tail' in the large bed and drew lots to see who was going to sleep in the middle. I lost, but insisted that the other two kept their feet well away from my face. Pat and I had great fun on that trip.

On we flew with the coast of Italy on our left. I opened the map and tried to make out some of the cities, hoping that I might see the seven hills of Rome. It was hazy and we were too far away. As we neared the coast of Sicily I could see a wisp of white smoke obscuring the top of Mount Etna. This active volcano had recently erupted again. The known history of the mountain went back to 396 BC when the fiery lava kept the Carthaginian army from reaching the town of Catania. Now, apart from the small plume of smoke it all looked calm and peaceful as we flew over the slopes and looked down on the orderly vineyards and plantations of citrus fruit and olive groves. Two bridges connect Sicily with the toe of the Italian mainland.

The town of Augusta nestles in a long sandy bay off the east coast of Sicily. We flew low over the island and landed smoothly on water that sparkled in the early-afternoon sun. It was a relief to go ashore and walk round the pleasant lawns that went right down to the water's edge. The boys made a beeline for the water and wanted to paddle, but I wasn't sure how long we would be staying. They cheered up when I took them into the cool dining-room of the rest house, where the steward served us with real Italian Cassata ice cream. Bill managed to consume that without any difficulty.

John had talked about the happy times he spent in Augusta water-skiing, while the crews waited for the next service. He had bought me a beautiful Italian silk scarf, and I was keen to see the little shop where he'd found it. The shop was full of lovely things, a joy to look at after the scarcity of luxury goods in England. The other passengers were swooping down on gloves, fine leather handbags, and silk blouses. I was tempted, but I only brought one thing – a tie for John.

As there was a crew change here I said goodbye to Uncle Glover and thanked him for his care. The Southampton crew passed on the message that we were on board, so the new purser gave us a warm welcome when we stepped on board again feeling refreshed after the break.

I felt sure that the boys would sleep on the next leg but although I had given Bill another dose of medicine before we left the rest house, it seemed to have the opposite effect. He was more awake than ever.

The kind, white-haired gentleman who had chatted to me during lunch, got off at Augusta to visit his daughter, but Colonel Morris was still with us. He had moved to the window-seat and closed his eyes. Not wanting to disturb him, I took Bill on my knee, found the A.A. Milne books and settled down to read to the boys. They both loved these poems, and I could recite them with my eyes shut. I had kept a new Rev. W. Awdry engine book to bring out in an emergency and had a colouring book and crayons ready for Richard who always needed to be occupied.

The captain kept us informed of the various points of interest. We were flying at an altitude of 8,000 feet, a comfortable height in an unpressurized aircraft. The Mediterranean Sea, far below was azure blue and dotted with tiny toy ships.

When the white island of Malta came into view, I wished John was here to tell us more about this island where he had spent several months during the siege of Malta in 1940. As a Wellington bomber pilot with 99 Squadron, he had flown 13 raids from England over enemy territory. He applied for an overseas posting, and when it came through he was sent to Stradishall Air Base in Cambridgeshire. After waiting there several days, four brand new 'Wimpey' bombers were delivered. The crews were given instructions to fly these planes to the Middle East via Malta.

One inky black night they set off with full tanks. Just before take-off, each captain was given a Heinz baked bean carton containing a quarter of a million Maltese pounds, for the Bank of Malta to pay the troops stationed there. They flew due south over France, across the Mediterranean until they came to the north coast of Africa. Then they turned east for Malta. Flying over the Italian enemy island of Panteleria, they looked down and saw the Italian airforce CR42 Fighters parked at their disposal points. They fervently hoped they would stay there. As dawn was breaking they made out the white limestone cliffs of Malta.

John had said: 'It was difficult to see in the early light but three of us made a good landing at Luqa Air Base. The fourth Wellington bomber with the new air officer command designate for the Middle East on board, got lost and made a forced landing in Sicily where the crew was imprisoned and the aircraft destroyed. No one ever knew what happened to the Heinz carton of bank notes. The commanding officer of Malta met us and took us into the mess for breakfast. He told us we would not be flying on to Cairo. We were being retained in Malta to form a new squadron, No. 148.'

Malta fascinated John. I wondered if the friendly English-speaking Maltese girls had something to do with its attraction!

Millions of years ago, this island had been part of an upthrust of high ground in the vast land-bridge joining Italy to Africa. The Mediterranean wasn't a sea at all. It was part of the mainland where wild animals roamed the forest until the earth sank and the Atlantic Ocean began to roar through the western sluice gate, the Pillars of Hercules, now known as Gibraltar. As the land became surrounded by water, hundreds of animals on their wandering flight from Arctic Europe, to warm Africa, were cut off and died because there was no food for them. John had visited museums in Malta and had seen the delicately-boned fossilized fish, and the remains of the dwarf elephants found on the island.

Malta had a turbulent history of battles, sieges and romantic stories of the knights of St John. The most famous was the French grand master, Jean de la Valette who came to the island in the sixteenth century. The main town, Valletta, was named after him.

The months John spent there were no less turbulent. He didn't talk much about his war experiences but he once described to me an air attack on Malta.

'We were stationed on Luqa Airport,' he said, 'and one morning as we were getting dressed, there was an air-raid warning. Bombs began to fall all round us, I dived under my neighbour's bed and waited for a lull. When it came I dressed and got out to the deep shelter on the edge of the airfield. The raid by German dive bombers and M109 fighters had destroyed our Wellingtons. Then the Germans set about the British aircraft carrier *The Illustrious* anchored in the Grand Harbour. The intense harbour barrage of heavy flak hit many of the German bombers but they still kept on diving into this ring of fire. Those that got through were pounced upon by the island's Hurricane fighters and many were shot down. Although considerable damage was done no ships were sunk on that day.'

Because all the Wellington bombers were destroyed, a passage was arranged for the crews on the Royal Navy Cruiser *Bon Adventure* to sail to Egypt and collect more aircraft. It was an adventure – John's first sea voyage.

'We sailed out of the Grand Harbour in the evening and by midnight had joined up with the full Royal Navy Mediterranean fleet. Dawn revealed an amazing sight. There were ships everywhere, five battleships including the *Barham, Warspite*, and *Queen Elizabeth*, two aircraft carriers, and many cruisers. Fussy little destroyers kept everyone in their place. We sailed on towards Alexandria unmolested and unchallenged.

'The next day all the fleet, except our ship, turned to port and disappeared northwards. It was strange and scary to find ourselves on our own after being surrounded by ships of all shapes and sizes. We learnt later that the fleet had caught the Italian navy at sea and fought the Battle of Matapan when a large part of the Italian navy was sunk or damaged.

'We sailed into the Western harbour of Alexandria the following day. Britain was in charge of the defence of Egypt so our pilots were admitted straight away and entrained for Heliopolis RAF, to collect the new Wellington bombers. There we were given instructions to wait for 12 Hurricane fighters to join us, so we could guide them to their new squadron on Malta. When they didn't arrive at Heliopolis, we flew our 'Wimpeys' west to El Adam near Tobruk. After a day's rest, the Hurricane fighters joined us and we took off for Malta with the 12 followers holding back their speed. Our bombers only did 130 knots. Those 12 young fighter pilots had recently finished their training in Rhodesia and would be facing the fiercest of the enemy. It was a testing time for all of us.'

I suppose I must have dozed a bit as I remembered all this. When I next looked out of the window I saw below the coast of North Africa with its yellow sands melting into the blue sea.

The tiny harbour of Tobruk jutted out into the sea and there were a few twinkling lights coming on, as we sped over the desert sands where battles had raged backwards and forwards during the tussle between Monty (Montgomery) and Rommel. Tobruk was a dreaded name when we lived in South Africa because many of our friends' husbands were taken prisoner there.

The sun went down as a fiery ball and it was quite dark when the lights of Alexandria appeared on the starboard bow. This was my first night-landing and I looked down on the flare path of buoys. They were not very brilliant, and I hoped that captain knew where the water was when he came to put the boat down. Lower and lower we came. With a couple of bumps and a splash, we touched the water and skimmed along between the flare lights. The spray trickled down the windows, the boat settled comfortably and taxied slowly towards the jetty where the boatman was waiting to throw the rope to the radio officer, and moor the boat securely to the bollard on the pier.

Another crew took over here, and I wondered who would be taking us on to Khartoum. As we tied up to the wharf I looked through the window and was delighted when I recognized a tall familiar figure standing on the jetty. It was Athol Foster, one of my favourite pilots – after John – of course. He was a New Zealander with us in Durban, and often came to baby-sit for the boys in Southampton. When we stepped ashore, the boys ran to him and greeted him enthusiastically.

'What are you doing here, Vivienne? I didn't expect to see you.'

'At last, Athol, we're on our way to join John in Asmara. I hope he's arranged to meet us when we arrive in Khartoum tomorrow morning.'

'I'm afraid there'll be a delay here, Vivienne, because of an electrical fault in the aircraft. It will probably take about an hour and a half to fix, but we should be away by ten o'clock. Better let the boys run off some of their energy. You'll find refreshments in the little restaurant at the end of the pier.'

The boys were already chasing each other along the pier. When I caught them Richard said in a loud voice: 'Why are all the men wearing long nighties, Mummy?'

'Sshush, Richard. They're not nighties. In Egypt the men wear this loose-fitting garment called a *galabiah*. It's much cooler than a shirt and trousers.'

'Can I have one to wear in Asmara if it's hot?'

'Well we'll see. I don't think it's as hot there as it is here.'

I felt very hot and sticky by the time we reached the restaurant. I was glad to sit down at a table covered by a newly laundered white damask cloth, and feel the ceiling fan whirring above me. The waiter served us with iced drinks, Richard couldn't take his eyes off the red fez with a black tassel that the waiter had on his head.

'If I can't have a gal – white nightshirt,' he said, 'please will you get me one of those hats? I want one just like that.'

The waiter grinned all over his dark face and taking off his fez, he put it on Richard's head. It came right down over his fair curls and he looked quite dashing. But then Bill had to have a try and the fez swallowed his head and came to rest on Bill's ears. These had always been a sore point, and when he was a baby I used to try and stick them back with sticking plaster. But it hadn't done any good. They still stuck out. He looked a funny little chap in the red fez.

'I think you must give the man back his hat now, boys, and enjoy your drink and sandwich.'

The waiter brought a lovely bowl of fresh fruit and put it on the table. The boys' eyes gleamed as they saw the beautiful peaches and grapes. Bill had forgotten about his sore mouth but when some of the peach juice got into his cut lip he began to cry. Poor little man! It had been a long exhausting day. I wanted to get back on the boat and settle them down for the night.

'How long do you think it will be before we can go on board?' I asked the traffic officer.

'We should be ready to depart in about half an hour,' he said.

We walked outside. It was a clear night and the stars shone brilliantly in the blue-black sky. We sat on the edge of the wharf with our legs dangling over the water. I had my arms firmly round the two boys. I didn't trust Richard and had no wish to have him fished out of the water. We gazed at the stars and the lights bobbing up and down on the small boats out in the harbour. The time dragged by.

It was a relief when I saw the engineers leave the boat and the passengers come out of the restaurant. We stood up and joined the queue to get onto the aircraft.

Then the traffic officer came to me and said: 'I'm afraid you'll have to wait, Mrs Pascoe.' I went cold. 'I think it's all right but we can't be sure – until everyone is seated.'

Oh bloody hell! I hadn't given a thought that we could be turned off in Alexandria. What on earth would I do with the two boys if we had to spend some time here? That would be the last straw.

I stood back and watched the passengers file past. The uncertainty was killing.

'Let's go on board, Mummy,' said Richard tugging at my hand.

'We just have to wait a few minutes, dear, so be a good boy.'

The traffic officer came hurrying out. 'All is well, Mrs Pascoe, I'm sorry to have worried you. We've got three spare seats now you'll have room for the boys to sleep.'

'Thank you very much. Whatever would I have done if we had been stranded here?'

'Don't worry, we'd have looked after you. But I know you are anxious to join your husband. Please remember me to Captain Pascoe.'

He picked Bill up in his arms and we followed him thankfully. The cabin looked cosy and welcoming. Colonel Morris was no longer with us and his seat was occupied by an Egyptian in his *galabiah*. I hoped that there wouldn't be any more remarks from Richard about clothing. It was a relief when the door was shut and the engines started. We taxied out to the end of the flare path and rocked gently while the captain revved the engines, making the whole boat shake and shiver. The noise and vibration worried me, even though John had explained the engines were tested this way before taking off. We roared along the water and then up into the starry sky. The engines throttled back and settled into a comfortable purr. I tucked both boys in their seats, kissed them goodnight and the main lights in the cabin were turned off.

The purser came through the cabin. 'Would you like a drink, Madam?'

'I'd love something long and cool, please.'

He brought me a delicious looking iced drink with a cherry and a piece of pineapple floating on the top.

'Captain Foster sends his compliments and says you are welcome to go up on the flight-deck whenever you like.'

I gratefully sipped my drink, and opened my book hoping that reading would send me to sleep. After a while I put my reading-light out and shut my eyes. There was nothing to worry about. I couldn't be off-loaded now on this final leg. John would be at Khartoum to meet us when we landed in a few hours' time.

Although my eyes were shut, my brain was ticking over at great speed. I tried to relax my muscles, but first my fingers went to sleep and then my foot. I tried every possible position in the chair; my feet on the footstool, my head against the pillow on the armrest, but it was no use. I got cramp in my leg and had to get up and walk around. The boys were sleeping peacefully. I spoke to the purser and climbed the spiral staircase to the flight-deck. The crew greeted me pleasantly and the first officer got up and gave me his seat. He went back to have a rest in the cabin.

'I can't sleep, Athol, so I thought I'd come up here with you.'

'Did you see the lights of Cairo as we flew over it?' Athol said.

'I saw a lot of lights but didn't realize it was Cairo.'

'Now we're flying down the Nile to Wadi Halfa.'

I looked through the windows. It was a grand view from the cockpit and the stars looked as if you could pluck them in your hand. A full moon had risen and it was as bright as day. I could see the river below very clearly, but where the irrigation ended the green pastures on either side gave way abruptly to the sands of the desert.

I was happy sitting with Athol in the cockpit. Slowly the traumatic events of the day faded away. The sky with its wonder was all round us. The earth seemed far away. I understood how men who fly can forget, and divorce themselves from the petty troubles of life on earth. Life has a different perspective with stars, moon and clouds as companions. This was real! With enough fuel, you could go on and on never come down to land again. Sitting there on the darkened flight-deck and looking out into space, I felt a great sense of peace and tranquillity. The purr of the engines made me feel happy and relaxed.

'Thank you, Athol. Now I'll go and check the boys and hope I'll have a few hours' sleep before we arrive in Khartoum. Goodnight – or I suppose it's really good morning.'

All was quiet when I returned to the cabin and I slipped into my seat. The next thing I knew, I was being shaken by Bill who was wide awake and wanting to go to the toilet. I stirred myself quickly and went forward to the washroom.

The sun was just colouring the horizon when we came back and as I watched through the window, a hot, very orange sun burst into the sky. Down below the sands of the desert looked grim and forbidding, full of shadows and indentations.

'Orange juice, Madam?'

I took the glass of cool juice but I wasn't sure if it was a good thing for the boys to drink. Bill didn't want anything at all. He looked tired and was not his usual happy self.

'We'll be arriving in about half an hour,' the purser said when he collected my empty glass.

I found my spongebag and went quickly to the ladies' toilet to wash some of the night's dreariness away. My mouth felt furry and my teeth needed cleaning. Amazing what a boost clean teeth and a new face can do to the morale. I was tired, but at least I could try and look a bit groomed when I met my husband after a couple of months' separation.

The boys were jumping around in their seats and both wanted to sit in the window-seat as we flew over Khartoum. The flying-boat base was a few miles out of the city at Gordon's Tree on the Blue Nile. It looked far from blue in the early-morning light – dull, brown and sluggish. The winds had been favourable during the night flight and we had made up most of the time lost in Alexandria. The seat-belt sign went on, and as the boat gradually lost height and circled the alighting base, I peered out of the window hoping to see John waiting on the jetty. But all I could see were small launches fussing about clearing the flight-path which was very close to the sides of the river. There was a slight bump and we planed along the water like a duck coming into land with its feet down and its beak up. Then we nestled comfortably onto the water.

'We'll take you and the children off first, Mrs Pascoe.'

The purser took Bill while I tucked my violin under my arm and firmly took hold of Richard's hand. I knew one glimpse of his father and he'd be off like a bullet.

A wave of hot air attacked us when the door was opened. I was almost blinded by the bright light as we stepped into the sunshine and walked up the small gangway. I could see someone in khaki shorts, bush-shirt and peaked cap waiting at the top. As he came forward to give me his hand I almost stumbled into his arms. Then with desperate disappointment, I saw it wasn't John; it was the traffic officer who looked a bit surprised at the strange lady who had nearly leapt into his arms.

He recovered quickly. 'Good morning, Mrs Pascoe. I hope you've had a good trip. I've very sorry to disappoint you, but there's been a message from Aden Airways to say your husband has been delayed in Aden. We're not sure when the flight will arrive but we'll take you to the Grand Hotel where you can have some breakfast and a rest.' He led us to the small shed at the end of the pier. 'Please wait here until the luggage has been off-loaded.'

The boys were tearing round outside and didn't seem to notice the heat. How often this was the pattern of a pilot's wife. The tremendous build up of excitement and anticipation at the thought of seeing your husband again. The agonizing wait at a flying-boat base or an airport listening for the sound of the approaching plane. And then the disappointment of a delay or change of crew down the route. The man coming off the plane isn't your husband after all, but another pilot, whose wife's feelings of joy will in no way compensate for the sick disappointment of you having to wait until the next flight arrives – maybe days later.

Whoops of delight were coming from outside. I went to the door to see Richard and Bill in possession of the small red two wheeler and the tricycle, which had just been off-loaded from the aircraft. Bill was on his tricycle calmly plodding round and round on the hard-packed sandy path near the hut. But Richard was having difficulty. He didn't want to stay on the path but was trying to ride in the sand. The more he pushed, the deeper the bike became embedded in the sand. And the madder he got, the more bogged down he became. Then with a howl of rage that could be heard for miles around he collapsed with the bike on top of him.

I extracted him from under the bike, and carried him, still protesting loudly, into the shed. He had scraped his knee and it was bleeding badly. A Sudanese waiter rushed forward with a cold drink for him but at that stage nothing was going to placate Richard. The sight of strange faces around him only made things worse. I hugged him tightly, making soothing noises and took him into the rather primitive toilet to bathe his cut. There were no spare towels. I found my handkerchief and tied it round his knee. Then I noticed that in hugging him I had got blood over my new green linen suit. That made me want to howl too. So much for trying to arrive looking elegant and uncrumpled for the reunion with an adoring husband. I looked a mess. But what the hell! My husband was 'down the route', and we'd meet up sometime, I suppose. This is the next stage after the first disappointment – covering up your hurts with a non-caring attitude.

'Ah, there you are, Mrs Pascoe,' said the traffic officer, a bit put out with all this hullabaloo. 'The crew transport is ready to leave. Your luggage will follow later.' He was only too glad to get rid of us and hand over his responsibilities to the captain, who would take us into the Grand Hotel.

'Sorry about the noise, Athol,' I said as we climbed aboard an ancient looking vehicle.

Athol looked at me kindly and I knew he understood my disappointment. 'Never mind, Vivienne, this will give you a chance to see the famous Grand Hotel in Khartoum. You can have a bit of a rest before going on to Asmara.'

He was obviously tired after the night flight so we drove silently along the dusty roads. There seemed no relief from the sand. Sand – sand – sand everywhere, even the so-called houses were sand-coloured. But there were imposing looking buildings in the city centre. The streets were bustling with men in all kinds of clothes as they hurried to their day's work. We went down a tree-lined road leading to the banks of the Nile. As we turned the corner I saw the Grand Hotel. For years I had sent letters to 'Captain J.G. Pascoe, C/O Grand Hotel, Khartoum.' Writing the address I had tried to visualize this place where the crews spent several days. Well, there it was! A long low building with spacious cool verandahs looking across the road to the slow-moving river, where little boats sailed, and cows grazed on the other side.

'We may see you at breakfast,' Athol said as he helped me out of the car. 'I hope you meet up with John soon and enjoy your stay in Eritrea.' He took me into the hall and introduced me to the girl at the reception desk.

'Good morning, Mrs Pascoe. I'm afraid we haven't had any further word about the arrival of the Aden Airways service from Asmara. It may not be leaving until this afternoon.' She called to a tall black African who was standing by. 'Hassan, please take Mrs Pascoe to room one hundred and two. It's at the end of the corridor on the left. We'll send you luggage along when it arrives and will let you know as soon as we have any news of your departure time.'

I followed the red-fezed Hassan along the corridor. He unlocked the door and I went into a large high-ceilinged room which was deliciously cool after the hot drive from the air base. A large fan whirred away. I longed to have a shower and lie on the bed with the air moving above me. I felt hot, sticky, and oh, so very disappointed. The boys explored the room and opened the doors onto the verandah, but blasts of hot air came in so I hastily closed them. I was longing for a drink but although there was a thermos of iced water by the bed, I wasn't sure if it was safe to drink. I knew all about tummy-bugs caused through drinking unboiled water from my experiences in South Africa.

John had told me about the wonderful dairy herd in Khartoum which had been established by the Garfouri family. In such a torrid climate and with cows prone to tropical diseases, this was no mean achievement. Instead of powdered milk used throughout the Middle East, real fresh milk could be bought in Khartoum. Two interesting brothers, Gabs and Charles, ran the farm. They'd befriended many of the BOAC crews who stopped over in Khartoum. John made me envious when he described the wonderful dinners in their comfortable farmhouse on the other side of the Nile.

Just as I lifted the phone to ask for some fresh milk to be sent, there was a knock on the door. Richard rushed to open it. There stood Hassan and another boy, with not only our suitcases, but the red bicycle and the tricycle.

I looked in my bag for some money to give them for a tip but I had no local money. 'Thank you very much. That was quick. Will you leave the bicycles in the corridor, please?'

They brought the suitcases into the room. But the arrival of the two wheeler was too much for Richard. The long wide corridor presented an ideal race-track and before I could stop him he jumped on his bike and shot off. I held my breath when I saw glass doors at the far end but he came to an abrupt halt, turned round and came charging back again.

'Now that's enough, Richard. We're all going to have a shower before we go to the dining-room for breakfast. You'll be able to have a cool drink of fresh milk from those cows you can see on the other side of the river.'

I pulled him inside the room and stopped Bill who had mounted his tricycle ready to take off down the passage. He came in very reluctantly. The boys undressed and I turned on the shower. Shouts of glee came from the bathroom. I undid a suitcase to find clean clothes for them. I found Bill's red and white suit which had been made for Richard before we left South Africa and Richard's blue shorts and shirt to match. There was only a small swelling now around Bill's lip and he seemed to have forgotten about his fall.

'Right, out you come. You can play outside on the verandah in your shorts while I have a shower.'

Richard had undone the precious small suitcase containing his cars and he was charging up and down with the usual engine noises being uttered – brm-brm-brm. He could never just play with a car. He had to make the appropriate noises. I hoped the person in the room next door wasn't trying to sleep.

I went into the bathroom and tried to sponge the blood off my jacket. It was green linen. To get rid of the stain properly the whole thing would have to be washed. Now it looked a mess. As I was about to step into the shower the phone rang. I grabbed a towel and went into the bedroom to answer it.

115

'This is reception desk, Mrs Pascoe. We've just heard from the airport that the Aden Airways plane arrived twenty minutes ago. They want to take off as soon as possible so can you get ready immediately please? The car is waiting at the door.'

'Is my husband there?' I asked eagerly.

'No, I'm afraid not. There's a message to say your husband should be waiting to greet you when you arrive in Asmara.'

I put the phone down and looked around the room. Two opened suitcases, clothes strewn about, the boys outside in their underpants with all the Dinky toys out of the suitcase, and me wrapped in a towel. Damn, damn, damn, I thought. I haven't even had a shower. What kind of an airline is this Aden Airways? They don't seem to know if they are coming or going. My husband SHOULD be there to meet me! Unless of course he's been sent somewhere else in the meantime.

I was angry and fed up. I dressed hurriedly in the same clothes, curtly told Richard to put the toys back, pulled Bill inside and got him into his suit, shoved things back in the suitcases and tried to get the wretched things closed. Why is it that once a case is open it never wants to close again? It had been difficult enough to fasten before we left Minnie's flat but now it was hopeless. I struggled and struggled, getting hotter and hotter. Finally I plonked both Richard and Bill on top and managed to fasten one side. There was a knock on the door and Hassan appeared.

'Are you ready, Madam? The car is waiting.'

'Please can you help me close these suitcases?' He took over and I dashed out onto the verandah to finish collecting the toys. Why, oh why couldn't Richard finish a job instead of leaving it half done! The boys had already disappeared and were riding their vehicles to the reception foyer. I looked round the room and remembered the toilet things in the bathroom and stuffed them into my overnight bag. There hadn't been time to put make-up on but maybe I could do that before we arrived in Asmara.

I tried to smile sweetly at the receptionist when she apologized for the hasty departure. After all it wasn't her fault. I followed the boys, the bikes and the suitcases into the waiting car and we shot off with a jerk. The driver was obviously in a hurry. He was generous with the horn and regarded every other car, bicycle and pedestrian as obstructions in his path. Every nerve in my body jangled as we braked, jerked and slewed round corners. Richard was sitting in front, loving it all, thinking he had found a kindred spirit, happily brm, br-mming away in duet with the sudden revving of the noisy engine. I shut my eyes and clutched Bill which made us both hotter than ever.

'Look, Mummy, what a funny little aeroplane.' Richard's voice pulled me back into the present as the driver made his final triumphant rocket approach, pulling up just past the entrance to a small building that housed all the passengers leaving Khartoum. We bundled out of the car, thankful to be alive and able to continue our journey. The traffic officer appeared and gave instructions about the luggage. He looked surprised when he saw the bike and tricycle.

'Oh, I don't know if we have time to get these on board. The aircraft is waiting to take off now. You are the last passengers. We've been waiting for you.'

I felt like retorting tartly: 'And whose fault is that?' but I restrained myself. While seething inside I said as politely as possible: 'Oh, I'm sure my husband, Captain Pascoe, will be very disappointed if we don't arrive in Asmara with all our luggage. It's a shame he is delayed because I'm sure he'd have managed to find room on board for everything.'

'Well, come along quickly now and I'll see what I can do.'

We marched towards the aircraft waiting on the tarmac. It was as Richard said, a funny little plane. After the spaciousness and luxury of the flying-boat, the DC3 looked small and tatty. The boys thought it was great fun to have to go 'uphill' to their seats. Our arrival caused a bit of a flurry and the other passengers looked disgruntled after their long wait in a hot aircraft. The air-hostess did her best to get us settled as quickly as possible.

The door closed, the engines started and we taxied to the end of the runway. It was many years since I had been in a land plane. I found it frightening to be bumping along the uneven surface of the runway instead of watching the wave of water outside the flying-boat.

The flight passed by in a haze. I was too tired and too exhausted to even worry about the boys. The seat-belt sign came on as we ran into some turbulence and the plane starting bouncing about. Bill went very white and my stomach didn't seem to belong in the right place. Just my luck, I thought, if the boys are sick all over their clean clothes. I leaned forward to look for the paper-bag in the seat pocket. It wasn't there. I rang for the hostess and asked her to give me two bags. The air outside settled down and the engines droned on. The small plane gave me claustrophobia and I had a job to control myself. Wouldn't do for a new Aden Airways wife to start screaming and demanding to be let out of the aeroplane when we were flying at 7,000 feet. I shut my eyes and tried to imagine I was outside floating freely among the soft billowy clouds with space – space all around and nothing pressing down on my head.

'Mummy, Mummy.' My arm was being shaken hard. 'I want to go to the toilet.'

Richard was evidently in a great hurry so I staggered to my feet and we lurched up the aisle to the toilet. There never seems to be a standard height for a lavatory seat, and it's difficult to get a small boy's appendage at the right angle or height, so the flow of liquid can be directed into the bowl and not on the walls. The confined space of a DC3 toilet and the instability of the aeroplane made the operation almost impossible.

We returned to our seats where Bill had fortunately fallen asleep. I was in no state to repeat the toilet performance at that moment. I looked out of the small window. Down below the sandy waste had given way to hills. I couldn't see much sign of habitation. It all looked a bit dreary. The hills became mountains – mountains on mountains. There wasn't a flat place anywhere. I began to believe the stories about Asmara being 8,000 feet above sea level.

The hostess came forward with a basket of sweets. 'It won't be long now. We'll be landing in Asmara in about five minutes.'

In the mess in my handbag I found my powder compact and lipstick, but as I struggled to repair the damage of the last few hours, the aircraft started dancing about again. The lipstick in my hand jerked on the upper lip giving my mouth a lopsided smile.

From brilliant sunshine outside we suddenly became enveloped in thick cloud. Our safety-belts were on ready for landing but nothing could be seen down below. We circled round a couple of times coming out of the cloud into clear sunshine as we climbed over the mountains, but each time we turned and started to descend the inside of the plane went dark. I wondered if we were going to run into one of those mountains. Richard's impatient question 'When is he going to land this thing, Mummy?' didn't help.

Then suddenly there was a slight break in the clouds. We did a let-down and a few minutes later were spinning along the runway. When the plane came to a halt I found my heart was jumping up and down – not sure whether it was fright or excitement.

Richard was first to the door and when it opened there was a wonderful cry of: 'There he is, Daddy, Daddy.'

The hostess took Bill in her arms and put a restraining hand on Richard until the steps were in position. He had even forgotten his precious little case of toys in his excitement. I gathered them together, picked up my violin and the other bits and pieces and went down the steps. There at the bottom with a great big grin on his face, was John.

12

Asmara

First impressions of a place are not always reliable. They depend on the state of mind – the state of health – the state of the weather, and often on a particular set of circumstances. They remain vivid and lasting memories even though time may change or soften those initial impressions.

I was disappointed that the city of Asmara was not built on the side of a mountain with magnificent views. Instead it was a conglomeration of buildings gathered together in a basin on a large flat plateau.

At the airport we piled into a large, noisy Italian car, and drove a few miles along a dusty road into the city where wide tar-sealed streets were divided by a grass strip. Bill sat on John's knee, happy to have his father's arms around him. Richard chatted away telling John all about the journey in the flying-boat.

'I went up into the cockpit, sat on the first officer's knee and held the joy-stick. That was great fun. Do you really fly one of these tiny planes now, Daddy? I don't like them nearly as much as the flying-boats. They bump about too much.'

'The Douglas Dakotas or DC3s are wonderful old planes, Richard, and I do enjoy flying them. They're very reliable and ideal for these Middle East routes. Some of the trips are short, even one-day flights, so I'll be able to spend more time at home with you.'

'What kind of car is this, Daddy? Why does it make such a noise? Doesn't it have an exhaust pipe?'

'It's an Italian Alfa Romeo, Richard. You'll see a lot of old cars here – mostly Italian. No new cars have been imported into Eritrea since before the war.'

I was amazed when I looked around and saw the ancient vehicles. Most of the cars were 1928–38 vintage. That they survived to roar through the streets spoke well of them, and of the Italian mechanics who maintained them. But many times during the first few weeks I wished that the scrap-heap had claimed them.

When I could get a word in I asked: 'And where are we going to live, John? Have you managed to find a house?'

'Well, no!' John sounded a bit cagey. 'As yet I haven't been given permission to look for one because of the security restrictions. In the meantime we'll be living in the Aden Airways building, Palazza Valletta. Our flat's on the fourth floor of D-Block. (Sounds like a prison, I thought, but didn't say anything).

'I've found an Eritrean girl called Zitoo, to look after the boys and a cookboy, Ghabre, so you won't even have to do any cooking.'

'You mean to say I won't be able to find out how long it takes to boil an egg?'

'Well, maybe you can do that on a Sunday evening or on Ghabre's day off. You'll have a rest from household chores; play tennis and amuse yourself.'

It all sounded idyllic.

Palazza Valletta, where most of the Aden Airways crews lived was a large block of flats consisting of four sections, A, B, C, D, built round a central courtyard. It was four stories high with only one lift – in A Block. Although our flat was large and spacious, the kitchen balconies overlooked the central quadrangle and washing dripped from lines suspended from the railings. The courtyard was the children's playground. Round and round they tore on their bikes and tricycles. Coming in off the street was a hazardous operation as it meant running the gauntlet between the bikes.

Noises and smells! At first these two senses were over-exercised. It was an abrupt transition to be dumped in the middle of a noisy foreign city after the clean smelling, quiet countryside of England. The distinctive body smell of the Eritreans, of coffee, paraffin, foreign tobacco and sewerage were mixed with the smell of cooking oil. But I think my nose became acclimatized before

121

my ears. The cars were driven by maniacs practising to be racing drivers, who delighted in exhausts with no silencers. When one of these monsters started up under the window in the middle of the night, my eardrums were shattered and the hairs on my arms stood out like porcupine quills. Petrol was unrationed and cheap – only three shillings a gallon.

When the British took over the Eritrean Administration in 1941 they introduced the left-hand rule of the road. But the Italian cars still had the left-hand drive. The drivers gloried in the sport of overtaking without being able to see clearly any on-coming traffic. Richard thought all this was wonderful. It wasn't necessary for him to make traffic noises. They were there all the time.

I much preferred and felt safer in the quieter and more picturesque form of transport – the *carrozzina* – a type of horse buggy which was fairly cheap to hire and clip-clopped along the streets at a leisurely pace.

Before 1897 Asmara was an obscure Coptic village. The majority of the native Eritreans in this district, and in the highlands stretching south to Ethiopia, were Coptic Christians, a faith spread in the sixth century by Christian priests from Syria. Later the Muslim expansion threatened Eritrea and there were many converts to the Islamic faith.

At the end of the nineteenth century the Italians moved in, culminating with Mussolini's drive towards Ethiopia in the mid-30s. The municipality, hospitals and doctors were still run by Italians, who were Catholics.

The town itself had a somewhat unfinished appearance. In the centre were several large buildings where construction had ceased at the beginning of the war. Opposite the flats was an imposing shell of a building designed to be the Italian Fascist headquarters. Part of this had been completed and was now used as a garrison church for the two British battalions stationed in Eritrea.

Next to Palazza Valletta was the imposing, red-brick Catholic cathedral and its subsidiary buildings. The tower, full of jangling bells, dominated the city. I didn't really appreciate these, especially when they started ringing loud and clear at five-thirty on a peaceful Sunday morning.

Another sound that drifted up early in the morning was the cry from the newspaperboys. The first few mornings I couldn't make out what these strange cries meant. They were calling: *La Gi–or–nale–nale*,' the name of the daily Italian newspaper. The British information service put out a single sheet newspaper once a week. It was like reading the news bulletin on the notice-board of a ship.

A great mixture of races and creeds mingled on the footpaths. The Coptic women were easy to distinguish as they wore their black frizzy hair dressed in elaborate styles – sometimes 30 or 40 tiny, tight plaits going from the forehead to the nape of the neck, where it bushed out in an unruly frizz. The more plaits the greater their claim to beauty. Definitely not a hairstyle to try if you were running late for an appointment. But once done, the hairdo lasted for weeks. Some girls had the Coptic cross tattooed on their forehead. Their long coloured dresses were simple in style, and around their bodies and over their heads they draped a lightly woven cotton cloth, with a coloured border called a *futa*.

Instead of carrying a baby on their backs in a rug or blanket, like the Maoris of New Zealand, the Eritrean women carried their babies in a piece of hide with straps crossing over the breasts. Baby and all were then covered with the *futa*. The babies' hairstyles were cute. Sometimes the head would be shaved completely, except for a few tufts here and there. In small children a ridge of hair going from the forehead to the back of the neck would stand up – rather like a rooster's crop – or the latest 'punk' style.

Most men in town wore European dress. But those from the countryside were clad in baggy white trousers with a long shirt worn outside the trousers, and a white – or dirty white – *futa* draped over their heads and shoulders. It was easy to distinguish the Muslims as they wore a white turban, or if they had been on a holy pilgrimage to Mecca, they were entitled to wear a red turban.

There were beggars everywhere, pitiful creatures, maimed, mis-shapen and often blind. They sat on the pavements with their little enamel bowls beside them. Richard wanted to know why they had 'finished with their eyes' and couldn't pass them without demanding something to put in the bowl.

We arrived at the beginning of the rainy season. Ten months of the year it is dry, with an average temperature of 65 degrees. Then in July and August the rain descends. Such a thing as a gentle rain from heaven was almost unknown. Everything was violent and harsh. About two o'clock in the afternoon the clouds rolled up and gradually obscured the sky, until suddenly with a frightening flash of lightning and reverberating claps of thunder, the heavens opened. In a few minutes the roads were awash and the gutters full. The Italians built wonderful roads but their expertise didn't stretch to drains and plumbing. If you were caught outside during the deluge it was easier to take your shoes off and paddle. At four o'clock the rain stopped, the sun came out, the streets dried quickly and everything looked washed and clean.

At first, Richard and Bill eyed Zitoo and Ghabre with suspicion and bewilderment. They asked awkward questions. 'Mummy, why is Zitoo's face black? Why are our hands white and Ghabre's black? If he washes them enough will they turn white?'

I felt unequal to a technical explanation about the pigments of the skin. At first Bill objected to Zitoo doing anything for him, and wouldn't even let her bath him. He was just beginning to thaw a little when she arrived one morning with the palms of her hands hennaed a reddish brown. There was blood curdling shrieks from the bathroom. When I rushed in to see what was happening, Bill was struggling like a demon and wouldn't let Zitoo dress him.

'Mummy, Mummy, Zitoo's got prickly pear hands. Don't let her touch me!'

Poor Zitoo! She wanted so much to be helpful. For an Eritrean girl, putting henna on the palms and on the bottom of the feet was like a European lady painting her nails. I tried hard to explain to Zitoo in my extremely limited Italian what all the fuss was about, and persuade her to remove the henna. But henna is a dye and wears off gradually.

Richard gradually made friends with the cook who was always dressed in immaculate white. One day Richard wanted Ghabre to mend a punctured tyre. He came into the sitting-room looking very cross. 'Mummy, why doesn't Ghabre help me. I've asked and asked him and he doesn't understand what I want.'

Well might Richard ask! The Eritrean language is strange sounding. It is a dialect of the Amharic language known as Tigrian. But with years of Italian colonization, most of the natives spoke

Italian as well. For me, it was one more difficulty to try and overcome. The Italian dictionary was my constant companion. I would carefully work out a sentence and go into the kitchen to give Ghabre instructions about what we would like for dinner. The actual food that appeared on the table wouldn't bear any resemblance to what I had ordered. It was exasperating! I arranged to have Italian lessons and was determined to study seriously and speak correctly, but most of it was lost on Ghabre and Zitoo, because they spoke 'kitchen Italian.'

As I found communication so difficult I decided, after a few weeks that I would do some of the cooking myself. My presence in the kitchen was tolerated but certainly not welcome. That was Ghabre's domain. He did the shopping and didn't want to be questioned very closely about the cost of things. That was one of his perks. I hadn't a clue what things cost at that stage, so he was quite safe. Anyway my limited Italian didn't stretch to arguments about food prices.

In the kitchen was a new monster to deal with – a wood-burning black range like the ones used before the invention of electricity. The nearest coal mine was thousands of miles south, at Wanki in Southern Rhodesia (now Zimbabwe). Because of transport difficulties, it was virtually impossible to import coal. Electricity for Asmara was generated 70 miles away at the sea port of Massaua and was too expensive to use for cooking. I wondered where all the wood came from because there were very few trees round the town.

It took skill and patience to keep the stove stoked and the oven at an even temperature. There was no thermometer or thermostat and the altitude was blamed for things taking longer to cook.

I decided I would not be edged out of my own kitchen – I would master that monstrous range. I waited until it was Ghabre's day off and set about mixing a birthday cake for Richard. My recipe books hadn't arrived. The luggage had been held up and we were still managing on what we had brought out with us. How glad I was that we at least had the boys' bikes.

I got rather carried away with my mixture and kept adding this and that. But it tasted good and looked the right consistency by the time I was ready to put it in the oven. I stoked the range and had a good pile of wood handy. For the next five hours I was in and out of the kitchen, nursing that cake along like a clucky hen. Finally I decided it must be cooked and removed it from the oven. Except for a few burnt bits around the edge it seemed in a fairly stable condition. I had used all the wood so I put the cake back in the oven to cool and took the boys for a walk.

When I came back half an hour later I opened the oven door in great anticipation and removed the cake. Disaster! In my absence the precious cake had changed shape. It looked like a flat-bottomed boat with a sunken middle. I turned it upside down and for the sake of the birthday smothered its bottom with icing. It tasted like a sad, soggy Christmas pudding. Richard, although delighted about lighting and blowing out his six candles, declined to eat more than a small mouthful.

It was such a complete change in lifestyle. In England, where I never seemed to finish the daily chores necessary to keep a household in running order, the idea of a nanny for the boys and a cook has sounded absolute bliss. But it didn't work out that way. If the luggage had arrived, it would have been easier. I had my fiddle – but no music – as that was packed with the books and heavy things. I tried practising scales and exercises but living in a flat, I was very conscious of disturbing other people. A violin on its own doing technical things is an acquired listening taste and the flats were far from being soundproof.

The boys were still restricted to the little case of Dinky toys and the few books we had with us. I was tired of reading A.A. Milne and the engine books of Rev W. Awdry. I visited the little book shop nearby, but that was run by Italians for Italians. There were no children's books in English.

I couldn't sew because I didn't have my machine, couldn't practise properly without music, couldn't cook because I couldn't manage the stove, couldn't garden because there was no garden, and couldn't chatter to the servants because I was too dumb to understand their language.

Too little to do was as bad as having too much to do. That blissful 'leisure' was a snare and delusion. It needed to be treated as an 'art' and worked at, or it easily turned into that dreaded disease: 'boredom'.

The flat was completely depersonalized; the furniture – dull and basic. When a flat became vacant, a great game of swapping and acquiring furniture went on among the wives. If you needed a plate or pot, you applied to the Aden Airways man in charge of accommodation. Nothing in our flat seemed to match and the walls were bare, not even a calendar broke their virginity.

Then there was 'THE ALTITUDE'. If you had a headache it was because of the altitude. If you were depressed the altitude was blamed. Rows with husbands, shortness of temper with children were all blamed on the same thing.

I knew I would be better when I could get regular exercise and the tennis courts looked very inviting. I longed for my racket to arrive. Mavis, an engineer's wife, gave me cold comfort.

'Oh, you'll find it far too tiring playing anything as strenuous as tennis here. It's the altitude, my dear. You'll get terrible headaches, and you know,' her voice dropped several decibels, 'it affects you so badly when you have your period.' Mavis had been in Asmara for a year and her headaches were a by-word among the other wives. I was determined to give tennis a go as soon as my equipment arrived. I didn't want to turn into another bored, headachy Mavis.

But one thing did surprise me. I had always kept fit, and was used to bounding up stairs two at a time. Here, by the time I had walked up four flights of steps – one at a time – to the flat, my heart was pounding away and I had to stand still for a moment or two to recover.

I didn't like the feeling. Was it age or altitude?

I had to admit I was bored! Bored with living in a flat that had no feeling of home, bored with not having my own things around me, bored with the coffee mornings where I met other wives and listened to their aches and pains, bored with the dinner parties where the men talked of nothing else but aeroplanes – just BORED, BORED, BORED!

13

Villagio Paradiso

John was oblivious to my inner turmoils. He was thoroughly enjoying flying the little DC3s and working with his friend Steve again. He thrived on the challenge of nosing out freight to fill the plane if there were not enough passengers and enjoyed the bargaining process, which was part of life in the Middle East. Flying vegetables from Asmara to Aden was a profitable cargo. The port of Aden on the other side of the Red Sea was a desert where nothing green grew. Aden had no cold storage facilities so fresh produce grown on the Eritrean plateau sold easily.

I tried hard to pull myself together. It had been a long standby voyage to reach Asmara but I hated living in the flat.

One afternoon John came bounding into the flat and catching hold of me twirled me round the room.

'Steady on,' I said. 'Don't forget the altitude. What's all the excitement about?'

'Guess what? Our luggage has arrived at last. It's out at the airport – and – I've found a villa and – persuaded Steve to let us move away from these flats.'

'Where is the villa? How far away?' I asked practically. We still didn't have a car and hadn't needed one while we lived in the centre of town. Cars were expensive and not easy to find in Asmara.

'It's out at Villagio Paradiso – about two miles from the centre. I've been to have a look at it. I'm sure you'll like it. The boys will have a garden to play in and I can have a workshop in the garage.'

'It sounds fine. Anything is better than living in this rabbit warren. But is it safe to go so far out John? What about the Shifta?'

Shifta! I had never heard the word until I arrived in Asmara. Every day it cropped up in conversation with tales of the latest outrages. No one seemed able to define 'Shifta'. They were outlaws, Eritrean bandits, organized guerrillas, robbers who broke into houses at night, gangs who stopped trains and buses and took what they wanted. There seemed to be no end to their exploits. This was the 'slight trouble' that John had so airily talked about when he first mentioned the involvement with Aden Airways.

The 'slight trouble' now meant that two British battalions, the Berkshire and the South Wales Borderers, were stationed in Eritrea. It was their job to control the Shifta and maintain law and order. But the Shifta were difficult to capture, and escaped to the safety of their villages.

'Never mind the Shifta, Viv. Come on, where are the boys? I've borrowed Steve's car. Let's drive out and see the villa.'

I was delighted to know the luggage had arrived at last. Getting into the car I thought ' Villagio Paradiso' would be a good address to have at the top of my letters.

We drove out of the town and turned right onto a dirt road. I wasn't very impressed with the group of dull looking villas clustered round a Coptic monastery, and a boys' school. Hardly my idea of paradise! The villa John had seen was empty. Because people were afraid to live so far out, it had been empty for some time. John opened the door and we went inside. I noticed how dark it was and that all the windows had shutters with steel bars across them.

'Surely we won't have to keep those things?' I asked him.

'Well,' I could see him struggling for reassuring words. 'You'll soon get used to them. We're advised that as soon as it's dark the shutters should be closed and the bars put in place. It's best to do this especially when I'm away.'

I wandered through the rooms. As a house it didn't have much to recommend it. It was a square concrete construction. The kitchen had the usual horrible black cooker and water was heated in the bathroom by a wood burning geyser. The good-sized lounge had a fireplace at one end, but the large entrance hall would have to be used as a dining-room.

We walked out into the 'garden'. There were two straggly eucalyptus trees in one corner, and that was all. Still it was somewhere for the boys to play and ride their bikes. With care and water something should grow. It would be a challenge.

'There's a small flat across the road where Zitoo can live and as Ghabre has a bike he can ride out from town.'

'If we move out here I can't see Ghabre lasting long. He's too fond of his visits to the market and socializing with the other boys around the flats.'

Back in the house John was busy in the lounge with his measuring tape. 'The furniture from the flat will fit in quite well here. I'll build a bookcase and make the fireplace look attractive with shelves either side.'

His mind was at work redesigning the whole room, thinking it would be a good excuse for buying power-tools to set up a workshop. 'But first I'll have to build a workbench.'

I laughed. Wherever we went in the world, John constructed workbenches made to last a lifetime, and left them behind for other people to use. He was full of enthusiasm and I could see he had made up his mind.

'Come on, Viv, let's go back to the office and finalize the deal with the landlord, ring the airport and have the luggage delivered here. Then we can move in before the pilgrimage starts.'

'And when's that going to be?'

'Oh, probably some time next week. I'd like to see you settled before I leave. I won't be home much in the next few weeks.'

The pilgrimage of Muslims to Mecca was the busiest time of the year for Aden Airways. The wives were warned they wouldn't see much of their husbands during this period. For the past few weeks the pilots had talked of little else. They told stories of how last year 6,000 pilgrims died, or were trampled to death, as they fell fainting from the heat in the overcrowded mosques. It was big business for the airline. Deals were made between the company and pilgrim aid societies in Muslim countries to provide special flights to the port of Jeddah in Saudi Arabia. The planes flew pilgrims from Karachi and Kabul in the East, Teherãn, Baghdad, Turkey and Amman in the North, and as far away as Accra and Kano in West Africa.

The date for the commencement of the *Eid* varied each year and usually came at the hottest period of the northern summer. With the first sight of the new moon, a proclamation was made in Mecca.

The crews flew day and night to ensure the pilgrims arrived on time before the devotions began. It was spartan flying – no hostesses on board – and travelling over desert country in the height of summer, often meant very bumpy flights. Pilgrims were often sick and didn't understand the toilet facilities of the plane. There was hardly time to have the planes cleaned properly between flights, and the lingering sour smell was overpowering.

But the faith and the spirit of the pilgrims overrode all discomforts. It was the greatest ambition of their lives to visit the shrine at Mecca and the tomb of the Prophet Mohammed at Medina, where they received absolution and forgiveness for their earthly sins and misdeeds, and assurance of a place in the Kingdom to come. Old pilgrims hoped that death would claim them after the ceremonies were completed, so they could be buried close to their Prophet. Those who returned home after the pilgrimage were regarded as men of standing and entitled to dye their hair and beard with henna and wear a red turban. They were known as *hajiis*.

When the pilgrims got off the plane, they wore the simplest clothing – usually a towel draped around them – with sandals on their feet and carried an umbrella to protect them from the fierce sun. But the most important part of their sparse luggage was a kettle and water bottle. Water was necessary as part of their prayer ritual. A Muslim prays facing toward Mecca, five times a day. Before he prays, his hands and feet must be washed. Water was scarce and rationed. The Saudi authorities charged large sums of money for this purifier as they knew it would be bought at any price by the devout pilgrims. Sometimes they even charged the poor pilgrims for the privilege of sitting in the shade of one of the few trees in that deserty country.

We soon encountered difficulties over water restrictions. Before the war, the Italians occupying Eritrea imported everything from Italy – including water. When reservoirs were built outside the city, they were unfortunately constructed away from the main catchment area. Even in a good rainy season the storage of water wasn't sufficient for the town supply. The municipality controlled

131

the amount of water allowed for each household. This was turned on at 6 a.m. and started running into the tanks. If we were lucky we would have two hours' supply. But often this wasn't enough and it would have to be supplemented. Large tankers delivered water at a cost of one shilling and sixpence a cubic metre. The water from the municipality was filtered and chlorinated. It had a horrible taste and no amount of soap powder would produce a lather. Drinking water was boiled and kept in the fridge. We soon got used to drinking *aqua minerale* which came in large green bottles. The boys had to be taught not to leave the tap running while cleaning their teeth. Every drop was precious – as I found out later.

John tried hard to get us moved out to Villagio Paradiso straight away. He knew I was not happy about being so far out and he was anxious to see us settled before I changed my mind. It didn't help when some of the other wives expressed their fears and said they wouldn't dream of living in a villa while the Shifta scare was on.

There were the usual excuses and delays. The contract couldn't be signed because the landlord was away. The landlord returned but there were formalities about taking over the villa. You would have thought he'd be overjoyed at finding someone willing to rent the house. The luggage was still out at the airport and hadn't been cleared through customs. The furniture couldn't be moved until a truck was available … I was learning that *domani* was the most popular word in the Italian language, – and tomorrow never came!

John bought a second-hand red Morris Minor convertible in Aden and somehow it was squeezed into a freighter aeroplane and flown to Asmara. At least now we had transport .

The minute John came back from the office one morning I knew something was wrong.

'What is it this time? Has the landlord changed his mind?'

'No, everything's fine. The lease is signed and sealed and the move can be made tomorrow. But, he hesitated, 'I won't be here. Jim's gone sick and I'm standby captain. I take off at two this afternoon.'

I looked at my watch. It was nearly mid-day.

'When do you think you'll be back?'

'Goodness knows! We're flying to Cairo and then over to West Africa to pick up a load of pilgrims from Accra. And after that we'll be right in the thick of the chartered flying for the pilgrimage. What do you want to do? Postpone the move until I get back?'

'And go through all this *domani* business again! No thanks. Let's leave things as they are. I'll manage somehow.'

Tears weren't far away but I didn't want him to go off and remember me crying. I busied myself seeing to lunch for him and checking what he needed to pack.

'You've got the car now so you'll be able to use that to move some of the bits and pieces.' I thought of the four flights of stairs.

'The men will be here at nine tomorrow morning to move the furniture and they'll pick up the luggage from the airport in the afternoon. Sorry, darling. You'll be all right and you'll enjoy it once you get settled. Don't forget to go to the office and collect the key. Be sure you sign for it.'

Sometimes his faith in my ability to cope was maddening. When he went out the door in a flurry with the boys charging down the stairs to say goodbye, I went into the bedroom and couldn't stop crying. Why wasn't I a helpless little wife and have everything done for me? I thought bitterly.

When I had recovered from feeling sorry for myself, I sent Ghabre off to find boxes to pack the kitchen things, and started putting clothes into the suitcases.

There was no sign of any furniture removers at nine the next morning. Ten o'clock came – and went. At eleven I took the boys and walked over to the office to find out what was happening.

'Oh, I'm sorry, Mrs Pascoe,' the secretary said. ' The truck has had to take some freight out to the airport. It doesn't look as if they'll start moving any of your furniture until after lunch. Here's the key to the villa. I'll send a message to the flat if there's any further delay.'

We were just finishing a sandwich when the doorbell rang, and the flat was immediately invaded. There was no order about the way things were shifted. They were just taken. I called to Zitoo, '*Andiamo*, come quickly. We'd better get out to the villa and be there when the truck arrives.'

133

I rushed down the stairs clutching my violin and the others followed with their arms full. The boys wanted their bikes to go in the car but I drew the line at that. I saw them safely loaded onto the truck and drove off, leaving Ghabre in charge at the flat.

The villa looked pretty desolate when we walked in and I opened all the doors and windows. I wanted the terrazzo floors washed before the furniture arrived and Zitoo was armed with a bucket and scrubbing brush. She went into the kitchen and turned the tap on to fill the bucket. Nothing happened! There wasn't a drop of water. We tried the taps in the bathroom and the outside one with the same result. I walked across the road to one of the little villas where I'd seen a car. John had told me that one of the prison officers lived there.

'I'm sorry to trouble you, but we don't seem to have any water. Do you think you could let us have a bucketful please?'

'Certainly. I'll get it for you. I don't suppose the municipality has turned the water meter on yet. They won't do this until the office gives them instructions. Here's your water. Let me know if I can do anything.'

I thanked him and took the water. He looked strong and solid and it was comforting to know there was a police officer across the way.

The truck arrived before Zitoo had time to clean the floor. I decided we had better save this water for essential purposes. I had a job to make Zitoo understand as my flow of Italian deserted me. Ghabre, who arrived sitting on top of the furniture in the truck, was a tower of strength, ordering the removal boys around and giving instructions where to put things. I noticed he didn't do any of the heavy work himself but he got the job done. It was after four o'clock by the time everything was unloaded. I drove Ghabre back to town and went to the office to see about the water being turned on.

I asked the secretary to phone the municipality. She tried but got no reply. 'I'm afraid there's no one there now. They close the office at four-thirty p.m.'

'Surely there's some way of getting water tomorrow morning. Isn't there an emergency number?'

She tried the exchange. I waited impatiently. She rattled away in Italian. 'You won't get any water tomorrow morning, I'm afraid, because a man has to come out to the villa, read the water meter, and then give instructions to the water authorities.'

'Why on earth wasn't this done before we moved?' I said crossly. 'Will you please ring first thing in the morning and make sure that the water man comes out? We can't go on for days without water.'

I drove back to Villagio Paradiso. If we only had a telephone, I thought desperately, and if only I could speak enough Italian to make myself understood.

The beds were made up, the dining table and chairs were in place and the boys were tearing around outside on their bikes.

At least Zitoo was happy about having her own place. Her husband, Garensay, had a good regular job with the fire service. He always looked very smart in his immaculate uniform and his American haircut.

Zitoo went to put her house in order and I decided we'd have boiled eggs for tea – remembering, of course, that they took much longer to cook at this altitude. Richard ate his quite quickly and got stuck into bread and honey. Bill was only playing with his egg and didn't seem hungry. Most unusual! He didn't even want his drink of tea and when he got down from the table he went and curled up in one of the chairs. I cleared away the dishes. Suddenly I heard a cry from Richard

'Mummy, Mummy, come quickly. Bill's been sick all over the place.'

I flew out of the kitchen and rushed into the bedroom where poor little Bill was sitting in the middle of the floor. He had tried to get to the bathroom but hadn't made it and, as Richard so rightly said, he'd been sick over himself and everywhere else. There's no mess like a smelly sick mess. Bill was shivering so I quickly took off all his clothes and with a little water in the basin cleaned his face and hands. Richard ran to bring his pyjamas and we soon had him tucked up in bed. I left Richard sitting on his bed reading to him. He knew all the books by heart and could 'read' them with great expression.

I looked for some newspaper to clean the floor. In an English household there would always be plenty of newspaper but here we only had a single sheet bulletin giving us world headlines.

135

How ridiculous! No water, no newspaper, no old rags! How do I get rid of this mess? I sat on the floor and then I began to laugh. Once I started I couldn't stop. Perhaps it was hysteria or reaction to the whole overwhelming day, but suddenly it was funny to find myself stuck out in the blue in a strange house with two small children, surrounded by sick mess I couldn't mop up.

Richard came running in. 'What's the matter, Mummy, why are you laughing?'

'Oh, I don't know, darling. Better to laugh than to cry.'

I picked him up, gave him a hug and felt the comfort of his arms around my neck. 'Come on, young man. You'll have to skip cleaning your teeth tonight because we haven't enough water. They'll need an extra special clean tomorrow. Bedtime now. Let's have a story.' Bill was asleep and Richard cuddled down.

'The King asked the Queen, and the Queen asked the Dairymaid …,'

I finished the A.A. Milne poem, closed the shutters and put the bars across the windows. And so, I thought, here endeth the first day in Villagio Paradiso.

Our waterless state continued through the next day. Zitoo made friends with the girl who looked after Ralph, the prison officer, and there was a constant to-ing and fro-ing with buckets of water. Dukas' 'Sorcerer's Apprentice' would have been suitable music to play, although I wasn't suffering from a surfeit of water – quite the contrary. Zitoo scrubbed the floors with a strong solution of Dettol.

It was a lovely day, clear blue skies and a clean feeling in the air. I opened all the doors and windows and let the sunshine stream through the house. The Italians seem afraid of the sun and like to keep rooms as dark as possible. When no water-meter man had arrived by 11.30 a.m. I got the car out and drove into town. When I walked into the office, Maria, the secretary looked up from her typing with a resigned expression on her face.

' I'm sorry to bother you again, Maria, but the meter man still hasn't come. I just can't go another day without water. Would you please ring the municipality again for me and find out what is happening?'

She picked up the phone and a spate of Italian filled the office. If I'm going to live in this place, I decided as I tried to listen, I've simply got to learn this language.

'All is well,' she said as she put the phone down. 'Someone will be out there before lunch.'

I did some shopping and returned to Villagio Paradiso. When I turned off the main road I was overjoyed to see a motorbike outside the house and a man bending over the meter. Such a simple job. It only took about five minutes.

'*Va bene*,' I said using the few words I knew, '*Acqua domani?*'

'*Si, si adesso, tutto va bene.*' He grinned and roared off on his motorbike.

Later that afternoon there was a knock at the front door. David, one of the first officers who flew with John was standing on the porch with a large bunch of roses in his arms.

'Hullo, Vivienne. I saw John in Cairo and he gave me these to bring to you. He sends his love and felt you might need something to cheer you up. Sorry they're a bit wilted. It's been so hot and we had a delay before we left Cairo. No doubt they'll revive with a good drink of water. I can't come in. I'm flying again tonight so I must get some sleep.'

I thanked him and took the roses. Their heads drooped sadly. I looked for the bucket to give them a drink but it only had a drop of water in the bottom – not enough to help those poor rosebuds. Zitoo had gone home and I didn't like to go over to Ralph's and ask for more water. We must have used up most of his day's ration already.

Dear John! He knew I loved flowers. When we lived in South Africa he would arrange for flowers to be sent to me while he was away on his long trips. I hadn't seen any roses in Asmara so these ones from Cairo were special – beautiful pale pink ones. There was a note pinned to the green wrapping-paper but I decided I wouldn't read it until I was in bed. I felt frustrated not to be able to put the roses in deep water. Such a shame when John had gone to all this trouble. But my spirits soared with the gift. What a wonderful thing to be loved!

That was the turning point of our life in Asmara. At 6 a.m. the next morning I woke to the sound of sweet music – the trickle of water into the tank. We would be clean again and my roses could have a long drink. Later in the morning the luggage arrived from the airport and we had fun unpacking our treasures. I found my precious crystal vase – unbroken, thank goodness – and arranged the roses with a few pieces of grey eucalyptus from the tree growing by the garden wall. John's tools were in another box and I found his hammer and some picture hooks. How clever of me to remember to pack those, I thought. I'd never be able to find a shop here selling picture hooks. Even if I did I wouldn't be able to explain what I wanted. With a few pictures, books, music and coloured cushions scattered about, the villa changed from a grim concrete construction into a place we could call home.

With two battalions stationed in Asmara there was no shortage of social activities. The Aden Airways crews and wives were given membership to the officers club, and the children went to the British army school. There was plenty of opportunity for outdoor sport and the tennis club had three excellent courts in the palace park. They were 'chip' courts, a mixture of sand which soaked up the rain like blotting paper, and could be played on almost immediately after a shower.

With my tennis gear unpacked I hurried down to the courts but the first few games were very strange. We played with high altitude balls and it was hard to judge the fall of the ball when serving. And, boy, did I puff to begin with! The first day I had a game with Ann, Steve's wife, who was as fit as a fiddle. I only lasted 15 minutes.

'Goodness, I'll never be able to play properly at this altitude.'

She cheered me up when she said: 'Don't worry, everyone's the same at first. You have to play regularly, every day for short periods and gradually you will get acclimatized.'

I was quite happy to go to the park every afternoon and play tennis. The boys loved wandering over to the pony club with Zitoo and watching the horses. Bill was too small but Richard kept pestering to have lessons. I thought that could wait until John came back. I'd never been exposed to horse-riding and wasn't going to take on another responsibility.

Not far away from the villa the army had made a nine hole golf course. It was golf with a difference as there were more stones than grass on the fairways and the so-called greens were made of hard packed sand. It was quite usual for your ball to hit a stone and cannon back behind you. All good fun and exercise!

Because of the Shifta troubles we were virtually prisoners within the city boundaries, and the military guarded all the exit roads. We couldn't go far enough out of the city to see over the rim of the basin, to the mountains and valleys beyond. There was no blessed relief of 'lifting ones eyes unto the hills', because we were in a crater on the top of a mountain. And there was no river, no lake, no water at all to gladden and refresh the eye. It was difficult not to have a feeling of claustrophobia.

One day the bulletin announced that on Sunday, from 2 until 4 p.m. the road to Kherin would be opened and cars could drive along it for 10 to 15 miles to the reservoir. John was away but Steve sent a message asking us to join him and his family for a picnic. It sounded marvellous. He collected us just before two and we joined the long queue of cars waiting to be searched at the barrier. There was a gay, festive atmosphere and a great deal of noise as the Italian drivers revved their engines and took off in spurts to conquer those 10 miles in as little time as possible.

Steve, at the best of times, was not a patient man, and I was afraid that waiting in a long line of cars might make him change his mind. But the boys were so excited and thrilled to be going somewhere again that he didn't have the heart to turn back. It gave us all a glorious feeling of freedom to drive beyond the military post and into the country. About 5 miles out we turned off the main tar-sealed Kherin road onto a dirt track to the reservoir.

It was a beautiful day. The clouds formed castles in the air and moved quickly across the sky to let the sun shine through. Most of the Italian drivers had driven straight ahead and spent the two hours tearing up and down the permitted stretch of road. The cars stirred up the dust and it was difficult to see anything ahead. But suddenly, there it was! Water! Glistening and shimmering in the sunshine. The best sight I had seen for months.

Steve found a parking spot and we bundled out of the car. The boys tore towards the water with whoops of glee. Richard struggled to take off his shoes and socks.

I hurried after him. 'No, darling, I'm afraid you can't paddle in this water. It's a reservoir.'

'What's a reservoir?'

'It's a place for storing water. The water from here is piped into the city and supplies everyone with water.'

'But surely, Mummy, it wouldn't hurt just to have a little paddle. I won't go far in.'

Steve came to the rescue. 'Look, see if you can make the stones skim along the water.' He showed the boys how to look for nice flat stones and sent one jumping across the water, one, two, three, four, five times. Richard was excited when he managed two jumps but Bill was content to pick up the stones and drop them into the water where they made a satisfactory plonk.

Ann, always energetic, said: 'Let's go and climb that hill over there.'

It didn't look much of a hill, only great big stones and boulders. We clambered up helping Bill by pushing him from behind. I started puffing and realized how unfit I was for rock-climbing at this altitude.

I'm getting as bad as everyone else, I thought to myself crossly, blaming the altitude for everything.

Steve and Richard were well ahead and nearly at the top. Bill and I stopped and sat on a warm stone. It was calm and peaceful looking down at the water. I looked at my watch. 'Time for a cup of tea,' I shouted to the others. We started our rather hiccupy way back to the car. Bill was determined to navigate the rocks himself and refused to take my hand. The soles of his sandals were slippery and he decided it was safer to slide down on his bottom.

The car was surrounded by a crowd of small bedraggled Eritrean boys with dirty brown *futas* wrapped round them. They had appeared from nowhere and were obviously annoyed over the crowd on their land. Immediately they caught sight of me they began to shout, '*Baksheesh, baksheesh.*' I was quite relieved when Steve and Richard came running towards the car. The sight of a man sent the boys scuttling away. But not for long! By the time I had the thermos out and drinks ready they had closed in on us again, and were watching every mouthful the boys put in their mouths. Richard held out his sandwich to the boy nearest him and immediately a fight broke out. Poor little ragamuffins. Life was very hard for them and they were obviously hungry. We left a pile of sandwiches for them to scrap over.

We finished our drinks hurriedly and got back into the car. Steve started the engine and moved off with the boys scampering around on all sides, yelling and screaming for more *baksheesh*. It was a relief to get back on the main road and join the queue to the entry point where all cars were being stopped and searched. A rather pointless exercise as we had only been away for two hours.

But what a glorious two hours! To feel free again and unrestricted in our movements. Steve dropped us at the villa in Villagio Paradiso.

'Thank you, Steve, that was great. We all enjoyed the drive and it was wonderful to be on the other side of that barrier and see some water. Bless you for taking us.'

14

Operation – Tonsils

Italians in Eritrea were living under British army protection. Doctors, dentists, engineers and office workers in the municipality who originated from Italy considered Asmara their home. Under the British administration we enjoyed all the facilities provided.

The British governor, Sir Duncan Cummings, an Arabic scholar who had served in the Sudan, had a great knowledge and understanding of the Middle East. When he took office in Asmara Shifta gangs of several thousand terrorized the whole country. Although the army and the police were being successful in capturing many of the Shifta, a court sentence of death had to be ratified by the Foreign Office in London. This meant constant delays and reprieves. Prisoners who had been found guilty were released and returned to their villages to carry on with their harassment of the population. Sir Duncan travelled to London and demanded that he be allowed to confirm and carry out the death sentence without reference to the Foreign Office.

The first time a convicted Shifta was hanged, there was a tremendous uproar. The Eritreans would not believe the sentence had been carried out. A funeral was arranged, but on the way to the cemetery there were angry scenes. Finally the mob carried off the coffin and exhibited it around the country. There was speculation as to whether the authorities had purposely allowed this to happen, so it could be understood that in future a hard line would be taken on any banditry. It had an immediate effect of stabilizing control, and gradually restrictions for travel outside the city were eased, and guards removed from the city boundaries.

One morning, just before this first hanging, I was in the backyard pegging out some washing. I listened to the Eritrean boys in the little school next door chanting their tables, while another class sang 'Oh Clementine, Oh Clementine'. It was the only English song I ever heard them sing and I wondered how it came to be chosen. My washing-line suddenly broke and all the clothes fell down in the dust. I said a few bad words and walked round to the front of the house. Across the way, I saw Ralph in his police uniform coming out of his door to get into his jeep. He was carrying a coil of rope.

'Good morning Ralph,' I called out. 'Lovely morning. I wonder if you can help me. My washing-line's just broken and I need some new rope. Could you spare me some of yours? Have you time to fix it up for me?'

'Sorry, Vivienne, I'm afraid I can't let you have any of this. I'm just off to the prison and need this rope in place ready for the hanging at dawn tomorrow.' He went on to describe how it was done, how they had to calculate the weight of the condemned man and be sure the deed was carried out as humanely as possible.

But I couldn't listen to him. It made me sick to think I had asked for the rope that was going to kill a man. Casually he waved as he drove off, 'I'll see if I can find you some old rope and fix the line for you when I come back.'

Early in 1952 the United Nations became interested in the future of Eritrea and sent a party of officials to inquire about the wishes of the people. They reported to Headquarters in New York and an ambassador and staff were sent out. The ambassador came from South America, spoke fluent French and Spanish but very little Italian or English, no Arabic or Tigrian so his communication with the locals was limited. He was known as 'His Excellency' and took precedence over the British governor.

A plebiscite was arranged throughout Eritrea giving the people three choices: they could remain under British administration, become a state in their own right, or become a Federated State of Ethiopia under Emperor Haile Selassie. Everyone had the right to vote and there was a great deal of propaganda and preparation for polling-day. The majority of Eritreans couldn't read or write so the votes were marked with crosses. But when it came to counting the votes the results were very confusing. There were stories about villages with a population of 600 returning over a thousand votes.

Finally it was announced that the people had chosen to become a Federated State of Ethiopia and Haile Selassie, emperor of a land-locked country would get his sea port – the port of Massaua on the Red Sea. (All that happened over 40 years ago. Now, after continuous fighting, Eritrea has once more regained its independence.)

I shall never forget the ceremony in March 1952 when Eritrea was handed over to the Ethiopians. Stands were set up in front of the cathedral in the main street, from now on to be known as Haile Selassie Avenue. All the dignitaries were in formal dress. The princess, daughter of the emperor, her husband, the United Nations ambassador, the British governor, the colonel of the British regiment and the American consul and his wife were seated in the front row. The South Wales Borderers Band marched past and played the various national anthems. It was a poignant moment when the British flag was lowered for the last time, the silver crescent on blue of the United Nations and the two flags of Eritrea and Ethiopia were raised and fluttered in the breeze.

We wondered how this was going to affect our lives. Many of our friends had already returned to England. The Berkshire regiment had left several months before. There were farewell parties nearly every night for the officers of the South Wales Borderers who had played a big part in our social life. The emperor's daughter and her husband took over the palace and park grounds and the officers club became police head-quarters.

Elaborate preparations were made when the emperor came to visit Eritrea for the first time. Flags flew on newly constructed poles all the way from the airport. Roads were closed two hours before he was due to arrive. There were strict instructions that all animals had to be kept off the streets.

John came back from the office one morning and said: 'You'll have a great chance of seeing Haile Selassie this afternoon. I've just heard that he's coming out to Villagio Paradiso to visit the Coptic school next door. We'll have to be careful that Hamlet is shut up.'

144

Hamlet was the boys' pet dog. He was a white and black shaggy Heinz variety, and he'd adopted us when he was a small roly-poly pup. The boys loved him and he followed them everywhere.

Our villa was on a corner with a 4-foot concrete wall around it. At two-thirty that afternoon a large shiny new red car pulled up outside our gate. Two very tall men in military uniform got out, and stood either side of the door. One unfolded a large black umbrella and held it as a black-bearded little man stepped out of the car wearing a large toupee and a long khaki cape lined with red. He walked briskly down the side of our wall to the school where the boys chanted a welcome.

We hung around the garden waiting for him to return to the car. We wanted to take a photograph and have it on record that we had seen the emperor. Zitoo had been in the back garden waiting for him to come out of the school, and when she saw him leave she went through the house to call us. When she opened the front door, Hamlet dashed out, jumped over the wall, and barked ferociously. The imperial party, the little man in the large toupee, the two over 6-foot guards holding the umbrella halted momentarily. Then a very large foot shot out and Hamlet, barking even more fiercely, flew over the gate into the garden where the boys rushed to comfort him. The car turned round and drove sedately down the road.

When the British hospital closed, Aden Airways appointed an Italian, Dottore Mario Manfredonia as the official doctor. We became very friendly with Mario and his beautiful wife, Renato. I went to dinner in their house every Friday to give them English lessons. Renato worked hard and her conversation was good but Mario never seemed to progress beyond what he needed for his medical explanations.

I developed severe tonsillitis which kept on recurring. My throat was permanently sore, eating was difficult, and I began to look pale, wan, thin and scraggy. Finally Mario said he couldn't keep on giving me antibiotics and recommended that the tonsils be removed. I agreed to have the operation and arrangements were made for me to go into an Italian nursing home.

A childish complaint, I felt, wishing I had got rid of some of my bits and pieces at an early age. It's only a minor operation and I wouldn't know anything about it.

Joy, who was a nurse, came out to coffee the day before I was to go into the hospital. 'Have you asked Mario what kind of anaesthetic you'll be having?'

'No, but I guess it will a general anaesthetic. I certainly don't want to know what's going on.'

'I think you'd better ask Mario. Italian doctors seldom give a general anaesthetic in Asmara because of the altitude.' (That word again!) 'I'm pretty certain you'll have a local for a tonsillectomy as there's always the danger of bleeding.'

I began to have second thoughts about this 'childish operation'. I went into the surgery to see Mario and plead for a general anaesthetic.

'That's impossible here for such an operation,' said Mario, 'but I can assure you that you won't feel anything.'

'I mightn't feel anything but what about seeing and hearing?'

'Don't worry, you'll be all right. It's no good putting this off any longer. Is John home?'

'No, and he won't be back for several days.'

'In that case, I'll come and collect you at eight o'clock tomorrow morning and drive you into the nursing home.'

When he blew his horn the next morning I got into the car and wished he would turn right and take me for a ride in the country rather than left into town.

I didn't know what I was expected to do when I arrived at the hospital. A nurse showed me to my room and then left me. I changed into a nightie and dressing gown and sat in the chair waiting for someone to come and give me a pre-med injection to dull the senses. But nothing happened until a male nurse arrived and said, '*E pronto, Signora Pascoe,*' and beckoned me to follow him.

I walked along the corridor with my knees knocking together. So much for being doped and wheeled along on a trolley-bed. Mario, looking very unfamiliar in his operating gear was standing by a kitchen chair when we entered the room.

That kitchen chair! It was an ordinary brown wooden chair with a rounded back, a seat with small holes punched in it and a ring underneath the seat. The chair will never fade from my memory and I clung desperately to the ring as the operation proceeded. It was sheer torture as implements were thrust down my throat. I felt I would choke and had an overwhelming desire to bite hard on Mario's hands as they came near my open mouth.

My hearing was even more acute than usual – the clatter of the instruments as they were put back on the glass tray, the click of another one being picked up and the horrible, horrible squelchy noise inside my head when one gory tonsil was taken out and deposited in a nasty enamel bowl.

I fainted at the sight of it and had to be revived before they could get going again. One's anatomy has not one, but two tonsils and the beastly process had to be repeated. The male nurse held my head firmly. I tried to keep my mouth open. My hands clutched the rung under the chair.

'Just relax,' said Mario, 'we're nearly through.'

Although it is many years since that operation every detail and sound is etched into my brain. I can still see and hear it all clearly. The nurse helped me walk back to my room where I collapsed on the bed. Another nurse came in and gave me an injection of morphine which was to calm me down and put me to sleep.

Alas, I was beyond sleep. My whole system was in rebellion. They wouldn't knock me out for the operation and now, when they wanted me to sleep, every fibre of my body was jangly and on edge. I was vividly awake. I was aware, too of screams and moans going on in other parts of the hospital. In my dazed state I thought everyone must be having their tonsils removed.

How can they make such noises with their throats full of instruments, I mused.

Gradually I was aware of other sounds – the crying of newborn babies, and I worked out that another 'natural' process was going on all round me. Italian women's approach to motherhood is quite different from the stiff upper-lipped English lady. Members of the family are with the 'lady in waiting'. Her form of relaxed breathing is to open her mouth, make no attempt to disguise her agony and protest in the loudest possible way. A new life is a family concern and all must play their part to encourage the performer during the production. I fervently hoped there would be no tragedy because then the whole family would join in the wailing chorus.

It was a long, long day. Mario came in to see me around six o'clock in the evening and seemed surprised to find I'd been awake all day. He gave me another injection of morphine and one of penicillin.

Not long after he left I began to feel very hot and feverish. I touched my sore neck and face. There were burning blotches all over it. I looked at my arms where angry red welts had suddenly appeared. Then I started to itch madly and felt as if I was on fire.

During the day when I'd pressed the bell nothing happened but this time I kept my finger on it until one of the Eritrean helpers arrived.

'*Dottore, Dottore,*' I managed to whisper.

She went out quickly and came back with a nurse who took one look at me, broke into a spate of excited Italian and rushed out.

This is it, I said tearfully to myself, I'm going to die here all by myself with John miles away.

I tossed and turned, trying to find a cool spot in the bed and stop myself from tearing at my itchy skin.

I rang furiously again. The Eritrean girl came in. I wanted a bedpan. She didn't understand any English. I tried hard to think of a suitable Italian word but my brain wouldn't function. In my distracted state I grabbed the pencil and paper by my bedside, drew a chamber pot and pointed to the part of my anatomy that needed attention. She disappeared and then returned triumphantly bearing the required receptacle. I used it gratefully but I was so tormented by my itchiness I couldn't keep still.

Mario came through the door. 'Now what's the trouble?' He took one look at my face. 'You must be allergic to penicillin. I'm going to give you an injection. Turn over.'

I couldn't have cared by that time what he did to me. The needle went in. A wonderful cooling liquid seemed to rush through my whole body. It was amazing that anything could work so quickly. Mario put his hand gently on my forehead and the tears of relief flowed freely down my cheeks.

'Thank you,' I whispered. 'And by the way, what's the Italian word for bedpan?'

'*Vaso da notte.*'

I closed my eyes.

Left to right: Vivienne, Pat, Mother, Father and Betty in New Zealand

My favourite photo of John

The purple outfit I was wearing when I met John

Our wedding, 23 September, 1944 in Durban

50 years on. Our Golden Wedding with granddaughter Virginia wearing my wedding dress

John in the cockpit of the flying boat in Durban

John, Richard and I, Durban, South Africa

My sister Pat and I at her daughter Anne's wedding in Wellington, New Zealand

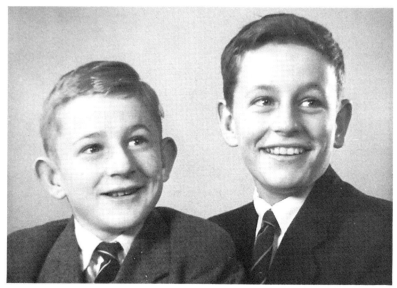

Richard and Bill

Two different modes of transport. John in Aden Airways DC3 in Aden and camel

Doing an Ikebana demonstration in
Wellington, New Zealand

Peter and Roz

Peter, Bill and Richard

Richard and Tina

Bill and Elizabeth

The eight grandchildren, seven girls and a boy

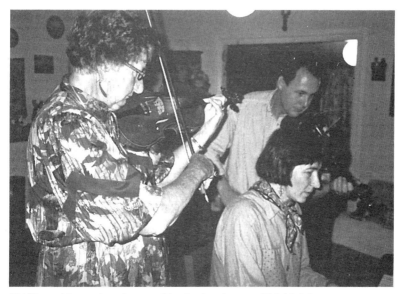

Fiddling with my niece Anne and her husband on my 80th birthday

All the family celebrating our Golden Wedding down on Bill's farm, New Zealand

In the driver's seat of Concorde

15

Departures and Arrivals

Life went on. Zitoo became pregnant and when Ghabre returned to the glamour of his town life, we found a wonderful girl, Zarah, to help in the house and look after the boys. I taught Zitoo to cook and was amazed how she remembered recipes when she could not even read. She only needed to be shown once.

As the Ethiopian princess was living in the palace where our tennis courts had been, we had to find other courts. I acquired a dashing Italian partner, Maurice Aleon. We played well together and won a number of tournaments. The Italians took their tennis very seriously and competed for silver cups. Soon there was an array of cups on the bookcase that John had made.

More United Nations personnel arrived and trading companies from other parts of the Middle East opened up offices. We formed a repertory society and had fun producing Noel Coward's *Present Laughter.* Willie, a representative of the Besse Company from Aden was a fine actor and made a wonderful Gary Essendine. There was plenty of talent among the Aden Airways wives to support him.

Zitoo produced a small son – an adorable little black bundle with pink palms and pink soles. I got all clucky and enjoyed showing her how to bath the baby properly and keep him clean. I gave her soap, nappies and clothes and he looked very cute – and black – in the white clothes. One morning there were shrieks from Zitoo's house across the road and Zarah came running over. 'Signora, Signora, andiamo. Zitoo's baby is sick. He's frothing at the mouth.' I dashed over. Little Totsie was indeed frothing at the mouth, but only because Zitoo in her enthusiasm to carry out my instructions had filled his mouth with soap. He was screaming with rage and distaste as he tried to spit out the soap suds.

Then I became a 'lady in waiting' and although I continued to play tennis for a while and take part in the repertory, my activities were curtailed.

With the closing of the British army school we faced a big decision over Richard's education. There was no other school – except an Italian one in Asmara. It meant him going away to boarding-school, either to Nairobi or back to England. I had put his name on the waiting-list at a preparatory school in Canterbury before we left. We wrote to the headmaster of Vernon Holme and had a reply that Richard could be accepted as a pupil when the new school year started in September.

I will never forget Richard's seventh birthday, September 7th, 1952. It was a heart rending day – the day he left Asmara to go to school in England. He put on his new uniform, grey shorts, maroon cap and blazer and we took a photo of him with Zitoo, who was in tears, in the garden of the villa. Bill couldn't understand what all the fuss was about, and we left him with Zarah. John drove us to the airport. Richard chatted away cheerfully, excited at the thought of going on an aeroplane. I couldn't travel with him because I was seven months pregnant – a rule of the airlines in those days. We had arranged with the governor's personal assistant, Sydney Miers, who was travelling back to England on the same plane, to look after Richard. He said he would take him to Victoria Station when they arrived in London, and put him on the train to Canterbury. My heart ached as we watched him climb the steps of the plane turn at the door and wave. He seemed so small, so young and so vulnerable to be going away on his own. I felt sick with apprehension, not only for the journey but for his arrival at a new school among strangers. John put his arm around me and gripped my hand hard.

'He'll be all right, Viv. He's a bright little chap with plenty of spunk.'

My heart nearly broke as I watched the plane take off. I prayed for his safe journey and that the school staff would be kind and understanding when he arrived tired and alone in strange surrounding.

We never heard the full story of that journey. There were delays due to bad weather and engine troubles, a night spent in Cairo and in Malta instead of Rome. This made Richard two days late arriving at school. It was a relief when a cable arrived from the headmaster saying he had arrived safely. We longed for his first letter, hoping it would give us some details of the journey. But what could you expect from a little boy of seven writing his first letter home?

> Dear Mummy and Daddy,
> I hope you are well. I was sick on the plane because it was so bumpy. Uncle Sydney put me on a train at Victoria but I had to change at another station. I was late getting to school. The headmaster was cross. Give my love to Bill and Hamlet. I love you.
> Richard.

I wept as I read it and longed to take him in my arms, love and comfort him.

Although the British army had left, there was a large American base established in Asmara, as a monitoring radio station to keep tabs on the Russian encirclement of the Middle East. It was, at that time, the only American base in Africa and it ran a popular radio programme which was listened to by all the English-speaking families in the area.

After my experience in the Italian nursing home with a doctor who didn't believe in general anaesthetics, I wanted to arrange for the American doctor to deliver our baby. He agreed to take me as a patient but I couldn't be admitted to the American-base hospital. He said he would be on call and bring his nurse to the Italian hospital – a different one from my tonsil episode.

Prospective mothers and fathers today have all kinds of courses available to them, – ante-natal care, post-natal care, breathing and relaxation exercises – stage one, stage two etc. etc. Fathers are keen to be present and take part in the birth of their child.

Even after producing two children in different parts of the world, I didn't have a very clear idea about the actual production procedure. My past experiences had been painful and prolonged. John had never expressed the slightest desire – quite the reverse – to be present at a birth.

Peter Jeremy burst his way into the world at 9 a.m. on October 20th, 1952. He had signalled his approach to landing about 3 a.m. I had been awake for some time trying to decide if this was really it, and if I should disturb John who was sleeping soundly. He had arrived back from Nairobi late that afternoon and I knew he was tired. The pains became more frequent so I shook him. 'I'm not sure, but I think it's time you took me into the hospital. Will you get dressed and go over and tell Zitoo where we're going. I'll phone the hospital.'

I got out of bed but felt I didn't want to walk very far or struggle into any clothes so I slipped my dressing-gown over my nightdress, gathered my toilet things together and put them in my suitcase which was already packed.

A sleepy Eritrean nurse sitting at the reception desk in the hall greeted us when we arrived at the hospital. She didn't understand English and couldn't find my name on any list. As there wasn't a chair in the hall, I sat on the concrete stairs while John tried to establish that I was booked, needed a room and attention, immediately.

It was cold. I felt shivery and apprehensive and longed to get into a warm bed. John was pounding the desk and I was amazed at his flow of Italian but he didn't seem to be getting anywhere with the receptionist.

'*Per favore, la prima signora, subito, subito.*'

It was a great relief to see an efficient looking Italian nurse coming down the corridor, 'What's all the noise about? Oh, yes, Signora Pascoe. Come this way.'

She bustled me upstairs – or rather she bustled and I moved with difficulty, into a comfortable room. John trailed behind. 'Please, dear would you go and phone the American base, get hold of Dr Gillespie and tell him that I'm now in the hospital.'

'But, Viv, it's four o'clock in the morning, He may not want to be disturbed so early. Don't you think it would be better to wait until seven?'

'No, I don't. This baby is not going to wait that long. I need him here right now.'

When John went to phone, I tried to explain to the sister that the American doctor would be attending me and not the resident Italian one. She seemed surprised but shrugged her shoulders, examined me and went out of the room.

It was ages before John came back. He hates telephoning at the best of times and this was not 'the best of times'. He came into the room looking worried. 'The duty officer says Dr Gillespie is away for the weekend but I spoke to the nurse and she said she'd come as soon as possible. I've just talked to the sister here and she says it will be some time yet. I'll stay if you want me too but there's not much else I can do.'

I was tearful at the thought of being left on my own and would have loved him to stay and hold my hand and stroke my forehead. But I could see he was like a fish out of water – he hated hospitals – and he was dying to get back to his bed.

'Be good, see you in the morning.'

I was left to get on with it as best I could. Time meant nothing; there were just periods of pain. The sister came in a couple of times, but as I wasn't her patient she wasn't really interested. I felt convinced that this baby had had enough of being cooped up inside me and was determined to make an appearance as soon as possible.

About eight o'clock John arrived back. 'They phoned me and said it was a false alarm and that you could come home. At least that's what I thought they said.'

'False alarm, my foot. It's any minute now. What's happened to the nurse – and the doctor?'

A girl came in with my breakfast, a cold cup of tea and two grissini.

John looked at it with disgust. 'That doesn't look very appetizing. I'll go and get you some fruit.'

'No, stay right here!'

As he pulled the bed table over for the tray, there was an explosion inside and the waters broke.

'Get the sister,' I gasped and he rushed out.

She came in and between the two of them I struggled along the hall to the labour room at the end. There was an excited agitated Latin panic going on as nothing had been prepared. Someone helped me up onto the table. John disappeared.

My brain was befuddled. I couldn't understand a thing that was said. They kept asking about '*Dove sono vestiti per bambino*' but I couldn't reply. Everything was heaving, pushing and pulling in an uncontrollable way. I had trouble breathing. I wanted to scream. More instructions – did they say push or stop pushing? How the hell did I know what I supposed to do?

And then – I heard a cry! It was all over. What a wonderful sound! There is no other sound like it in the world, no music has ever been composed to equal that vocal utterance – the first sound uttered by a newborn babe comforting the mother with the assurance that all is well.

I heard an American voice say. 'It's a boy.' The doctor and nurse had arrived in time to do their needlework – without a general anaesthetic. I might just as well have stuck to the Italian doctor.

Pity I had made that extra bit. It would have been nice to have a girl. But it didn't matter now. It was a safe, if bumpy landing. What else could you expect at this altitude!

16

Another Standby

It was early morning and the sun had only just begun to filter through the shutters. I stirred uneasily. Someone, or something had gently shaken my shoulder. Suddenly – I was wide awake.

Yesterday we had received a letter from New Zealand. One of my parents' neighbours in Wellington had written to tell me my mother was not at all well. As my father's letter – by the same post – had merely said Mother was spending a day in bed, I had not taken it too seriously. But all the same, it was disturbing news.

I sat up in bed. John was asleep. Call it premonition or what you will, but I felt as if my mother's hand had woken me. My mind cleared. I knew I must go to New Zealand to see her.

I was impatient for John to wake up. I nudged him with my feet. 'John,' I whispered.

'Ummm – what's the matter?'

'John, I've made a decision.'

'It's too early in the morning. Go to sleep.'

'I'm wide awake. When's your next trip to Cairo?'

'Cairo?' What on earth do you want to know that at this time of the morning?'

'Darling, that letter we received yesterday from Linda Clark. I'm worried. Something tells me that Mother is seriously ill. We haven't had a letter from her for some time. I feel I must go and see her as soon as possible. I know we can't travel until Peter has had his smallpox vaccination, but now he's three months old it could be done straight away. Bill's vaccinations are up to date and Richard won't be coming home from school for another six weeks.'

'Now hold on.' John sat up and looked at me. 'Travelling all that way with a three month old baby and a child of four is a bit of an undertaking. Wouldn't it be better to wait until we get some more news? Surely your father would have said something more in his letter if it was really serious?'

'Well, you know Father. He probably doesn't even realize how ill mother is. Something woke me this morning. I have this very strong feeling that I must go. I'd like to send a cable immediately to Mother. I want her to know I'm coming. You'll be all right. Zitoo and Zarah will be here to look after you.'

John sighed. This was the second time I had made a spur of the moment decision to return to New Zealand. 'Well, you'd better think about it very carefully today. When I go into the office this morning I'll have a look at the flight timetables. You'll have to fly to Cairo on Aden Airways, BOAC to Singapore, and if the BOAC flights there don't connect, you'll need to travel Qantas to Sydney and across the Tasman by flying-boat. And you understand, those four flights will be on a standby basis.'

'Yes, I realize that, but I'm willing to risk it.'

As soon as the surgery was open I rang Dr Manfredonia to make an appointment for Peter's vaccination.

'*Si, si, va bene*. Come in at ten o'clock. You know you can't fly with him for ten days after the injection. That's the limit set by the international health authorities.'

John came home for lunch and said he was trying to rearrange things so he could operate the flight to Cairo in 11 days' time.

'You're quite sure you want to make this trip now, Viv, rather than wait until we hear again from your father?'

'Quite sure. I've got to go before it's too late.'

That settled it. We sent the cable to New Zealand and for the next ten days I didn't have time to think or question whether I was doing the right thing or not. I was still breast-feeding Peter but in case anything happened to the milk supply, I would have to take bottles with me – and nappies. I'd need two dozen towelling ones as well as muslin. It was going to be a long journey and somehow the washing would have to be done along the route. As it was summer in New Zealand clothes were not a problem.

John, who had replaced Steve as Operations Manager, did everything he could to help. I was relieved when he told me he had changed the roster and would be taking the service to Cairo. At least, I would be pretty sure of a seat on that leg of the journey.

Zarah was upset about our going. She loved Peter and I don't think she trusted me to look after him properly. '*Oh, povero bambino ... povero bambino*,' she kept on saying. There was a tearful goodbye when she handed him over to me at the airport. How I wished I could take her with me.

We climbed into the DC3, the door shut and we raced along the runway. The wheels left the ground with a bump, and we flew over the edge of the basin where Asmara clustered like a pocket town tucked away on the top of the world. As we went over the rim I looked down on the jagged mountains underneath.

We bumped a bit as we hit pockets of hot air over the mountains. Bill went very quiet and still. I watched him anxiously, ready to grab the paper-bag from the pocket in front. Peter was asleep on top of all the nappies in the carrycot at my feet.

I was sitting in the front seat so I could feed Peter without disturbing the other passengers. But across the aisle from me was a very sophisticated looking young lady, with sleek dark hair. She wore a smart off-the-shoulders black linen dress. In my loose-fitting, nursing mother garment, I felt like a plum pudding beside her. When the plane stopped bouncing around I went through the door and into the cockpit to see John.

'Who's the dishy looking passenger in the front seat?'

'Oh, she's the girlfriend of the famous American archaeologist. He chartered Aden Airways to fly them – and all their gear – up to Wadi Hadramawt, north of Aden, where the ruins of the Queen of Sheba's palace is said to be. He's making a film as well as doing an archaeological dig.'

'I can't see her doing much digging in that outfit. I wouldn't think the Muslims approved of all that exposed flesh.'

'Now, Vivienne, don't be bitchy. She's quite a character – intelligent, well-put-together, and acts as his secretary.'

'Some act!'

The flight was restful and uneventful. This was a big enough adventure without any emergencies.

We landed at Al Maza Airport, Cairo at 4 p.m. A torrid wind blasted us with hot sand as we walked down the aircraft steps. Inside the airport building the ceiling fans cooled the air a little. John had told me to go ahead with the immigration formalities. He said he would join us as soon as he had cleared his aircraft. He warned me he would only have an hour before setting off on his return journey to Asmara.

Because of the Suez crisis, the political situation in Egypt was fragile and tense. There was no telling what kind of reception a British passport holder would get from the immigration authorities.

I joined the queue and stood behind the lady in black. When the official took her passport and looked up her name in the little book on his desk, he got up from his seat, and went over to talk to two other immigration officials. There was a lot of noisy discussion and argument. The lady remained remarkably unperturbed until an officious military gentleman beckoned her to follow him and escorted her to a room across the passage.

As I was carrying Peter and hanging onto Bill, there was a certain amount of juggling to be done before I could get my papers out of my handbag. The official looked at my passport and flipped through the pages of Peter's new health document.

'Where's the smallpox vaccination certificate?' he demanded.

I took the yellow health document book and found the pages stamped by the Asmara health authority. I handed it back to him.

'Is not right,' he said, tapping the book hard.

I carefully pointed to the date on the stamped page. He took no notice and called another official who peered at the book and shook his head.

'No correct,' he said. 'Not enough time. You can't stay.'

'But,' I said politely, although by this time I was feeling extremely annoyed, 'the vaccination was done eleven and a half days ago. The health authorities state you can travel after ten days.'

He shook his head. 'In Cairo, different. Here, must be twelve days. You all right and your other son, but baby must go into quarantine.'

'But I'm not staying in Cairo. I'm in transit and am flying out tomorrow –'(I hope, I said under my breath.)

158

At that moment John appeared and looked surprised to find me still at the desk. 'I thought you'd be through by now. What's the trouble?'

'You might well ask, 'I snapped 'This *gentleman* [big emphasis] says that health regulations for smallpox vaccinations are different in Cairo.'

John turned to the man at the desk and said mildly: 'I think there must be a mistake.'

'No mistake. Sorry, Captain, these documents not correct.'

John asked to see the airport doctor and we were taken to the same room where the lady in black sat in a chair, patiently reading a magazine and showing a lot of black silk-stocking leg.

We waited and waited.

'I'll have to go soon. It's nearly time for my departure.'

When the doctor came in John explained what had happened and said he was sure there was some mistake. 'I'd be very grateful if you can help my wife.'

But the doctor was adamant that the Egyptian authorities demanded a period of 12 days after the vaccination before anyone could stay in Cairo. 'It's only the baby who has to be quarantined,' he explained. 'The other two documents are in order.'

I exploded. 'Don't you understand? I'm breast-feeding the baby, so wherever the baby goes, I go. It's no good saying it's only the baby who's in quarantine – we'll all be in quarantine. It's just absolutely ridic –'

John interrupted firmly. 'Now steady on, Viv, getting upset won't do any good.'

The doctor ignored me and spoke to John, 'Your wife and children must either return to Asmara with you, or the baby stays at the airport in quarantine, until tomorrow morning.'

John turned to me, 'Well, what's it to be? It's your decision.'

I was furious. 'Well, I'm certainly not going back to Asmara. I'll just have to stay at the airport.'

'All right. I'm sorry, darling, but I'll have to go now. We take off in ten minutes.' And with those cheering words, he stood up, smiled at me reassuringly, hugged us all – and went back to his aeroplane.

I was left with the doctor. I tried again to reason with him, using all the charm I could muster. But it was hopeless.

'I'll arrange for you to be taken over to the quarantine quarters as soon as possible. You and your little son can come back to the airport for a meal this evening. But don't bring the baby.'

Stupid man, I thought. How can I do that when I don't even know how far away the quarantine quarters are?

During all this time, on the other side of the room, the lady in black was having a heated argument with a different official. Voices were raised, arms flung about as they shouted at each other in Arabic. I watched her being escorted away and wondered what crime she had committed that her name was recorded in the little black book. What was going to happen to her? Was she going to be flung into a damp rat-infested dungeon, or maybe whisked away to some sheikh's harem?

A young soldier arrived and abruptly told me to collect my luggage and follow him outside to a jeep. He didn't offer to help. We rattled across the airport and finally stopped in front of a corrugated tin hut. He got out and unlocked the door.

I looked around. 'Surely this can't be the right place? There must be some mistake.'

He shrugged his shoulders, threw the luggage out of the jeep and drove off.

I put Peter back in his carrycot and Bill helped me drag the luggage inside. What a night! It was hot and airless in the hut, and when I opened the small window, an army of mosquitoes invaded the room. I quickly shut it again. The narrow army iron bedstead had a lumpy mattress and I tried not to think who had slept on it before me. Bill tossed and turned trying to find a cool spot to lie on. I longed for the morning and was glad when Peter woke and demanded his feed. I needed the comfort of cuddling him and the soothing noise of his sucking, as much as he needed his breakfast.

In one corner of the hut a curtain hid a makeshift shower – cold water only. I turned the water on and was just about to step underneath it, when two monster cockroaches popped their heads out of the drain. I screamed and rushed back into the room. I had a horror of cockroaches and had no wish to share my shower with them. There was a knock at the door.

160

'Just a minute,' I called and hurriedly pulled on my skirt and buttoned my blouse. I opened the door and was surprised to see the doctor standing there, immaculately dressed in well-ironed bush-shirt and shorts. The sight of him early in the morning filled me with loathing and anger.

He gave me a toothy smile. 'Good morning, Mrs Pascoe.' I waited for him to ask me if I'd had a good night. 'I've come to take you back to the airport for breakfast. We have made arrangements for you to be taken into the Heliopolis Palace Hotel until your flight this evening.'

What a turn around! I hoped his conscience had given him a bad night! Now he was all smiles and bows – couldn't do enough for me. He stood patiently while I threw things into the suitcases, helped me shut them, and then carried the bags – and Peter out to his car. He drove us back to the airport and stopped outside the restaurant. Handing me some vouchers he said: 'These are for breakfast. A car will be at the entrance to take you to the hotel at nine o'clock. Have a pleasant stay.'

'Two-faced so-and-so,' I muttered under my breath. It took an effort to smile and thank him. But oh, the relief to get away from that hot, horrid hut, and to sit and have a strong cup of coffee.

I enjoyed the drive into the Heliopolis Palace Hotel. When I walked into the spacious, exotic reception lounge the staff rushed forward to help me. Oh, the bliss of a lofty room – with bathroom and hot running water! I filled the bath and let Bill wallow in it while I lay and fed Peter. When he was asleep Bill and I wandered downstairs to find the BOAC desk.

The receptionist looked up with a smile. 'I was just about to call you, Mrs Pascoe. I'm sorry about what happened at the airport yesterday. It was very unfortunate. You're listed for the flight to Singapore tonight and as far as we know at present, the flight is wide open. Transport will be leaving for the airport at seven o'clock. Let me know if there's anything I can do for you. If you'd like to go to the swimming pool I'll arrange for someone to keep an eye on the baby.'

'Thank you, that sounds wonderful.' After the shattering experience yesterday at the airport, when John left me, I doubted if I had enough courage to tackle the journey on my own.

Bill and I dashed back to the room, checked that Peter was still asleep, grabbed our swimsuits and went down in the lift to the pool. It was a delightful spot, surrounded by emerald green lawns, beds of brilliantly coloured canna lilies with bougainvillaeas in purple, red and orange shades trailing over the walls. I played around in the water trying to get Bill to kick his feet and extend his arms but he wandered off to splash in the paddling pool. I lazily swam a few lengths and got out and relaxed in one of the pool's comfortable lounge-chairs. I called the waiter and ordered long glasses of ice-cold, fresh lime juice.

It was a pleasant non-hassled day. I was packed and ready well before seven o'clock and went down to wait in the reception hall. I was ready to face the next part of the journey. But my spirits wilted as I saw a queue of guests waiting at the counter to settle their accounts, and then move to the BOAC desk where porters were struggling with piles of luggage.

The BOAC officer came over. 'I think you'll be all right, Mrs Pascoe. We don't seem to have many passengers for Singapore.'

'Where are all these people going?'

'Oh, most of them are returning to England and some going down to Africa. We're sending you out in the crew transport so you'll have plenty of time for check-in.'

'Do you know who the captain is?'

'It's Captain Williams. Here's the crew coming now. I'll help you onto the bus.'

Captain Bill Williams had been in Durban with us but in those days he had been clean-shaven. I didn't recognize this bushy-bearded man in uniform who came out of the hotel and climbed aboard. When he saw me he exclaimed: 'Goodness, what are you doing here, Vivienne? Are you going on our flight tonight? How's John? Haven't seen him for ages, not since he went to Aden Airways.'

We exchanged news and I told him I was going to New Zealand because my mother was ill. I certainly hoped to be on his flight to Karachi.

'See you on board,' he said cheerfully as he got off the bus with his crew.

I called a porter and followed him into the building. The girl at the desk was very polite. 'Good evening, Mrs Pascoe. We won't

162

know what seats are available until the flight is closed. Leave your luggage here and come back at eight-thirty p.m.

This was before the days of portable folding pushchairs and baby knapsacks. Peter was too heavy to carry for long and too active to leave in the carrycot unless he was asleep. Bill dashed around getting rid of his energy. Time passed slowly. I watched the desk and hated every passenger who booked in as I knew it meant another seat occupied.

Just before 8.30 p.m. the traffic officer came over to me. 'It's OK, Mrs Pascoe. You're on, anyway as far as Singapore. I'll see you through immigration now.'

My legs felt like jelly. It had been an effort to sit calmly waiting when inside I was seething like an active volcano. I hurriedly followed the officer and couldn't get out of the building quick enough. I didn't want to see any of the obstructive immigration men who had been on duty yesterday.

It was a smooth take-off and soon we were sharing the skies with the galaxies. After Peter was fed and settled I enjoyed a leisurely meal. Bill seemed to lose his appetite when he got on an aircraft, and after a drink and biscuit, he curled up in his chair with his favourite koala bear and was soon sound asleep.

When the cabin lights were turned off I gazed out of the window and saw a slim, sliver of water glistening below – the Suez Canal. The stars shone brightly in the blue-black sky. They looked so close it was hard to think they were millions of miles away. What wonderful friends stars have been to travellers through the ages. The Wise Men followed a bright star to Bethlehem. Polynesians, in their long canoes, paddled across the Pacific Ocean, with only their knowledge of the stars to guide them to a South Pacific Island – an island they named 'Aotearoa' – the Land of the Long White Cloud. And now men in their flying machines used a bubble sextant to make celestial observations and fix their position so they would arrive safely at their destination.

Daylight saw us flying over uninviting country – a barren land lacking in colour. Bill woke and looked out of the window

'Mummy, what would happen if we crashed down there? It looks so rocky. I can't see any roads, water or trees. Would it be very hot?'

'Yes, very hot. But don't worry Bill, I'm sure the captain is not thinking of landing there. We'll soon be at Karachi.'

The hostess came through and told us we would be landing in about 20 minutes. 'Another crew takes over here so we'll be leaving you. There will be transport to take you to the BOAC rest house for breakfast and a shower.'

When we walked through the scruffy looking airport I was glad we didn't have to spend any time there. The rest house, in contrast, was spotlessly clean and the breakfast excellent. Bill, now his feet were on the ground was ready to eat anything. Our waiter knew who I was.

'How's the captain, Madam? He hasn't been through here for some time. I remember him when I worked in the mess at the flying-boat base here. Captain Pascoe always enjoyed his meals and it was a pleasure to serve him. Please tell him that Ahmed was asking after him.'

Ahmed must have grown used to the likes and dislikes of the various crew members. No doubt he was fully aware of John's insistence that the correct sauces be served with the right meals.

I had a shower and looked longingly at the bed but we were called back to the bus and taken to the airport. Even though I had been told in Cairo we were booked through to Singapore, I had unhappy thoughts about being put off. But all was well. The Indian hostess in her attractive sari in BOAC colours, helped me on board. We were back in the same seats and the carrycot was securely fastened to a shelf in front of me.

The rest of the flight passed in a daze. Food and drink appeared but the constant change in time had messed up Peter's feeding schedule and I fed him when he demanded it. Bill was happy with the colouring book the hostess had given him and he was absorbed in doing – and undoing – a jigsaw puzzle of the Constellation aircraft. I watched the clouds building up in front of us – great billowing castles of cotton wool. As we flew into them the aircraft began to dance and buck. Bill sat very still.

The captain came through the cabin and stopped to talk to me. He knew John and asked how we liked living in Eritrea. He was thinking of applying for a posting there. Suddenly the aircraft dropped with a sickening thump – or it may have bounced upwards.

164

Which ever way – up or down – it played havoc with one's tum. Crockery and glasses crashed around and the stewards rushed to repair the damage in the galley. Bill, whose face had gone very white, looked up at the captain and said: 'Why don't you go back to your driver's seat?'

'Not a bad idea, young man. Don't you like these bumps? I'd better get back to the cockpit and see what's happening.'

When all was smooth and calm again Bill went back to his jigsaw puzzle. I sat back and closed my eyes – but not for long.

'Mummy, Mummy.' Bill was shaking my arm. 'That man. Look, he hasn't got any eyes.'

'Sh-shh, Bill.'

I looked up and watched a very tall man walk down the aisle with his hand on the steward's shoulder. Where his eyes should have been were two hollows and I could understand Bill's agitation.

'Mummy, what's happened to his eyes? Where have they gone? How can he go to sleep if he hasn't got any eyes to close?'

There's nothing so devastating as a child's logic and I couldn't think of an explanation. But I found out from the steward that the man was a well-known New Zealander, Sir Clutha Mackenzie who had devoted his life to helping blind people. With such a physical handicap there must have been a reason why he wasn't wearing dark glasses. It was an awesome sight to look at those empty sockets – especially for a child with Bill's imagination.

When the steward came through again I asked him if he would look in the ABC timetable to see when the next service left Singapore for Sydney.

'I'm afraid there's no BOAC service for four days. This flight terminates in Singapore. We only go to Sydney twice a week, but Qantas has a service every afternoon.'

This news meant a night in Singapore. John had told me if I got stuck, to book into the Raffles Hotel where the crews stayed. At least it would give me a night in a bed. This famous hotel had been named after Sir Stamford Raffles, an agent for the East India Company in the Far East. Realizing the importance of the island's location for British trade, he had made an agreement with the Sultan of Johore in 1819 and took possession for Britain, of the Singapore harbour.

165

The sun was setting as we flew in through the Singapore Straits where little fishing-boats bobbed about. We came in low over the harbour full of ocean-going liners and busy cargo vessels. We touched down smoothly and taxied to the airport building, where polite and courteous Chinese officials stamped our passports and health documents without any fuss or bother.

It was hot and sticky even at that time of night and I was very tired. The bus pulled up at the impressive portico of the hotel where everything was taken out of my hands – including the baby. A charming girl greeted me at the reception desk. 'Good evening, Mrs Pascoe. Welcome to Raffles. I hope you'll have an enjoyable stay. We've given you an air-conditioned room at the end of the corridor. Would you like a cot for the baby?'

The dark-panelled room was fairly cool, but stuffy, and the only window heavily curtained, opened onto the corridor. I started to unpack and sort out the nappies. What a difference disposable nappies would have made to my journey!

Bill was overtired and grizzly. Peter was screaming. I didn't know which one to tackle first. I rang for some milk and biscuits for Bill and sat in a chair to feed the baby. But he wouldn't settle and when I put him in the cot he had worked himself into a fine old rage and cried as if he had a pain. I tried to remember where I'd put the bottle of Gripe water – a great settler of tummy pains. I felt wuzzy and peculiar and couldn't remember where I'd packed it.

Suddenly Bill rushed to the bathroom and was sick in the basin. Poor wee chap. He looked so white and miserable. I washed his face with cold water and took off his clothes. He lay on the large bed, exhausted. I thought an aspirin might help and fossicked around, pulling things out of the overnight bag, desperately trying to find the bottle. Then I remembered I'd put it in my handbag. Bill took the pill and lay quietly, gazing up at the ceiling with his eyes wide open.

Peter was another matter. He was beside himself – didn't know if it was day or night – breakfast or dinner – thoroughly fed up with being messed about. Picking him up, I paced up and down the room, patting him on the back and singing anything I could think of.

'Three blind mice, three blind mice…' No that wouldn't do. It might remind Bill of the man in the plane.

'Hush a bye baby on a tree top When the wind blows the cradle will rock, When the bow breaks, the cradle.…'

It became a competition between his sobbing and my singing. 'Hush a bye baby…' Gradually his little chest stopped heaving and he nuzzled his head into my shoulder. I sat in the chair and rocked him gently backwards and forwards murmuring, 'Hush a bye baby…' Finally he succumbed and I put him down gently in the cot.

I was dying for a drink – something long and cold – but I didn't want to leave the room until I was sure that Peter was asleep. I soaked in a relaxing cool bath, brushed my hair, dressed, and took time over my make-up. When I tiptoed back into the bedroom, all was quiet, but when I went over to look at Bill, he was still staring up at the ceiling.

'Darling, I'm just going along to the restaurant to have something to eat. I won't be long.'

I walked along the corridor until I found the famous bar – the Tiger Bar. Legend has it that one day – many years ago – a tiger walked into the bar startling all the ladies sitting in their expensive clothes drinking Singapore gin slings. Now was the time, I felt, to find out what was in those potent drinks. I sat down at a table and looked at the murals of the tigers painted on the walls. Hoping that I looked very sophisticated and 'with-it' I asked the waiter to bring me a gin sling. I didn't think much of it when I tasted it – far too sweet and pink – but I drank it all and felt better.

The fresh lime I ordered with my meal out in the Palm Court was much more refreshing. The menu frightened me – a great selection of curries and spicy Malaysian dishes – all very exotic sounding and very expensive. I played safe and ordered a mushroom omelette with salad and then worried in case the lettuce and uncooked vegetables gave me the 'squitters' – one of John's descriptive words. Which reminded me that I mustn't let Bill drink the water from the tap. He was always so thirsty after a long flight.

I walked back to the room keeping my fingers crossed that all would be quiet. But when I went in I was horrified to find Bill crouching on the floor near the door, sobbing his heart out.

I gathered him in my arms. 'Bill, Bill darling, whatever's the matter? Sh-shsh, now come on back to bed. You're very, very tired. I'll lie down beside you and we'll both go to sleep.'

I stroked his forehead and moved my hand down towards his eyes to try and shut them. He brushed my hand away roughly.

'What's wrong, Bill? Come on, be a good boy, shut your eyes and try and go to sleep.' He started crying again. 'There, there, Bill. Tell me, darling, what's upsetting you?'

'Mummy, I'm frightened. That man in the plane – won't he ever be able to get his eyes back so he can shut them and go to sleep? If I shut my eyes maybe they'll go away too and I'll never be able to see again. I'll be blind just like that man without eyes.'

I held him tightly trying to find words to comfort him. 'Try not to worry, dear. It doesn't happen like that. Perhaps that man on the plane had an accident, or was very sick, and they had to operate and take his eyes away. But that doesn't mean that he can't sleep. You're a very healthy little boy and there's nothing wrong with your eyes.' I switched on the light beside the bed. 'Now watch, I'll shut my eyes and open them again. Look – shut – open – I can see you perfectly. You try now. Let's do it together – shut – open – shut – open. I'll read you a story.'

I picked up one of his favourites, *Hesperus – The Unwanted Car*. He listened with his eyes wide open, but gradually he relaxed and before the end of the story when the poor battered Hesperus found a family to love and care for him, he heaved a long, shuddering sigh, closed his eyes at last, and fell asleep.

17

Singapore

Poor Bill! I lay on my bed thinking about this upsetting experience. It was strange that a man, so well-known for his compassionate work with the blind, hadn't realized the effect he might have on a small child. Maybe he did wear dark glasses as a rule and had taken them off before going to the toilet.

I felt better after a night's sleep and bustled about sorting out clothes and nappies ready for the long flight to Sydney. I wanted to be at the Qantas office in the hotel as soon as it opened, to make sure our names were listed on standby for today's flight. When I got to the office there was already a queue of young people waiting. I joined the queue but stood for a long time before handing my tickets to the girl at the desk.

'It's pretty hopeless for this afternoon's flight, Mrs Pascoe. I've put your name down but I'm afraid it's not worthwhile going to the airport. There are too many full-fare passengers waiting.'

I pleaded with her. 'Please see what you can do. I'm desperate to get to New Zealand as my mother is seriously ill. I'm staying in this hotel – Room Sixty Eight – and can be ready to leave at half an hour's notice.'

I filled in the morning – went for a walk along Beach Road. But it wasn't much fun in the steamy heat, carrying Peter and holding Bill's hand. He was dying to have ride in the bell-ringing trishaws, a colourful tricycle with a sidecar. But in case there was a call from Qantas, I didn't want to be away from the room for long. There was no message. After lunch I phoned the clerk: 'Sorry, nothing

169

available today. We're absolutely full. Come into the office at eight o'clock tomorrow morning and see the officer on duty.'

'Are we going today, Mummy?'

'No, dear, I'm afraid not. Too many people want to go to Australia. We'll have to wait until tomorrow.'

At the hotel reception desk I booked the room for another night and asked for an Amah to look after Peter for a couple of hours. I needed to find a shop to buy some drink for Bill who was continually thirsty. The hotel was expensive and my Singapore dollars were dwindling rapidly.

Outside, a gaggle of trishaws clambered for trade. Bill tugged at my hand and happily climbed into a bright-red sidecar. The driver peddled slowly along the road ringing his bell furiously. When we turned into Stamford Road, I saw the Anglican cathedral standing in its grassy square, away from the busy streets and crowded shops.

I asked the driver to stop. He argued about the price and he shouted at us when we walked away. I wish John were here, I thought. He's much better at haggling than I am.

We walked across the grass and up the path to the door of the cathedral. A special paint had been used on the outside of the church – pure, white paint mixed with the white of egg. It glistened in the sunlight. Sir Stamford Raffles had chosen the site for the cathedral in 1823 but the building was twice struck by lightning and declared unsafe. The present building was consecrated in 1862 and it stood, serene and proud as a memorial to those men and women who had made this place a little bit of England. Before the fall of Singapore in 1942 it had been used as an emergency hospital.

It was reasonably cool inside and as we sat down in one of the pews I picked up a pamphlet from the seat and read the little prayer: 'Dear God, I am in much trouble. I have no one to turn to. There is no human being who can help me. Please reveal yourself to me and remove my trouble.' Could have been written specially for me in my present situation.

My heart was full of concern for my mother who had been such a loving influence in my life. All the years I had been away from home, her weekly letters had comforted and sustained me. She felt very near in that time of quiet. I knelt and prayed that she would

170

be saved from pain and discomfort. But oh, how I longed to see her again, watch her face light up with her special smile and hear her voice – the voice that had brought comfort to so many people during her years of ministry.

I was brought down to earth when Bill shook my arm and said: 'Come on, Mummy, I'm thirsty. I'm hungry and I want a drink.' We walked across the grass to the cricket club pavilion with its verandahs overlooking the cricket pitch. I imagined I could hear that hollow sound of clapping from the spectators as a good catch was taken or a player hit a six.

We wandered along the road by the water and I bought two bottles of orange fizz and some bamboo skewers of satay – meat cooked over charcoal and dipped in a sweet peanut sauce. Bill wasn't sure he liked those but was enthusiastic when we stopped at a fruit-stall. We walked away carrying large slices of delicious pineapple, mangoes and some prickly red rambutans, sat under a tree and enjoyed our dessert. Bill wanted a trishaw ride back to the hotel, but I was not letting myself in for another argument. Peter was asleep when we got back into the room. I thanked the Amah and flung myself down on the bed, leaving Bill to amuse himself with the suitcase of Dinky toys bequeathed to him by Richard.

And so day number one passed. It is a good thing I did not know then how many days I was going to be stuck in that hotel. Day number two found me up early and outside the Qantas office well before eight. I was first at the desk but a different clerk was on duty. I had to go through all the details again.

'I didn't get on yesterday's flight so I should be near the top of the list of standbys for today.'

He ran his fingers down the names. 'Yes, your name is here but there are a lot of people in front of you. Are you Qantas staff?'

' No, I'm the wife of Captain Pascoe BOAC.'

'I'm sorry. There are still full-fare paying passengers on standby and a number of Qantas staff waiting to go back to Sydney who have a higher priority than you. I can't see you getting away today.'

I felt I had been pushed around and asked to see the manager. 'He's engaged just now and I can assure you it won't do any good. But if you'd like to wait…'

I sat down and watched the people coming and going. After half an hour the manager came out of his office looking tired and harassed. 'You wanted to see me?'

I started to explain why I needed to go to New Zealand urgently but he interrupted me. 'Yes, yes. I know about you but it's quite impossible today. We have all these students going to Australia to start their university courses. They didn't get away yesterday and their new term starts tomorrow. I'm very sorry. I can do nothing to help you at present.'

So that was that! Another day messing about. Hotel expenses and food were running away with my dollars and I didn't have an unlimited supply of travellers cheques. Even if I cabled John – or New Zealand – the money would probably arrive after I had gone. If only I knew how long I would be here? If only I knew how Mother was? The anxiety and the uncertainty was shattering.

During the afternoon I left Bill with Peter and went out to buy some food to eat in the room. From a dusty little shop I stocked up with biscuits, chips and chocolate. The biscuits were soft and the chocolate had white marks on it where it had melted in the heat – but the chips were OK.

In the evening when the boys had finally gone to sleep, I wandered out into the lounge with my book and sat down in one of the comfortable chairs.

A group of men were at a nearby table drinking beer. I recognized one of them. He was an ex-flying-boat skipper who lived near us in Southampton – a tall, good-looking young man, amusing, but a bit of a line-shooter. When he looked up and saw me he came over. 'Hullo, Vivienne, what a surprise to see you here. Is John with you? Can't stop now as I'm in the middle of a meeting. I'm on the inquiry board about the Constellation aircraft that crashed here last week. Stick around and let's have a drink later.' He breezed back to his companions.

It was some time before the meeting broke up and when Mark came over he had a young lady with him. 'Oh, Vivienne, meet my new girlfriend, Susie. She lives in Singapore.'

I gulped a bit. I knew Mark's wife and wasn't sure how to take the 'new girlfriend'.

When I told him why I was in Singapore he said I had better get in touch with the BOAC representative to see if he could pull any strings with Qantas. 'Why don't you give Maggie Mollard a call? You remember Roger, our manager in Durban? He's now manager of Malaysian Airways. I was with him today on this inquiry. I've got his telephone number somewhere. Here you are. I'm sure Maggie would help you – give you a break with the boys.'

I wrote down the number and finished my drink – which I had enjoyed to the full – as I wasn't paying for it. I got up, thanked him and said goodnight to them both. I went back to my room wondering about pilots and the possibilities of girls in every port – or airport!

Next morning when I went to the Qantas office, I was horrified to find it fuller than ever. I recognized some of the students who had been there the day before.

'What happened?' I asked one of the girls who was sitting on her rucksack.

'Oh, we didn't get away yesterday. Nobody did, because the aircraft didn't arrive. It's stuck somewhere in India waiting for an engine change. They don't seem to know what is happening so we're just sticking around.'

This news made me feel terrible. The Chinese clerk recognized me when I went to the desk. 'It's quite hopeless today, I'm afraid, Mrs Pascoe. We don't know when the aircraft will arrive and now we have an even bigger backlog of passengers.'

I went back to the room and sat on the bed wondering what I should do. Maybe I had better give the whole thing up and go back to Asmara. Maybe it was already too late to see Mother. And yet, I had cabled I was coming and she would be expecting me. If only I could get away from this damned hotel which was beginning to feel like a prison.

I picked up the phone to call Maggie. I didn't know her very well but she had always seemed a kindly person and I was desperate to talk to someone. The lines were busy and it was sometime before I got through. Fortunately Maggie answered the phone herself or I might have given up.

'Hullo, this is Vivienne Pascoe. I don't know if you remember me from Durban days?'

'Of course I do. I'll always remember John. He was a special favourite of Roger's. What are you doing in Singapore?'

I poured out my tale of woe. She listened patiently. 'What a shame,' she said. 'Look, I'm busy this morning but I'll call for you at two o'clock and take you to the Tanglin Club for a swim. See you then.'

A swim – and a drive away from this hotel! What a wonderful idea!

I called the BOAC representative but he was very non-committal. 'This is a busy time of the year and we've had so many delays recently. There's not much I can do for you, but I'll contact Qantas and call you back.'

I messed about in the room waiting for the call but nothing happened. Then the receptionist phoned to say Mrs Mollard was waiting for me. After walking in the heat looking for something to eat, it was bliss to sit in an air-conditioned car and be driven through fascinating streets full of small stalls selling all kinds of local foods. Maggie was sympathetic and as an airways wife knew all about the uncertainties of standby travel.

'I know we're fortunate to have the privilege of rebate travel and I'm grateful,' I said, 'but oh, this hold-up seems endless. I'm so anxious about Mother and feel so helpless. I tried phoning New Zealand but it's impossible to get through.'

We drove into the entrance of the Tanglin Club. 'I'll keep an eye on the baby, Vivienne. You take Bill and have a swim. You'll feel better after that.'

It was wonderful to get in the water and sit under an umbrella and sip a long, cold Tiger Beer. I spread a towel on the grass, removed Peter's nappy and he lay there kicking and cooing happily. A lovely peaceful afternoon. Maggie said when she left us: 'I'll call for you again tomorrow if you don't get away. I'll ask Roger if he can do anything for you. He knows the Qantas manager quite well.'

As I walked in the receptionist called me. 'Oh, Mrs, Pascoe, we've been looking for you everywhere. There's a gentleman in the lounge waiting to see you. He didn't give his name but said it was important. Give me the baby and I'll arrange for him to be looked after.'

'Are there any messages for me?'

She looked in the pigeon-hole and shook her head. 'No I'm sorry, there's nothing here.'

I handed Peter to her and walked along to the lounge where a serious looking young man was sitting in a chair. He stood up when he saw me. 'Mrs Pascoe? I'm Ted Griffin, the BOAC station manager. Do sit down.'

I felt cheered that the station manager had come to see me personally and waited for him to give me the good news about my onward flight. He held some papers in his hand and was rather quiet and hesitant.

'Mrs Pascoe, I'm afraid I have some bad news for you. We received a message this afternoon from your husband in Asmara.' He handed me a piece of paper.

My mind went numb and I sat down with a bump as I read: 'Darling, cable from your father – "Mother died peacefully Sunday. Funeral Tuesday. Looking forward to seeing you. Love Dad." Today was Tuesday! It was too late to see Mother and too late for the funeral! It was a useless journey. I might as well go back to Asmara.

Poor Father! He would be lost without Mother to love and care for him. What should I do? It was such a terrible shock to receive this news so abruptly. I couldn't think straight.

I read the cable again. 'Looking forward to seeing you and the boys.'

He would need me more than ever. I couldn't let him down now. I would have to carry on.

I turned to Mr Griffin sitting uncomfortably on the edge of his seat. 'This is very distressing news as I'm sure you realize. I've been desperately trying to get a flight to New Zealand and it's been so hopeless. Now it's too late.'

' Please accept my sympathy. I'm very sorry about this. If we'd realized it was so urgent we would have tried to do something.'

That made me see red and feel very, very angry. How often grief and anger get muddled up! For days I'd been hanging round in this hotel pleading for a seat on an aircraft explaining again and again that my mother was desperately ill. And here was this man telling me that if he had realized it was serious, he might have been able to help. But it was no good being mad at him… bad enough for him that he had to bring me the cable.

'What do you want to do, Mrs Pascoe. Carry on to New Zealand or return to Asmara? Perhaps you need time to think about this?'

'No, for my father's sake, I'll go on to New Zealand as soon as possible.'

'As the Qantas flights are so full, I think it would be best if you go down on our BOAC flight tomorrow night. I'll see that you are booked to Sydney and send word to TEAL to get you on the flying-boat Service to Auckland on Thursday morning. Is there anything else I can do for you?'

'Thank you. Perhaps you could arrange for me to sign a personal voucher on my husband's account. I don't think I have enough dollars to pay the hotel bill?'

'Don't worry, Mrs Pascoe. I'll see to that and fix transport for you to the airport. What about your husband? Do you want me to send a message to him saying that you've decided to continue your journey to New Zealand?'

'Yes please. I'd be grateful if you'll do that… and give him my love.'

I said goodbye and went to my room. It wasn't easy to tell Bill that he wouldn't be seeing Minga. He knew Minga was sick and this was the reason for our trip to New Zealand. But he was amazingly matter-of-fact and philosophical and wanted to know where she had gone.

'What's Heaven like, Mummy? Will Minga be dressed in white flowing robes like an angel and ride on a cloud. I hope she'll be happy when she meets God, but I wish she could have waited until we'd arrived.'

As I lay on my bed with my eyes closed that night, memories came tumbling over me. Mother's whole life had been one of service to others. In 1903 she left New Zealand and went to England to train as a deaconess in the Methodist church. She told us many heart-breaking stories of her work among the poor in the slums of Leicester and London – the appalling poverty and the hardships caused through drink. She was quite fearless, and wearing her blue uniform and bonnet, would go into local pubs and threaten the innkeeper if she thought he was breaking the regulations and serving alcohol to anyone under age. Her smile could melt the wildest man, but if she felt an injustice had been done, her eyes would flash and her explosive words would reduce the bravest to a humble penitent. She ran a soup-kitchen for the children, begging bones from the butcher and made a gruel with vegetables in a large copper. She described the joy on a child's face when he – or she – found a piece of meat.

How I loved her! As a family we were secure in her loving understanding of all our problems. Her wonderful sense of humour made life fun. She had a gift with flowers – even the humblest blossom looked just right when she put it into a vase. When Betty and I played at a concert there was always a posy or a bouquet from Mother presented to us at the end.

Tears streamed down my face as I suddenly realized I would never see her again – never find a letter from her in the mailbox. (Alas as far as I knew there was no postal service from Heaven.) I longed to hear that dear, soft-toned voice – a voice able to move an audience to tears – or laughter.

And then, almost in answer to my prayer, I thought I heard her whisper in my ear one of her favourite quotations from the Bible: 'Darling, in my Father's house are many mansions... I go to prepare a place for you.' I imagined the house and smiled because I could just see her inside taking a quick look round and deciding the colour scheme needed changing. She had transformed the colours of many a parsonage during her life as a minister's wife.

(Years later – on my seventy-eighth birthday – I was in Singapore with John and Richard. As it was a Sunday we went to the nine-thirty service at St. Andrews. It was an emotional experience and brought back all the feelings I had on my first visit. The text for the sermon was Mother's quotation: 'In my Father's house there are many mansions.' In the modern Good News Bible it says: 'In my Father's house there are many rooms.' Mother loved space and even in Heaven I think she would enjoy a 'mansion' rather than a 'room'. I had difficulty in keeping back the tears when we stood to sing Mother's favourite hymn: 'Dear Lord and Father of Mankind, Forgive our foolish ways.')

But it was her hands that I remember most; small beautifully shaped with long tapering fingers. The details of her face might fade – but hands – never.

I was getting drowsy. The thought of Mother's hands soothed me – as they had often done as a child. Angel fingertips seemed to touch my forehead and a great peace descended on me as I slipped away from the sadness of the world into the soft embrace of Mother's love. Dear, dear Mother.

The rest of the journey passed by. I kept going with the rhythm of feeding, bathing, changing nappies, wondering how to wash nappies, and answering Bill's endless and searching questions.

The station manager saw us onto the plane at Singapore and again expressed his regret. Friends met us in Sydney, fed us and took us to Rose Bay where the flying-boat rocked gently on the water. Relations collected us in Auckland, rang Father, fed us and put us on a plane for Wellington. It had all taken such a long, long time travelling – or not travelling – for over a week. As we began our descent into Wellington an upsurge of emotion engulfed me. I had hoped for such a different home-coming. Now I must think of Father,

We touched down, turned and taxied to the airport building. I dabbed my eyes and fought for control, busying myself with checking all the bits of luggage.

Carrying Peter and holding Bill's hand, I stood at the top of the steps hunting for the familiar figure of my father. There he was, standing just outside the door, waving his hat and looking a little shrunken and stooped. I hurried down the steps and ran towards him. He enfolded us all in his outstretched arms. There were tears in his eyes as he welcomed us. 'My darling Vivienne, Bill and little Peter, thank you for coming.'

18

Wellington

Bir Salem! This was the name Father gave to the house he'd built on Seatoun Heights in Wellington. It was an anagram of the letters of his name 'Blamires'. Translated from the Greek it meant 'Well of peace'. It amused me that my parents who were strict teetotallers lived in a house with a name starting with 'Bir' pronounced 'beer' on 'Beerehaven' Road.

Father had lived all his life in church houses. First as a minister's son in Victoria, Australia, and later as a Methodist minister in New Zealand. When he retired he was determined to build his own house – his dream house. When he bought the Seatoun section in 1938, no one thought he could build a house on such a steep hill. He reckoned it was the closest to heaven he would ever get.

Mother and he designed it and a nephew, who was a builder, agreed to construct it. There were big plate-glass windows, unusual at that time, along the front of the house and every room had a view of the sea. Mother could lie in bed and watch the ships – big ships and little ships – sail in from Cook Strait, past the jagged Pinnacle Rocks at the entrance and round Point Halswell, on their way to a safe haven at Wellington wharfs. At the weekends the water was alive with trim little yachts sailing out from Worser Bay ready to do battle with the gusty harbour wind.

Because the plot had no flat land, the building of a garage presented a problem. Finally it was constructed on stilts and bolted into concrete above the house with a hazardous approach from the road. Father was warned that such a building would not stand the mighty gales that tore around Wellington hills. (At the time of

179

writing, over 50 years later, it had defied all elements – even the gales that sank the steamship, *Wahine*. It still stands perched on its stilts.)

Our parents wanted this house to be a wonderful home-coming surprise for Betty and me when we returned to New Zealand after four years' study in London. No mention was made of it in their letters. We knew the family had moved to Wellington but we didn't know where they lived. When we arrived by ship in Wellington in September 1939, the family met us and drove us through the city, past the Basin Reserve where we had so often watched Father play cricket, through the Haitaiti tunnel, past Kilbirnie to Strathmore Park. Father stopped the car outside a rather dull looking government house. After all the excitement of the arrival we tried not to look too disappointed.

Father opened the door of the car and started to get out. Then with a twinkle in his eye he said: 'No I don't think we'll stop here after all,' and got back into the car.

'Where are we going?' I asked, not able to bear the suspense any longer.

'You'll see.' Father drove on through the Seatoun Tunnel and turned left up the hill. We passed the Star of the Sea Convent standing proudly on the hill. As we topped a rise into Beerehaven Road, Father slowed the car. 'I don't think we'll go much further. What do you think of that for a view?'

It was breathtaking! Far below us the blue green water sparkled and the sun glinted on the sandy shore. In the distance we could see the Upper Hutt Valley and across the water the Orongorongo hills above Eastbourne Bay stood out sharply against the vivid blue sky. There were few houses to be seen but at the side of the road, Tararua daisies, periwinkles and nasturtiums ran riot.

Father switched off the engine at the entrance to the garage. I got out and looked down at the 20-foot drop to the path below. In the years to come I would have a recurring nightmare about driving the car over that drop. I would find myself falling, falling, falling … until I woke up with relief and found it was only a dream.

All that was a long time ago. Now as we topped the rise after the short drive from the airport, I remembered how thrilled Betty and I were when we saw the house, and how proud Father was to show us around. He had cleverly fitted the Frigidaire flush with the kitchen wall – even though it bulged out in the wardrobe behind – and his bed in the study folded back into the wall when it was not in use. Mother had taken the sea as her colour scheme and the soft blues and greens melted into the panorama. It did indeed live up to its name of a well of peace. I was suddenly tearful at the thought that Mother was no longer there to greet us.

'You take Peter and I'll see Bill safely down the steps. I expect Pat is wondering where we've got to. I'll come and get the rest of the luggage later.'

I climbed down Jacob's ladder – the tortuous steps that Father had built, carrying Peter while Bill followed behind holding his grandfather's hand. Pat stood at the open door with arms outstretched ready to welcome us. For a moment I thought it was Mother. They were so alike – the same build, colouring and expression. It was wonderful to see her again and her little son, Johnnie, who was just a little older than Peter. Pat and Roger had returned to New Zealand in 1949 and were now living in Napier.

It wasn't easy to walk into the house full of memories of Mother, and I gripped Pat's hand hard. We were both too near tears to say much. I didn't even know the cause of Mother's death but I felt it was too soon to ask questions. Betty and family had been down for the funeral but had returned to the farm.

When the three boys were in bed, Father, Pat and I sat at the table and looked out at the lights around the harbour. Pat had prepared a wonderful meal – New Zealand lamb, fresh vegetables including silver beet from the garden – but I was too tired to enjoy it.

As we sat quietly enjoying the view I turned to Father. 'Daddy dear, can you tell me about Mother. I'm heartbroken that I didn't manage to get home in time to see her – not even in time to be with the family for the funeral. When did she die?'

'Last Sunday morning. I took her an early morning cup of tea and thinking she was still asleep, left it on the table by her bedside. She looked so peaceful lying there. As I got to the door, I had a strange feeling and went back to her bed. I realized then that something had happened in her sleep. She had been ill for several weeks and had trouble in keeping any food down. We'd tried all kinds of things to tempt her. I even went into a pub and bought her a bottle of beer because she said she fancied something bitter to drink. But even a sip of that drink didn't stay down.'

It must have been quite an ordeal and taken courage for Father, when he was so well known, to go into a pub and buy beer. But he did it for the lady he loved and felt sure that the Lord would forgive him.

'But what was the cause of her death? Did she have pneumonia?'

'No, it was heart failure caused through pernicious anaemia. Our new family doctor, Dr Alan Moynaugh and his wife, Joy live just behind us. He wasn't happy about Mother's condition and suspected pernicious anaemia. His diagnosis was confirmed last Thursday when the blood tests came back and he immediately gave her an injection but it was too late.'

'But surely she must have had blood tests before she had the bladder repair operation in Palmerston North Hospital just a few months ago. Why didn't they discover this anaemia then?'

'Goodness knows. They probably only did a haemoglobin test before the operation and weren't looking for anything else. Vivienne darling, I know it's difficult for any of us to understand. But now we must accept it and be happy that she is at peace and free from pain. Mother wouldn't want us to grieve for her. She loved us all. She was so happy when she received your cable and knew that you were coming. I'm sad for you that you travelled all this way and then missed her. But for me, it's a great comfort to have you here and I'm so grateful to John for letting you come.'

Pat returned to Napier the following day making me promise that I would drive Bumpa (how quickly because of the grandchildren, we slipped into calling him 'Bumpa') and the boys up to see them as soon as possible. I didn't know how long I would be able to stay in New Zealand. I'd have to wait until I heard from John. Bill followed Bumpa like a little shadow and loved to go out in the garden with him to feed the hens.

When someone dies, especially a member of the family, one of the most upsetting tasks is to have to go through clothes and personal belongings. I knew it had to be done and was glad that I could save Bumpa a little bit of anguish by sorting through Mother's wardrobe – most of the clothes she had designed and made herself. At the back of the wardrobe I found a bottle of unopened beer and that sent me into floods of tears. How desperate she must have been to ask for that. She had worn her little white temperance badge so proudly on the lapel of her coat for many years.

Every mail brought letters of sympathy from the many friends who had known and loved her. Father had a card printed with her photo and a poem that Leslie Weatherhead – the well known Methodist minister – had quoted in one of his books. He had found it in the flyleaf of his mother's Bible when she died. The author was unknown but we felt that Mother could have written it for us. The words helped and made her feel very near.

> If I should die and leave you here awhile
> Be not like others sore undone, who keep
> Long vigils by the silent grave, and weep.
> For my sake, turn again to life, and smile,
> Nerving thy heart and trembling hand to do
> Something to comfort weaker souls than thine.
> Complete these dear unfinished tasks of mine
> And I perchance may therein comfort you.

As the days passed and the tension eased, I never tired of the view looking across the water to Wards Island and the hills beyond. Bumpa was still keen on his bowls and it was good for him to play as much as possible with his friends.

Betty rang from the farm. 'When are you coming up to see us? The girls are longing to meet Bill and Peter. What about next weekend when the holidays start. Has Peter been christened yet?'

'No, not yet.'

'Well, why don't you let me arrange a little service here at Bog Roy on Sunday and we'll get Pat and Roger to come down.'

It took me by surprise. I hadn't thought of a christening for Peter without John being present. But Bumpa had christened Bill when they came to England to visit us in Southampton and it seemed right that he should christen his other grandson.

'I think that's a great idea. I'll discuss it with Bumpa.'

So it was all arranged. We drove to the farm one sunny afternoon and met the three girls, Jayne, Billa and Mary, who were excited to be home for the holidays. Such a reunion! Betty and I never stopped talking. We had been very close during all the years we played together. In a concert, if I made a mistake and skipped a few bars, Betty would know immediately and follow. We had given many recitals up and down the country and produced a varied programme of violin, piano, drama and folk songs in costume.

It was a great wrench for me when she married Don and moved to Feilding. It wasn't easy to find another pianist to accompany me.

Now I had to realize she was a married woman – a farmer's wife – with three little daughters. It was strange that after being trained as musicians and artists we had both married men of the land. Don was a meticulous farmer, as was his father before him, and all John's family were connected with farming. Bog Roy was a lovely sheep farm where they had built a house on a similar plan to Bir Salem. Betty never did things by halves and was a fanatic gardener.

I sensed that she had been determined to be a good farmer's wife. I think she almost tried too hard if only to prove to Don's parents, who had rather disapproved of their son marrying a musician, that she could do all the things a farmer's wife was expected to do. So she gardened, bottled fruit and hoovered the house every day. I found it hard to accept this new Betty – so different from the sister of our student days when housework and keeping everything spotlessly clean and tidy were not a priority.

Bill was very happy to be on a farm and transferred his allegiance from Bumpa to Don. He developed a passion for gumboots and stumped around in an old pair of Don's until I bought him a new pair. Then he wouldn't be parted from them and even took them to bed. He and Mary, a dear little dark-haired girl a bit younger than Bill, had great games together and wandered over the fields looking at the sheep and cattle.

'I think you've got another farmer in the family, Vivienne.' Don said to me one day. 'You'll have to send him out to New Zealand when he grows up.'

Sunday dawned a beautiful day. The grass in the fields glistened in the early-morning sun and the sheep, looking snowy-white against the emerald-green grass, munched contentedly and baa-ed occasionally. The house was spotless, the windows shone and there wasn't a weed to be seen among the riot of colour in the flower beds.

It had been a long time since we three sisters had been together. It was sad that John wasn't with us. Betty had invited some friends and neighbours to the service and prepared a sumptuous tea: small sandwiches, Anzac biscuits, peanut biscuits, butterfly cakes oozing with jam and cream and – of course – a light airy delicious cream sponge – something every farmer's wife in those days had to bake to prove their worth. She had washed and ironed the family christening gown but Peter was no longer a small baby and couldn't be fitted into the flowing robe. He was all gurgles and smiles when Bumpa took him in his arms. Just as Bumpa was reading the responses from the christening service, Peter reached up and took a firm hold of his grandfather's spectacles twisting them off his nose. He wouldn't let go and there was a pause in the service until I managed to prize open his little fingers and put the spectacles back on Bumpa's nose. There were no further hitches and Peter Jeremy was duly christened by his grandfather.

For Bumpa it was a time of healing and adjustment – easier to do away from the home he and Mother had created together. He revelled in being with his daughters and grandchildren, played cricket on the lawn with Bill and Johnnie, chatted to his sons-in-law, showing lively interest in all things happening on the farm and in Roger's engineering business in Napier. He enjoyed being fed, cosseted and fussed over.

Pat and family returned to Napier and we spent a happy week on the farm. Betty was envious of all the travelling I had done while she had stayed put on the farm during the war. But she had kept up her music and played the piano better than ever.

At the end of the week I drove Bumpa and the boys up to Napier. As we drove along Bumpa recalled his journey from Masterton to Napier just after the bad earthquake in 1931. Because there had been so much damage to buildings and the water and electricity cut off, the authorities had called for outside help. Bumpa set off early in the evening after the quake with his car full of meat, vegetables and fruit. Just after Hastings he had come across a man whose car had overturned in ditch because, in the dark, the driver hadn't seen the fissure in the road caused by the earthquake. The man was unhurt but his car, which had been loaded with dozens of eggs and cartons of honey was an indescribable mess.

Now, as we approached Napier along the beach front, one would never had known it had suffered such devastation. There was a warm welcome for us from Pat, and Roger. Bill and Johnnie were soon roaring around together playing with Johnnie's bike and toys. At bedtime Pat cuddled up beside them both and read a story. Bill was enthralled – not only was it a new book – but Pat read stories so beautifully. With her great gift of drama and story-telling the book came alive.

It was interesting to compare the homes of my two sisters – both so talented and yet so different. When Roger was demobbed from the army they returned to New Zealand and had to start from scratch. Betty and Don, on the other hand, were established on a farm before the war began and providing food was an essential part of the war effort. Through Don's constant hard work, the farm had prospered and it was evident now in their home that money was not a day to day problem.

In Napier there was a more relaxed atmosphere and values were different. The hoover didn't appear every day and dishes could be left if there were more interesting things to do. It was more important to them to have a good record player and lots of music than a comfortable chair. Although I love music, I also enjoy sitting in a comfortable chair. But I was happy to feel at home and the stresses and strains of the last few days slipped away from me.

The phone rang early one morning and I heard Roger say: 'Just a minute and I'll get her. It's a cable for you, Viv.' I got out of bed hurriedly. Cables always frighten me and I wondered if anything had happened to John. I picked up the phone.

'Hullo, this is Mrs Pascoe speaking.'

'Good morning, I have a cable here for you. Do you want me to read it out to you or shall I post it?'

'Read it please.' I gripped the phone hard.

'It's from Captain John Pascoe.' I let out a breath. The girl on the other end of the phone continued. 'The cable says: "Plans have changed. Job finishing with Aden Airways. Returning to BOAC, England. Alter tickets to arrive Heathrow end of month. Letter following. Love John." '

I sat down on a chair with a thump, completely stunned. Roger looked up from eating his breakfast and said: 'Are you all right, Viv? What's happened? Is it bad news?'

'Well I don't know. John's OK, but he's returning to BOAC. The boys and I won't be going back to Asmara but flying direct to England. I feel a bit shaken – not sure what has happened.'

I made a cup of tea and took it back to bed. As I sipped it I tried to imagine what had brought about the sudden change of plan. Before we left Asmara there had been all kinds of rumours about moving crews down to Aden because of administration difficulties under the new government. But no one had taken them seriously. Asmara had a good climate, but Aden...! Perhaps the rumours were true. John knew I'd always been against the idea of living in Aden and he would have had to decide quickly whether to give up the job with Aden Airways or return to BOAC. Now I was longing to get his letter and decided we had better get back to Wellington ready to make new plans when I heard from him.

Every day at Bir Salem I dashed out to the mailbox when I heard the postman's whistle. Yes, in those days the postman blew a whistle when he put mail in the box. Sad how many things we have lost over the years. But then we have gained others, disposable nappies, folding pushchairs, glad wrap and plastic bottles.

I spent as much time as possible with Bumpa trying not to let him see my impatience and anxiety. And every evening when the boys had gone to bed we played two-handed bridge. Mother and he had always played this game after their evening meal and I knew he was missing the evening relaxation. I am not a card player at the best of times and except for the bridge I played with the three young men on the boat going to England, I had always avoided card-games. It was an effort for me to concentrate but it took my mind off 'things to come'.

The days passed in a flurry of preparations. I thought – yes, with envy – of Betty on the farm. Her life was so stable and secure compared to this nomad existence of mine, rushing hither and thither round the world without even the satisfaction of knowing when I would arrive at a destination.

I wrote to our friends in Sydney, Marie and Lyn Evans, to ask if we could spend the day with them. The BOAC flight that we hoped to take from Sydney to London didn't leave until ten o'clock at night. I asked Marie if she could take me shopping. I hadn't had a chance to buy anything in New Zealand and I wanted a new hat to wear when I arrived in England. In the 50s, hats were a great source of joy – a wonderful morale booster.

Bumpa cabled them when we left New Zealand and they were on the wharf when the flying-boat landed at Rose Bay. Lyn was a tall skinny man – a professor at the Sydney Conservatorium of Music – a fine pianist and a skilled raconteur. He was a better story teller than he was a driver and we had a hair-raising drive through narrow city streets, across bridges and out to the lovely suburb of Hunters Hill where their home had views of the harbour and a path led down to a swimming pool.

'I've found a hat shop close by,' Marie said, 'so you can go and try some on while I keep an eye on the boys. I know you said you wanted shoes but that's more difficult to find in this area.'

I had a wonderful time in that shop, trying on all kinds of creations: small, big, with veil, without veil, but I finally fell for a lovely primrose linen hat with a large brim turned up at one side. As soon as I put it on my head I felt a million dollars. Of course it was quite unpractical; a ridiculous hat to try and manage in a wind. But I didn't care. It was my hat and I had to buy it. Marie, bless her, only expressed mild surprise at my choice and hoped the racks in the aeroplane would be big enough to store it.

Strangely enough, apart from the excitement of buying the hat, I don't remember much about the journey. It just went on and on. Up, down, up, down, Darwin, Singapore, Calcutta, Bombay and even Baghdad. By this time I didn't know what I wanted to eat or drink. I remember ordering a tomato juice in the airport café during the refuelling stop at Baghdad, but it was the foulest dark-coloured, non-tasting tomato concoction I've ever tasted. One sip was enough.

In the aircraft Bill got whiter and whiter and didn't want to do anything except sleep. Peter, after Baghdad refused to go to sleep, got more and more tired and more and more fractious. He fought and screamed and by that time I was past caring what he did. Finally as we began our descent over the English Channel he fell asleep in my arms, exhausted and a dead weight. He wouldn't wake when we landed. The hostess came forward and held him while I packed the belongings into the overnight bag, jammed my precious hat on my head grabbed my violin and Peter, and prepared to leave the plane.

It was a typical English welcome, blowing a gale and drizzling with rain. As I walked down the steps onto the tarmac, a gust of wind caught the hat and sent it sailing away until it landed on the wet ground in front of a tractor. At the bottom of the stairs John stood laughing his head off at my dilemma but as he came forward to take Peter, the laughter turned to joy as he hugged me tight. The hostess ran to retrieve the hat. Plonking it on my head I stepped once again onto English soil and marched to the airport building.

19

House-Hunting

Our homecoming was traumatic! After we'd been in Eritrea for two years we sold the Southampton house so we were without a home. John had four months' leave and he felt we should take our time and enjoy wandering around England looking for the ideal place to live. Four months' leave! It sounded wonderful. To be together again, on holiday and away from aeroplanes. Idyllic! But finding somewhere to live had to be our first priority.

As we drove away from the airport I was surprised when John took the South Circular road instead of the road to Oxford. I knew his parents had moved back to the Cotswolds and were living in a cottage on one of his relations' farms. I had expected we would be going to stay with them.

'Where are we going? You've taken the wrong road. Aren't we going to Blaythorne to see your parents?'

'We'll go up and see them in a day or two. Father hasn't been well the last few weeks. The cottage is very small and it hasn't electricity. It isn't really convenient for us to stay there at present.'

'What do you mean "no electricity"? Blaythorne farm is only a mile from Chadlington village. Surely there are electric cables to the farm? There are very few houses in New Zealand without electricity. It's like going back to the Dark Ages. However is your mother managing? Anyway, where are we going now?'

'To Sidcup, to see our friends the Rutters. I called in to see them on my way down to Canterbury to take Richard out on exeat.'

'Richard! How is he? I'm longing to see him. When can we go down to the school?'

'Rich' is fine and seems to be enjoying school. He's mad on cricket and swimming. I hope he's as keen on his school-work. We'll go down and see him next weekend. In the meantime we're going to stay with the Rutters. They've very kindly offered us the flat in their house, until we find somewhere to live. They're looking forward to seeing you again.'

'Oh John, it's very kind of Betty and Allan. They're wonderful friends, but you know how you hate living in a flat. You loathe being confined, and wander round the place like a caged lion.'

'Well, we have to live somewhere and this will give us a base. I've contacted a number of land agents and they'll be sending us information about properties available within an eighty-mile radius of Heathrow Airport. I'm sure we won't have to stay in the flat for long.'

Famous last words! The four precious months' leave were spent looking for a place to live.

John had visions of buying a small farm. He had never really recovered from the shock of hearing the family farm in Shipton-under-Wychwood had been sold just before the war ended, when we were still in South Africa. He enthused about all the things I could do on a farm while he was away flying – what fun I would have running a poultry business and growing flowers and vegetables for sale.

I pointed out very firmly that I was a town girl, and didn't know anything about farming – and what's more – I had a horror of feathered things – couldn't stand anything fluttering around me – so I'd be no good at looking after poultry. I wasn't comfortable on a horse – the ground was too far away – and apart from Hamlet, our 'bitser' dog in Asmara, I'd never had anything to do with animals.

But he hankered after owning land and wanted a place where the boys would have space to play and develop their interests. With a few acres he could grow things, have some animals and build a workshop – another workbench!

Every day the brochures arrived from the agents with glowing descriptions of ideal homes, farms with thatched cottages, houses of character set in spacious grounds within easy distance of a delightful village. The pile got bigger and bigger. Every evening we sat down and tried to sort out the ones that might be possible – and in our price range. We would mark the places on the map and plan the next day's tour carefully. In the morning I packed a picnic lunch, and rain or shine – and being England, it was more rain than shine – we took off, full of hope that today we would find the ideal home, just waiting for the Pascoe family to move in.

It was a time a of great disillusionment. I developed a hate of all estate agents whose chief aim in life was to mislead the would-be buyer. The ideal home turned out to be a conglomeration of dreary rooms, the 'natural garden' described in one brochure was a mass of overgrown weeds and a rockery full of couch grass, and the 'easy distance' from a village was over 3 miles.

Bill and Peter trailed along patiently. But one day Bill said tearfully to me, 'We'll never find a place to live, Mummy. If Daddy likes the farm, you don't like the house, and if you like the house, Daddy doesn't think much of the farm.'

Gradually the idea of a farm faded. They were either too expensive or too far from the airport. We became desperate because Richard's holidays started in a few weeks and we had to find somewhere soon. The upstairs flat would be hopeless with three boisterous boys roaring around.

John decided to go up to Oxfordshire and look around there. His father had suffered from asthma for years, and John felt that, having been away for years, it was time he lived nearer his parents so he could help his mother.

He said he would spend a week looking round and sort out five or six suitable houses. I could drive up to Chadlington on the Sunday with the boys, and we'd look at them together.

That was a nightmare Sunday! I had details of a 'colt' house near High Wycombe and on the way up to Oxford, I went to see it. Having spent my childhood in New Zealand, I was used to wooden houses and this one appealed to me. It was light, spacious and had a good garden. In fact it was almost all that the brochure said it was – and what's more, it was in our price range. But when I arrived at the farm and started to enthuse about the design and the grounds, John's father soon flattened me. I hadn't realized before what a prejudice the English had about wooden houses.

'A terrible fire hazard – no resale value – no good at all. Quite out of the question,' he declared.

And so, leaving the boys with their grandparents, John and I set off to look at the houses he had selected.

The first house was a little box with no character at all, no trees or view, and a miserable kitchen. The second was in a delightful village but it was large and rambly and the front door opened straight onto the street.

'I wouldn't have a moment's peace in that house,' I said when we got back into the car. 'I'd never be able to have the front door open in case the boys made a dash out into the road.'

The third one was picturesque with a thatched roof – which needed attention – but the rooms were so small and the ceilings so low I felt claustrophobic.

The morning wore on and I got more and more depressed. There was nothing that I felt happy about. I'm sure houses develop their own special character and you get a feeling as soon as you walk in. The 'vibes' certainly were lacking in anything we had seen and I was pretty quiet as we drove back to the farm for lunch. I could feel disapproval in the air when we sat down at the table. John's mother pointed out how much time and thought John had put in during the week to select something I would like. I could imagine the enthusiastic conversation each evening when John came back, describing in glowing terms what he had seen, and what he would do to improve the property. In his mother's eyes John could do no wrong, and I felt a bit mean not to be carried away with all his ideas. But I was the one who was going to live in the house and so far I had seen nothing that appealed.

As we drove round the lovely Cotswold villages in the afternoon, John was full of stories about his childhood, and knowledgeable about the history of the district. I began to realize how attached he was to this part of England. This was his homeland and he loved it.

The first house we saw in the afternoon was called Rose Cottage. We found it tucked away in a dead-end in a tiny village. I felt happy as soon as I went through the door. It had everything. Built in mellow Cotswold stone, with roses climbing up the walls, it had a reasonable kitchen and a cottagey garden. I liked the couple who owned it. The husband had even built a special oriel window in the main bedroom for his wife to sit at and enjoy the sunsets. I was carried away with the whole place and there was a spring in my step as we walked back to the car.

'Oh John, that's delightful. It's the dearest little house – quite wonderful. I love it.'

John seemed rather taken aback by my enthusiasm and drove slowly away. Then he pulled into a layby and turned to me rather soberly. 'Yes, Vivienne, its very charming and in excellent condition. But before you get too carried away with it's beauty, let's be a bit practical. It's only got three bedrooms and I don't see how it could be extended. The lounge is small and you wouldn't be able to get a piano into it. There's no room for the boys to play. They couldn't kick a ball round in that neat little garden and the garage is tiny. It would only hold one car and there'd be no room for a workshop. And alas, the price is too high. We'd have to carry a very large mortgage. It's an ideal home for a married couple – but with three growing boys...'

I exploded, 'If it's not suitable why did you even bring me here?'

'I'm sorry, dear, I thought you'd like to see it but I didn't expect you to be so keen. Come on, we'd better see the rest of the houses.'

It began to rain. In fact it poured. All my enthusiasm had gone and I didn't want to see any more. About five o'clock we drove along a dull looking street in a small town.

'I've kept the best till last,' said John. 'This house has a large beautifully kept garden, a Cotswold stone garage, and five and a half acres of ground with it.'

'What's the house like?' I said wearily.

'Oh, it needs redecorating – but you'll love the garden.'

'I'm not so interested in the garden. I want to know about the house.'

We drew up at a gate which was off one of its hinges and difficult to open. Just inside was the garage, stone – as John had said.

'This must have been the original hayloft of a farm. Look, it's got some windows upstairs. I'm sure it could be converted into a delightful cottage.'

Hear we go again, I thought. John couldn't see any place without wanting to tear down walls and rebuild the whole thing. He stopped the car when the drive petered out a few yards past the garage.

'Now we walk up to the house under an archway of roses.'

'You mean to say we can't drive up to the front door? How do you carry groceries from the garage? Just imagine trailing up this long path in the rain, with a small boy and arms full of parcels.'

I wasn't impressed when I saw the house. The main walls were dirty, off-white stucco, and on one end was a wooden verandah. We rang the front doorbell and waited. We pushed it again. Nobody appeared. 'I did tell them we'd be here in the afternoon but perhaps we're a bit later than I expected. The owners said we could look around.'

We peered through the glass in the front door and looked down a long dark passageway divided by a beaded curtain. Most of the rooms we saw through the windows looked dingy and depressing. But there was a large lounge with corner windows and a big window-seat.

'The old man who lived here was a keen musician so he built the window-seat specially for rehearsing his choir. You can get fourteen bottoms on that seat!' John had got all the history of the house from the couple, the housekeeper and gardener, who had looked after the old man until he died. The property had been left to them in his will.

'I suppose he rode a bike and didn't hold with new-fangled machines like motor cars. Is that why he didn't bother to have a drive up to the house?'

'As a matter of fact, he rode a tandem. He and his wife cycled all over Europe but he must have had lots of train journeys because he's got a collection of rail tickets pinned to the back of the study door.'

We walked across the lawn, past the rockery and round to the back of the house. I looked through the kitchen window, – and exploded! 'Look at that old black range,' I spluttered. 'Is that the only way of cooking? I might as well have stayed in Asmara. At least there I had someone to clean the beastly thing.'

I refused to look at any more and marched off in the rain towards the rose-walk. I stopped to look back at the house as John caught up with me. Suddenly I burst into tears.

'I couldn't possibly live here,' I sobbed. ' The house is horrible. It's dark, dreary and miserable. I can't drive up to my front door and I don't care about the garden. There are acres and acres of lawn to be mown when you're away on your long trips.'

John put his arm around me and tried to comfort me. 'Darling, I'm sure we could make this into a wonderful home. With all this ground the boys would have lots of fun and plenty of space for doing things. I know the house need decorating but I'm sure you'd enjoy doing that. We'll get rid of the old stove and I'll build a new kitchen and put in all the latest equipment. There are all kinds of possibilities, Please think about it.'

I thought about it – all the way back to London! John stayed another night with his parents as he had to be at Heathrow the next morning to start his flying course on Constellations. Our four months' leave had finished and he'd be back to his aeroplanes. I was hopping mad with him because he hadn't returned with me to Sidcup, and at least helped me put the boys to bed after such a long disastrous day. I was lonely, miserable and utterly frustrated. I phoned him about ten-thirty and said I didn't care what he did. He could do what he liked. We had to have somewhere to live and if he wanted to make an offer for the house called the 'Bungalow' – horrible name – he'd better go ahead and do it.

He made the offer. It was accepted. And that is how we came to live in Chipping Norton for the next 28 years in a house we called 'Anakiwa.'

20

Hawaii

The mail had just arrived and I was sitting at the dining room table reading a letter from my sister in New Zealand.

John burst into the room waving a letter and said: 'How would you like to go to Hawaii for three months?'

'What did you say?'

'I said, how would you like to spend three months in Hawaii?'

'What do you mean – three months in Hawaii? Have you won the pools or something?'

'No, but BOAC are hoping to open a round-the-world route. Once America has granted the landing rights in Hawaii, crews will be based in Honolulu for short periods. They asked for volunteers some time ago and I put my name down. Here's the letter saying my application has been accepted. It could be fun.'

'Whew! And when does this happen?' I sighed. Typical of dear John to get carried away with the thought of flying in a different place without realizing what it would mean, familywise.

'Ah, we don't know that yet. Although the first crews are already out in Hawaii they can't start operating until President Eisenhower signs the American authority giving landing rights to BOAC. At present there seems to be some hold-up.'

I sighed again. It had taken a long time to make Anakiwa (the home of the Kiwi) – into a home. When we bought it, it was a house, that like 'Topsy', had just grown without any real planning. John bubbled over with ideas he dreamed up when he was far above the earth among the clouds. Trouble was, that putting them into practice was another thing, and one simple job usually led to half

197

a dozen more difficult ones. But it did have plenty of space and the two older boys played cricket tests on the lawn, and football matches in the field behind the house.

We had worked hard for four years and I was just beginning to feel settled and part of the community. I was playing my violin again and teaching and I didn't feel I was ready for another upheaval – even for three months. But the more I thought about it the more it sounded like a wonderful idea. Honolulu – lovely sunshine, warm sea and nothing to do but lie on a beach. What more could a girl want!

But days went by and nothing more was heard from BOAC operations. 'I suppose it's just another rumour,' I said, now feeling disappointed. 'We'd better forget the whole thing.'

'No, I don't think so. It may happen quite suddenly and we'll have to be prepared to go at short notice.'

John went off on a long trip and the boys, Richard and Bill came home for their summer vacation. When John returned he said that the three crews who had been sitting in Honolulu doing nothing for three months had come home, because the landing agreement had still not been signed by the President.

Listening to the six o'clock news a few nights later, I heard the announcer say: 'BOAC has been granted landing rights in Hawaii and the round-the-world service will come into operation in a few days.'

I dashed out to the workshop to tell John and as he came in the telephone rang. He answered it. 'Yes, we've just heard the news on the radio.' There was a pause and I hovered near the phone. 'Whew, that's quick.' There was another pause. 'Yes, we'll go – wife and three children. When do we fly out? OK – Heathrow at five a.m. on Thursday.'

'Thursday morning!' I exclaimed when he put the phone down, 'That's the day after tomorrow.'

'Well I told you we wouldn't get much warning.'

'Couldn't the boys and I come over a bit later?'

'No, because all the crews and families are flying out together in the Britannia 312 which we'll be operating on that sector.'

That night I tossed and turned with my mind whirling with all the things that would have to be done next day. John was up early and when he brought me a cup of tea, he was already dressed in the protective clothing ready to go out into the field to remove the shallow bars of honey from the beehives – one of his latest projects. When he came in for breakfast, in spite of the netted hat and all the precautions, he'd been stung several times on the face, and one eye was already swelling badly. I remembered Mother's old-fashioned remedy for bee stings. She rubbed the place with a Reckitts bluebag, used in those days to keep clothes white. I ran out to the laundry and luckily found a bluebag on a saucer near the washing machine. I grabbed a towel, wet the bluebag and applied it to John's eye.

'What on earth do you think you're doing?'

'Sit still. This should take the swelling down.' As I held the bag in position John cheerfully told me that he had always been allergic to bee stings. Once he'd been really ill with a very high fever and had to spend several days in bed.

'Now you tell me. You must be mad! If I'd known this I'd never have agreed to you keeping bees.'

Breakfast was hardly a happy meal. Bill and Peter were quiet, didn't want anything to eat and complained about tummy-aches. 'Viv, you'd better make an appointment with the doctor this morning and ask for a supply of medicines to take with us. Be sure to remember to ask for Enterovioform for tummy trouble. Richard, I want you to do the honey. I'll show you how to put the bars into the centrifugal machine, but you'll have to watch what you are doing or you'll get honey everywhere. Bill…'

Richard, who didn't like doing jobs on his own, interrupted: 'Can't Bill come and help me?'

'No, Bill's job is to sweep out the workshop and put all the tools away. Peter, you'd better sort out the games and toys you want to take with you.'

'And what are you going to be doing – now you've sorted us all out?' I asked.

'I'm going to help Malcolm move his piano up here. There's no time now to get a removal van from Oxford and anyway it's too expensive.'

Malcolm, our New Zealand pianist friend had agreed, when the posting had been first talked about, to look after the house while we were away. He'd already moved his belongings out of his flat and into our end bedroom – except for his piano. Over coffee John and Malcolm discussed their plan of action and finally set off down the rose-walk with the little trailer and some strong ropes. They were both optimists and didn't think the job would take long, but it proved more difficult than they expected. There was a bend in the stairway of Malcolm's flat and the piano got stuck when they tried to manoeuvre it round. Somehow they managed to get it down the stairs and out into the garden where they balanced it on the trailer and then pulled it along Albion Street and up the path to Malcolm's room. But the move had taken its toll, as Malcolm had wrenched his back getting the piano down the stairs. It was quite painful so I gave him a couple of aspirin and he lay down.

What with John's swollen eye, the boys' tummies, and now Malcolm's back, I didn't think much of the male members of the household. I thought even less of them when I went out into the back kitchen, and found that Richard had escaped after extracting the honey, without cleaning up the sticky mess. All day was occupied with domestic chores: cleaning the fridge, washing and ironing, seeing the doctor, and packing. We fell into bed about midnight – absolutely exhausted. But it was a short rest. At 3 a.m. we were packed in the car and ready to leave. I had to drive as John's eye was almost completely closed and Malcolm wasn't comfortable sitting and he would have to drive back to Chipping Norton after we'd gone.

'At least when we get to Heathrow we'll have our own aeroplane and there'll be none of the standby nonsense' I said thankfully.

But when we went into the departure building with all our baggage it was very quiet. There were no other passengers to be seen and the desk wasn't manned.

'I'd better go and ring the office and see what's happening,' said John. But just then a BOAC duty officer appeared.

'Captain Pascoe? I'm sorry, we tried to phone you to tell you that your flight was delayed because of an engine change. You must have already left home. Your new departure time is about sixteen hundred hours. Can we offer you some breakfast?'

After the concentrated rushing around of the past 24 hours it was an anticlimax to sit consuming bacon and eggs and know we had to mess about for the rest of the day.

'What do you want to do?' John asked.

I thought for a minute. 'I know. Let's have a real family day out and go into London to Madame Tussauds. The boys have never been and it must be years since you were there.'

'Actually I've never been there.' John admitted, 'when I was a boy there wasn't any money for outings to London.'

It was a great bonus day. The boys thought it was fun catching buses and tearing up and down the escalators in the Underground stations. We were early enough not to be bothered by crowds at the Waxworks. The boys were fascinated by the figures in the Chamber of Horrors but I preferred the historical section with all the magnificent costumes. John enjoyed looking at the figures of war heroes and politicians. He decided to take the boys to the Planetarium nearby but we'd just missed the eleven o'clock showing and the next one wasn't until half past two. We walked down to Lyons Corner House at Marble Arch for lunch, and then returned to the airport. John went off to the operations office to find out what was happening. He looked quite cheerful when he returned. 'It won't be long now,' he told us, 'We're going to fly to Montreal, then right across Canada to San Francisco for a night. Because the previous crews had to give up their accommodation in Honolulu there's some difficulty in finding enough apartments for us all, as it's the high holiday season. This has to be sorted out before we arrive in Honolulu.'

I recognized several of the wives and went to chat with them – found they'd all been taken by surprise at the suddenness of the departure but most of them had been warned about the delay.

We boarded the aircraft at half past four and everyone breathed a sigh of relief when the door was shut and the engines started. We taxied past the statue of Alcock and Brown – at that time near the runway, but now moved to the central area near the little airport church. Those two intrepid flyers crossed the Atlantic in a Vickers Vimy Aircraft with two engines in 1919. This was my first Atlantic flight, and the powerful noise of the four Bristol Proteous engines was a comforting sound.

Windsor Castle, where the Royal Standard fluttered in the breeze, stood out clearly as we climbed steadily. We passed over West London where miniature cars and lorries rushed along.

Billowing clouds blotted out the countryside, but when the air cleared and the sun shone, we looked down on sparkling blue sea – miles of it. The children on board were quiet at first, but after a few hours they got restless and wandered about vying with one another in helping the stewardess serve food and drink. When they got more obstreperous the fathers, unable to keep the peace, drifted towards the flight deck, keen to escape what was turning into an airborne Sunday-school picnic.

As the sun was setting the magnificent sight of Greenland's Icy Mountains appeared on the starboard side and everyone rushed over to have a look. Landing at Montreal after flying for ten hours gave us a chance to stretch our legs and breath the fresh night air before setting out across the vast area of Canada. The children, exhausted, quietened down and were soon asleep.

I was engrossed in reading my book, Neville Shute's *No Highway*. It was an exciting story but hardly a good choice for a long flight as the plot was woven around the dangers of metal fatigue in aeroplanes. I'd just got to the part where the aeronautical engineer had suddenly discovered he'd made some bad miscalculations and the aeroplane was likely to fall out of the sky at any moment. With this thought in mind I drifted off to sleep.

The stop in San Francisco was a blur except for the joy of a bath and the comfort of stretching out on a hotel bed. No one knew how long we'd be there. The chief pilot and his wife were busy phoning Honolulu trying to find sufficient accommodation for the 80 people on board. They were having all kinds of difficulties. John and the other pilots went back to the airport to do their landing procedures known as 'circuits and bumps' and get checked out for landing at San Francisco airport. Mid-morning they rushed back to the hotel with the news that we'd be taking off in an hour's time. As most of the children were having fun in the hotel pool there was a great scurry to get everyone ready and bags packed. But when we were in the air again, everyone relaxed and sat back, looking forward to the next stop: Honolulu, on the island of Oahu.

We approached the airport over the mountains where the Japanese planes had flown on the fateful morning of December 7th, 1941, swooping over Pearl Harbour and taking the Americans by surprise.

An official party gave us a warm welcome when we walked into the airy arrival lounge. Attractive Hawaiian girls in colourful dresses and red hibiscus flowers behind their ears kissed us on both cheeks and garlanded us with beautiful purple orchid leis. The men loved it and the children drank large cups of fresh pineapple juice.

The joyous word *Aloha*, which in Hawaiian can mean both hullo and goodbye rang through the reception lounge. We'd arrived!

As we stood in the baggage hall waiting for the luggage to come off the aeroplane John came over and said: 'Sorry, dear, the pilots have to stay here and complete familiarization flights for this airport. Transport has been arranged to take the families to the apartments. We're booked in at one called Coconut Palms. Here's fifty dollars for groceries. Take a good look at the money because the twenty dollar note is very similar to the one dollar. I don't know when we'll finish but I'll come and help you settle in as soon as I can.'

We piled into one of the large black limousines and drove through the streets of downtown Honolulu, past the docks where luxury ships were tied up, and along the waterfront to Waikiki. Coconut palms lined the street where the car dropped us. But our apartment, 'The Coconut Palms', didn't have any view of the sea. It faced the other way, looking over a dirty looking canal to the mountains.

'Let's go and have a swim.' Richard, who could never wait for anything was rummaging in the overnight bag for his swimming togs.

'Hold on. First we must buy some food before the shops shut.' I was busy looking in the kitchen cupboards. There was plenty of china, cutlery, coffee-maker and saucepans. But I couldn't find a kettle, teapot, or any eggcups. The apartment had only one bedroom and the three boys would have to sleep in the lounge where they'd already scattered things about. 'You're going to have to be very tidy.' I said firmly and allotted each boy a drawer in the bedroom closet. 'Put these things away right now before we think about swimming.'

I sat down and made a list of the basic groceries. Stocking a kitchen in a new country is always difficult. Familiar items have unfamiliar wrappings. The currency, until you get used to it, is always a problem.

I gathered up my list and the precious 50 dollars. 'Right, let's go and find the shops.'

'But we want to swim.'

'You'll have to wait until we've done the shopping. Then we can find the beach.' We walked round the corner and into the mainstreet, Kalakau Avenue. It was full of tourist shops displaying colourful dresses and attractive bathing-suits. We ran into Jean, one of the other wives, with her arms full of brown-paper parcels.

'You look as if you've been successful and found a food store.'

'Yes, there's a supermarket just around the corner.'

'Have you got a teapot and eggcups in your kitchen?'

'No, Americans seldom drink tea, so you won't find a teapot, and I believe if they want to eat a boiled egg, they cut the top off and empty it into a cup.'

'What a messy way to eat a simple egg.'

We found the supermarket and I wandered around clutching my list. There was plenty of lovely looking fruit: bananas, and huge piles of pineapples. 'Richard, see if you can find the Marmite while I look for some custard powder.' Marmite sandwiches and banana custard were always popular with the boys. Richard came back empty-handed and I hadn't been successful either. When I found an assistant she looked vague when I asked about Marmite. 'Never heard of it,' she said. 'We've got beef extract. Will that do?'

Funny people, these Americans, I thought. Everything seemed expensive but by this time I was feeling light-headed and not capable of working out the difference between pounds and dollars. When I came out of the supermarket there weren't many dollars left. I hope I hadn't got muddled with the notes.

'All right, let's get this stuff back to the flat and go for a swim.' The boys raced ahead and bounded up the three flights of stairs. They didn't take long to get ready, but I had to put the food away before we could leave the flat.

The beach was only three minutes' walk away. It was so much smaller than it looked in the pictures I had seen of the famous Waikiki beach. It was cluttered with brown bodies. Richard and Bill tore into the water but Peter, who couldn't swim, sat down at the edge and waited for me. The warm water was bliss with gentle waves lapping on the sand. Some distance out huge breakers crashed onto the coral reef where surfers crouched on their boards waiting for the right wave to carry them into shore. Richard went off to inquire the cost of hiring a surfboard but I said he'd have to wait until his father was with him before he hired one.

John hadn't arrived when we got back to the apartment. The boys ate scrambled eggs, moaned about the spongy white bread, but enjoyed the juicy slices of pineapple. Food quietened them down and as soon as I'd made up the three beds they crashed. The kitchen was part of the living room so I cleared up quietly and then tumbled into bed. I was nearly asleep when John crept in. He sat on the bed. 'Everything all right?' he asked. 'This apartment seems small for the five of us, but we'll try and find something larger when I get back from Japan. We're leaving at four tomorrow morning.'

'Oh no. You're not going away as soon as that, are you? I thought at least you'd be with us for a few days.'

'All the wives are in the same boat, so get in touch with them. I've left the phone numbers by the telephone. You'll have some fun together.' John always reckoned I should have fun wherever I was.

Honolulu was all we'd ever hoped for – after we'd got over the tiring journey and difficult start. There was a happy relaxed atmosphere. It didn't matter what you wore. The more colourful the better. You could pick a hibiscus flower as you walked along the road, wear it behind your ear and feel wonderful. The men, when they returned from their flying, discarded their formal white shirts and relaxed in colourful Hawaiian shirts with large floral designs.

Everyone was reading James Mitchener's book *Hawaii* which had just been published. It was the first of his sagas and gave a great insight into the history of the islands and the development of a multi-racial society, caused through the importation of labour for the cultivation of sugar and pineapples. In 1959 when we were in Honolulu, there was already talk of how commercial and synthetic Honolulu was becoming, and objections were being made because successful Chinese landowners were building more and more high-rise apartment blocks on the beach fronts.

But for us, it was great. The boys never tired of swimming in water so warm you could stay in for hours. Hiring surfboards was expensive – and quite dangerous in those days because they were made of wood and very heavy. Some nasty accidents occurred when inexperienced surfers lost control of their boards which then rushed towards the beach and struck unsuspecting swimmers nearer the shore. It was thrilling to watch the beachboys on their boards, and the canoes and catamarans skimming on top of the waves.

We found a Japanese swimming instructor for Peter and his friend Simon. Meiko taught survival swimming and after ten lessons the boys swam two lengths of the Olympic-size swimming pool. It took them nearly all morning to do this but, as they'd been taught, when they felt tired, they lay on their backs in the water and rested. They were very proud when they were presented with a certificate and a badge to wear on their swimming trunks.

It was a carefree existence. Twice a week we walked along the beach towards Diamond Head to watch the show of Hawaiian dancing put on by the Kodak company. For an hour we were entertained free of charge – except for the expensive films bought – by dancing girls stamping their bare feet to the rhythm pounded on gourd drums by men in Hawaiian costumes. The girls' skirts made of ti-leaves rustled as they twirled to the lilting songs sung by slim ladies in formal dresses, or *muu-muus* as they were called. Six large elderly matriarchs, standing in front of the pseudo-Hawaiian hut accompanied them on their ukuleles. In the early days of Hawaii, to be big was to be beautiful. A wife weighing 300 pounds – or over – was a real treasure.

The men in the audience never failed to react to the Tahitian dancers – beautiful girls with crowns of creamy, sweet-smelling frangipani on their heads and green raffia skirts worn well down on their hips. As the music got faster and faster the girls swung their skirts and violently gyrated their hips. The men watched avidly, waiting for the skirts to fall. But they never did. The show ended by everyone being invited to come down to 'have a go'. Amid great hilarity all shapes and sizes attempted to follow the instructions given by a 250-pound beauty, Nellie.

She wore a large straw hat on her head decorated with flowers and a long *muu-muu* which she flicked over her knees as she showed her pupils how to 'go round the island'.

Not to be outdone, Jean and I went along to one of the hotels where free lessons were given in hula-dancing. This was another tourist attraction. But it was much harder than it looked. So much depended on the suppleness of the fingers. At an early age, children were taught the movements by learning to roll a pencil between the fingers and thumb. The songs and chants are pictorial and in a fluid, flowing rhythm the hands describe the 'island' the 'hut' or the 'girl'. Early Hawaiians had no written language so hula-dancing and chanting took the place of their literature and history, as well as their religious ceremonies. Our teacher told us: 'There is a hula for life, a hula for death, hulas for kings and common people and hulas for joy and sadness. It is the heartbeat of the people.'

One afternoon we had a sobering launch trip around Pearl Harbour. There had been a sudden tropical storm. Heavy clouds hung over the mountains where – on that fateful December morning of 1941 – Japanese planes suddenly appeared out of the sky and in a short time caused terrible devastation. The American flag fluttered over the area where 1,100 sailors lost their lives in the wrecked ship, the *Arizona*. As we cruised around the harbour we went out to the narrow entrance which the Japanese pilots had tried to close by sinking a ship across it. The grey water and heavy air lent atmosphere to the story the commentator told as he vividly described that morning which brought America into the war.

After a glorious month's holiday, Richard and Bill had to return to England and start another year at boarding-school. I flew to San Francisco with them to make sure they caught their connecting flight to London. They left Honolulu in their gay *aloha* shirts with orchid leis around their necks and were very reluctant to change into school uniform at San Francisco for the journey back to England. They insisted on wearing their leis when they boarded the plane to London and were determined to arrive at school with them around their necks – even if the flowers had died on the way.

While John was away on a trip to Japan I found an upstairs flat in a private house near Diamond Head. It was ideal for the three of us – quiet, with a sea view and a little path that led down to a private beach. We had arranged for Peter, now six years old, to go to a primary school nearby. When he came back for his first day he was full of chat.

'We've got a very pretty teacher in our class.'

'What's her name?'

'Miss Nakamura. She's got long black hair and today she was wearing a lovely *muu-muu*. She asked me to tell them about school in England and they all laughed because I speak differently. But Miss Nakamura thinks my accent is cute. My friend Lim is Chinese and his father gives lessons in archery every afternoon in the park. Please can I go tomorrow at four o'clock? It's free! You don't have to pay anything.'

' We'll see. What did you have for lunch?'

'Chicken, salad and a Coca-Cola. I couldn't eat all the salad. Some of it was set in jelly and I thought it should have been pudding.'

Peter, like his father, was conservative about his food and I could imagine his reaction to carrots set in jelly and served as a salad.

The archery lessons were a great success and Lim's father, a patient man, had a wonderful way with small boys. No matter where we were, or what we were doing, when four o'clock came Peter insisted on going to the park. For the next hour he was completely absorbed in pulling the string of the bow – which seemed bigger than he was – and trying to hit the target set up on a bale of hay.

It was a good thing that John was kept busy flying. He was never much of a beachcomber and always had to be doing something. The flight to Japan was confusing because on each trip they crossed the date-line. When they flew to Tokyo, stopping briefly at Wake Island to refuel, they lost a day. Leaving Honolulu on a Tuesday and flying all night, they arrived in Japan on Thursday morning. After twenty-four hours, they flew back, this time arriving in Honolulu almost before they began – timewise. He had a job to know what day of the week it was.

Flying out of Wake Island one morning, on a return journey to Honolulu, John and his co-pilot saw a very bright light flash across the sky and disappear into the sea. Thinking it might be a plane in trouble they radioed Wake Island immediately and asked them to investigate. They were thanked for their information and told to proceed. But on arrival at Schofield Airport in *Honolulu*, journalists were waiting to interview them and asked the pilots to describe what they had seen. Their report appeared the next day in the paper, the *Honolulu Advertiser*, with speculation that they had sighted the end of the flight of the first long-range intercontinental missile, fired from Cape Canaveral earlier that day. After the paper was published the two pilots were summoned to BOAC's office and informed that this had to be treated as classified information. Later the American government published a statement which said the pilots had been mistaken and had not seen anything. But whatever it was they 'hadn't seen' made a tremendous impression on the two pilots. They both said that such an awe inspiring sight was something they would never forget.

One morning I switched on the radio to listen to the news and the announcer said: 'The Goddess of Fire, Pele, has been playing up again on the island of Hawaii – the Big Island. The volcano, Kilauea has erupted and fountains of lava are shooting up in the air and pouring down the mountainside. It is a spectacular sight.'

It was big news! Programmes were interrupted during the day giving the height and intensity of the eruption. The newspaper published photos and stories about people who claimed they had sighted Pele, the Fire Goddess with her long flowing hair, just before the eruption began. Some even said she knocked on their door.

Even though many Hawaiians had been converted to Christianity, at heart, they were still animists. They feared and respected the gods of nature. Though the frequent outbreaks of the volcanoes caused devastation on the island of Hawaii, the locals, in a strange way, took pride in the eruptions and flocked to watch the river of lava flow down the sides of the mountains.

Later that day, Jean and I were lazing on the beach, reading the newspapers. 'Look,' she said, ' they're even running special night flights from Oahu to Hawaii to view the volcano. Why don't we try and go over and have a look? Everyone else seems to be going.'

We called in at a tourist office on our way back to the flat and found we could get a flight at ten o'clock the following evening, just after John arrived in from Tokyo.

'Come on, let's book now,' said Jean. ' We won't get another chance. The volcano might stop erupting at any minute.'

I wasn't sure how John would feel about getting straight onto another aeroplane after his long flight. But it was too good an opportunity to miss.

Fortunately John arrived from Tokyo on time and didn't seem too put out when I met him and told him of our plans. He'd been listening to reports on the radio during the flight. 'The volcano is supposed to be shooting up higher than the Empire State Building, according to the last news I heard,' he said.

We boarded the small Hawaiian Airways plane and John immediately fell asleep. But he didn't miss much. It was an inky black night and as we dipped down through clouds over Hawaii, just after midnight, nothing could be seen of the spurting volcano. The tourist office had arranged with the hire firm, Avis, to have a car available at the airport.

'You've got a few miles before you take a turn off to the left.' the Avis receptionist told us. 'Then you'll find your journey will be slow as you'll join a queue of cars waiting to drive down to the viewing-spot. A traffic officer will direct you. He only lets a certain number of cars through at a time. Drive down the hill, turn and then park near a ridge overlooking the crater. A few minutes' walk through the bush will bring you to the edge. Everyone is allowed twenty minutes for viewing. Then you must return to the cars immediately so other people can drive in.' It all sounded extremely organized – like a military operation.

As we sped along the dark road we caught a glimpse of the red glow of the fire through the trees. We joined the queue of cars before we turned off. It seemed that everyone in Hawaii was out that night to gaze at their own special volcano. The cars came to a standstill and there we waited. Jean and I had brought thermoses of soup and coffee and we were glad of a hot drink. There was an air of expectation and excitement as the cars crept forward. The eruption must have had a special fascination to make so many people leave their beds and spend the night creeping slowly along the road. It was nearly three hours before we were able to drive down to the turning place and up the hill to the path that led to the cliff-face. I had put a special night film in my cine-camera but as I'd never used this type of film before I was uncertain how it would work. I wasn't likely to have another chance of filming an active

210

inferno at night. Although it was quite warm the air was damp. We put on our raincoats as we left the car and hurried along the track.

As we came out of the bush the sight was fearsome and a hush fell on all those watching. Earth and great boulders belched out of the mountain, high up into the air, and with a curious roar crashed to the ground, forming a river of lava which poured at great speed into the crater just below us.

In the few days the volcano had been blowing up, the landscape had been altered. A 400-foot high hill had been formed behind the main eruption and below where we stood a deep crater had been filled in. Twenty minutes flashed by. We were silent and awed when we returned to the car.

'Let's go back and rejoin the queue at the top so we can come and have another look,' said John. The cars had thinned out a little and we spent the time talking to one of the guards from the seismic research station. He'd been on duty for many hours and his job was to take samples of the lava in the crater and test the heat. If it rose above a certain temperature the area would be closed and no more viewers allowed near.

The dawn was just breaking as we parked the car for a second time. The view wasn't as spectacular as looking at the fireworks in the dark. But through the smoke and the haze we could see how the contours of the mountains had been changed. It was overwhelming to realize how insignificant and vulnerable we were. The crust of the earth was so thin here and the stupendous power of fire could pour out fast flowing rivers of lava and engulf the area around. It was a silent drive back to the airport. John was asleep and Jean, Ted and I were overcome with the adventures of the last few hours.

'I've never imagined anything like it,' Jean said as we landed back in Honolulu in time for breakfast. 'I'm so glad we made the effort and flew over. It was absolutely fantastic.'

That evening, just after the local news bulletin there was a special announcement. 'The volcano eruption of Kilauea on the island of Hawaii has now stopped and all is quiet. No lives were lost although a great area of land has been affected. The seismic research station will continue to monitor the area to ascertain the possibility of further eruptions.'

211

'Goodness, I'm glad we went over last night, John, even though you were so tired. It's something I'll never forget.'

The days rushed by. Lovely warm sunny days tempered by the trade winds. Soon it was time to pack and return to winter in England. Peter had a special farewell from his class when the boys solemnly shook hands and the little girls, 13 of them, kissed him on both cheeks and smothered him with leis.

Hawaii has always been a favourite calling place for the luxury liners cruising in the Pacific. On arrival passengers disgorged themselves from the ships anxious to enjoy the many blessings of the islands. They basked in the sun and swam in the warm sea fanned by the offshore breezes. They sampled the favourite drink, *Mai Ta*, and ate ham steaks with pineapple, *Teriyaki* steaks, served with delectable salads in pineapple halves. *Luau* were arranged where pork, and *poi* – made from the taro root – were cooked in the true Hawaiian way. After several halcyon days it was the custom, when the ships left the docks, for the passengers to throw their flower leis onto the water. If they floated to the shore it meant that a return visit would be made by the sunburnt, overfed, over-indulged passenger.

Aeroplanes make no provision for this casting of leis onto the water. On the day of our departure, soft Hawaiian melodies filled the air as we walked sadly through the airport gardens and went up the steps into the confined space of the cabin of the aeroplane. I took deep breaths of the frangipani lei round my neck and made a big wish that it wouldn't be too long before we returned. I murmured to myself as we took off and flew along the coast past Diamond Head, '*Aloha, Aloha, Aloha.*'

21

Another Posting

My wish was granted – but in rather different circumstances.

When we came back from Honolulu, John, as enthusiastic as ever, applied for a Honolulu posting for the next summer holidays. We didn't really expect anything to come of it because the postings abroad had become very popular.

One morning in June a letter arrived from BOAC by the early post. I waited impatiently for John to open it. 'Oh, great! We've got it.' He went on reading. 'But – they're moving the operation base from Hawaii to Japan. I suppose that's why I've been given another posting.'

' Oh, what a shame. I did want to go back to Honolulu and soak up that lovely sun and sea. We had such a good time there. I don't know that I'm keen to go to Japan, especially if you're based in a great city like Tokyo.'

John was still reading the letter. 'There's another snag. This posting starts from the beginning of July which means I'd have to go out there first and leave you to fly out with the boys when they break up from school. What do you think?'

I didn't know what I thought. 'Why don't we go and have a nice quiet holiday down in Cornwall away from flying and without any anxiety about getting on aeroplanes. You must have some leave due to you?'

'I suppose I have,' said John, 'but this is really a great opportunity for the boys to see another part of the world. It seems a pity to turn it down. There are lots of things we can do – climb Fuji-San – and you can have lessons in – what do they call it – *ikebana*.'

'And what's that? Some kind of martial art?'

'No, it's flower arranging – the Japanese way. Last year, on one of my trips to Tokyo, I met the BOAC manager's wife and she's a keen student at the Sogetsu School – one of the many flower-arranging schools in Tokyo. She says it's a fascinating art. It would be something different for you to study. Wasn't Bill invited to spend part of this holiday in Tehran with his friend, James Pearson?'

'Well, yes. But I've already written to Mrs Pearson, thanked her for the invitation but said Bill wouldn't be able to visit this holiday.'

'How about writing again and suggesting that James comes back here for a few days when school breaks up and then Bill and he could fly to Tehran together.'

'And what happens when I get them to the airport, if James is booked and Bill – being standby – doesn't get on?'

' If you wait a few days after all the schools have finished and most of the children have gone, I don't think you'll have any difficulty. Bill can spend a few days in Tehran with the Pearsons and then catch the service to Hong Kong. I'll arrange my trips so I can meet him there.'

He went off to find the BOAC timetable. I sat at the table chewing my piece of brown toast and marmalade. It was no use! I could see that John had already decided to accept the posting. I admit I always loved travelling and the chance to see other countries. I understood how John was delighted at the thought of flying a different route. But it was such an upheaval for the household, such a kerfuffle (one of my father's favourite words) to get away and I dreaded the uncertainty about flying as standby.

John came back to the table and sat flicking through the pages of the timetable. 'It looks OK for Bill. There's a weekly service from Tehran to Hong Kong. How about you? Which way do you want to fly?'

'If we have to go, I don't want to fly east about. I'd rather go across America and spend a little time in Honolulu. We won't get much swimming in a big city like Tokyo.'

'According to this timetable if you want to do that, it looks as if you'll have to spend one night in New York and the next day fly on to Honolulu. I'm not sure how long you can stay there. I'll have to work that out when I get to Tokyo. I'll collect Bill in Hong Kong and we'll all meet up at Narita Airport in Tokyo.'

I couldn't take it all in. It sounded so complicated. The odds on the whole Pascoe family coming together after flying around the world in different directions seemed pretty remote.

The remaining days before John's departure flew by in a flurry of activity. Vital jobs were done around the house, lawns mown, the garage-cum-workshop tidied, and business things like insurances and bank checked. Malcolm, who still lived with us, agreed to look after Anakiwa. He was excited at the thought of his fiancée, Judith, arriving from New Zealand at the beginning of the month.

I always sensed the change in John's personality as soon as we drove through the tunnel at Heathrow Airport. The smell of the fumes from the aeroplanes, the noise of the engines and the bustle of the airport changed the loving, caring husband into the airline captain. Flying was John's life and the aeroplane his ever demanding mistress.

'Don't wait, darling. I know you've got a lot to do. I'll go and see about the tickets being issued for Bill to Tehran and yours through to Tokyo. Ring Staff Travel if they don't arrive within the week.'

He cheerfully waved his uniform hat as I drove off slowly. I felt a sense of loss and was reluctant to assume all the responsibilities of the family. But at least Peter was at home to help me overcome the unhappiness of yet another farewell. Now seven years old, he went to the primary school in Chipping Norton.

Peter had a great friend known as My Friend Bry who lived in one of the terraced houses down the road. One night Peter made a fuss about having his usual bath. 'I don't see why I have to have a bath every night. My Friend Bry hasn't even got a bath in his house so he never has to bother. They don't even have a lavatory inside the house. It's down the garden path.' I didn't think such things still existed in England. It seemed so primitive. Although Peter and My Friend Bry were inseparable we could never persuade him to stay and have a meal with us. 'He doesn't eat vegetables or any salad stuff,' Peter told me knowingly.

'What does he eat?' I asked.

'He has his lunch at school and then in the evening they have baked beans or fish and chips. He loves fish and chips.'

It sounded rather a monotonous diet to me but he seemed healthy enough. I knew his mother was away all day at work.

A few days after John had flown off, there was a frantic hammering at the back door. I rushed to open it. My Friend Bry stood there looking very white. 'Come quickly,' he said, 'Peter has fallen out of the tree up in the quarry and is lying on the ground and can't move.'

My heart turned over. We ran up the lane to the quarry where the two boys had been playing. It was the longest run of my life. I imagined Peter lying there with a broken back and never able to move again. He was lying at the foot of the apple tree, but his eyes were open and he smiled weakly at me. 'It's my leg, Mummy. It hurts so much if I try and move it.' In my anxiety I forgot all those things they tell you about not moving anyone who has been injured. I wanted to get him home as quickly as possible and ring the doctor. I picked him up gingerly and held him as still as possible. 'Here, Bry, you hold his leg very carefully and we'll try not to jerk him.' It was a long slow, careful walk back to the house. I carried him upstairs, laid him gently on the bed and rushed to the phone.

We were very fortunate with our doctors in Chipping Norton. I spoke to Dr Leonard and he said he would come immediately. When he arrived and examined the leg he explained things very carefully to Peter. He and Peter were good friends. 'It looks as if you have fractured something down here and the sooner you get to the hospital in Oxford the better.' He turned to me: 'It will need to be X-rayed and more than likely put in plaster. I don't think it's a very bad break.'

Just then Malcolm, who was teaching music at the local High School, came home and said he would come to Oxford with me. He carried Peter down to the car and made him as comfortable as possible in the back seat.

All the way into Oxford Malcolm read a Noddy story – one of Peter's favourites – to try to take his mind away from the pain caused by any bump in the road. I drove as carefully as I could but was glad when I drew up at the casualty department of the Radcliffe Hospital.

'Malcolm, will you go and see if you can get a wheelchair and take Peter in. I'll go and find a park for the car.'

I hate hospitals. Especially casualty. (I feel 'casual' would be a better description.) Everyone's so busy. There are endless forms to fill in, questions to be answered and nothing to sit on but hard uncomfortable chairs. You just wait – and wait. I hadn't even bought my knitting with me. Somehow if my hands are busy – it helps to calm me. Peter was very quiet. Malcolm read him another story.

Finally a nurse came and put Peter on a stretcher. 'We'll take this young man to the X-ray department now but you may have to wait some time for the results.'

Another wait! Malcolm went to find me a cup of coffee. It was nearly an hour before the nurse came back with Peter. 'The doctor would like to see you now, Mrs Pascoe.' I followed her into a clinically clean and impersonal surgery.

'It's not a serious break, Mrs Pascoe. There are two minor fractures which means the leg will have to go into plaster for six weeks.'

I did a rapid calculation. I realized that if the plaster stayed on all that time it would be awkward travelling and there wouldn't be any swimming for Peter in Honolulu. I explained the situation to the doctor who was kind and understanding. 'We'll just have to see how quickly the bones knit together. Children this age have a great capacity for healing. Now we'd better send Peter to have the plaster put on.'

It had been a long day. I was glad to have had Malcolm's help and support. He was tall, calm and resourceful and had become a very good friend over the years.

After the initial shock, Peter quite enjoyed being a wounded soldier and quickly learnt to get down the stairs on his bottom. He collected everyone's signatures and soon the whole plaster was covered with writing and drawings.

When we went down to Canterbury for Bill's last speech and sports day at the preparatory school, Vernon Holme, Peter's leg was still in plaster. As he couldn't walk we were given permission to drive the car down onto the sports field so we could watch the events. It was a beautiful warm sunny day and the grounds and

217

gardens of Vernon Holme were immaculate. All the little boys looked scrubbed and clean. There was keen competition for the running and jumping events.

For Bill, it was an exciting day. He ran like a demon and bounded over the hurdles. But the thrill came when it was announced that he had won the coveted Victor Ludorum cup for the best overall sportsman. As Richard had won the same cup in his last year at the junior school I was very proud when Bill went up to receive his prize.

If only John could have been with us, the day would have been perfect, – or almost perfect! When the prize-giving was over, tea was served on the terrace and the boys consumed large plates of sandwiches, sticky buns and gooey cakes. They certainly made the most of their last meal at the school and were reluctant to leave. But I was anxious to get going because we still had to collect Richard from the senior school and load the trunks onto the car.

'Bill, you and James help Peter back to the car. Here are the keys. Be as quick as you can because it's time we got going.' I said my goodbyes to the headmaster and other teachers and walked back to the sports field. James and Peter were already in the car but Bill was busy talking and saying goodbye to his friends. I got in, started the engine and began to back slowly up the hill. Suddenly there was a shriek from Bill, 'Stop! Mother, wait!' He came running over to the car looking very upset.

'What's the matter, Bill?' I asked

'You've just run over the silver cup.'

'But how? Where was it?'

'On the grass behind the car.'

'What a stupid place to put it.'

'I'm sorry. I didn't know you were going to back up the hill. I thought you'd turn round on the sports field. Whatever will Mr Rattenbury say?' He burst into tears.

I got out of the car and sure enough, there on the ground, was a very squashed silver cup. I felt terrible and tried to comfort Bill. But I had to go and find the headmaster to confess. I felt like a naughty child when I knocked on his study door. He looked a bit surprised to see me as I'd only just said goodbye. I explained what

I'd done and if the cup couldn't be repaired we would present another one to the school. He took it all in good part.

'It's all right, Billy,' I said when I got back into the car. ' It was an accident. You still have your prizes and we'll get another cup. Let's go up to Kent College now and collect Richard.' It took some engineering to heave three large school trunks onto the roof-rack, pack all the sports gear in the boot and find room for four boys and me inside. Poor car! It was always overloaded. It was a long drive from Canterbury to Chipping Norton – about 160 miles. There were no motorways in those days and although we'd tried various routes, we found the quickest way was to go through Maidstone, Rochester and up the Old Kent Road straight through London. It was late when we got home and the boys were too tired to bother with anything to eat. They had a hot drink and fell into bed.

There are times when it's not easy to be an airline pilot's wife. This was one of them.

The next morning it was back to normal, trunks unpacked, clothes sorted, washing done and hungry mouths fed.

The next trip was to take Bill and James to the airport. James, with his firm booking to Tehran went straight through into the departure lounge. ' See you on the plane Bill,' he said as he left us.

Bill and I stood round waiting in the staff travel office. Staff seats were not allocated until the flight was closed – usually about quarter of an hour before take-off time. It was a tremendous relief when I heard 'Pascoe' called and went to the desk to collect Bill's ticket. Then it was all rush. I made sure he had his passport and boarding-pass ready before going through immigration. He went off happily enough although there was a look of apprehension on his face when he turned to wave goodbye. 'See you in Tokyo,' he called out.

The day before we were due to leave for New York, I drove Peter back to the hospital in Oxford. The doctor, after X-raying the leg, decided that the plaster could come off.

'You'll have to be very careful, Mrs Pascoe, to keep the leg covered when you're on the beach. The skin is very tender and shouldn't be exposed to sun, but swimming in the salt water will help to strengthen the muscles.'

219

It was a relief to know that Malcolm was going to stay in the house again while we were away. I didn't have to clear out the fridge, turn off the hot water or lock up. When he drove us to Heathrow the next morning he agreed to wait until he was sure we'd got away before returning to Chipping Norton.

Before Terminal 4 was built, BOAC departed from Terminal 3 and the staff travel office was in a different part of the building. That morning, when we arrived, the office was absolutely packed. Everyone had the same idea – to get away from England for their holidays. Although Peter's leg was out of plaster it was stiff and he couldn't walk very far. 'Rich, see if you can find somewhere outside for Peter to sit down and look after him while I find out what's happening.' I stood in a long queue waiting to hand in my tickets and find out what chances we had on the New York flight. It's a test in control not to appear anxious as you stand waiting, to smile at the girl at the desk, who is only doing her job, and not to feel hatred of other people wanting to get on the same service. Over the years BOAC has lived up to its name and taken great care of us. Financially it was a great way to travel but you never get anything for nothing and the price we paid was the uncertainty and anxiety of not knowing if we were on or not.

But this time all was well – even more so when I found that our captain was Athol Foster, the New Zealand pilot who had taken us by flying boat to Khartoum all those years ago. After take-off I asked permission to go up front to have a chat with him. I was delighted to find that he would be taking the service on to Honolulu. John had made arrangements for us to go to the New Western Hotel in Forty-Second Street where the crews stayed on their stop-overs in New York. Athol said we could have transport with the crew into the hotel and he would take us back to the airport the following afternoon.

It had been a long day. There was a message from John for me at the desk when we booked in, saying that if we wanted to meet up with him in Japan, we could only have one day and a night in Honolulu. It was disappointing as we'd hoped to spend three or four days there. With the five hours' time difference between London and New York, added to the early start from Chipping Norton and the long flight, we were all a bit crotchety by the time we got into our room. Peter, who was never enthusiastic about eating on an aircraft was feeling hungry, so we went downstairs to find the coffee-shop. The boys wanted bacon and eggs. Everything was clean and efficient. Immediately we sat down the waitress brought us glasses of iced water and set the table with knives and forks wrapped in white linen napkins. It was a good cup of coffee and really hot. I wondered if they'd ever learn to serve such coffee in England.

I hoped we'd sleep late the next morning, but by 6 a.m. the boys were chattering away and ready to get up and explore. I tried to think of the best way to spend the morning. As our pick-up time was at two p.m. there wasn't much time for sightseeing. I knew that Peter's leg wouldn't stand up to much walking. One of the crew members in the bus had suggested we take a trip on the Hudson River and see Manhattan Island from the water.

I packed all our things before going down to breakfast and then we took a taxi down to the Ferry Wharf on the Hudson River. There was an excellent commentary given as we sailed along the fascinating foreshore of this famous river. *Man-a hat-ta* was an Indian name meaning 'The Island of the Hills'. It was bought by the representatives of the Dutch West India Company in 1626 for beads, cloth and trinkets worth about $24. But it was an Englishman, Henry Hudson, employed by the Dutch West India company, who explored the river that now bears his name, and found the natural harbour which has become the gateway to the West.

But the boys weren't so interested in the history of the area. They wanted to see the famous Statue of Liberty. 'Gosh, isn't she huge?' Richard said as the small ferry chugged near Liberty Island and we gazed up at that proud lady with her right arm extended to the sky holding the torch of liberty . The French sculptor, Frédéric Auguste Bartholdi travelled to New York in 1870 and seeing Liberty Island at the entrance of New York Harbour declared 'Here … my statue must rise … here where people get their first view of the New World.' He returned to France and designed and created, with the help of his friend Gustave Eiffel, this statue. In 1884, on July 4th – American Independence Day– the French presented it to the United States Minister in Paris as a gift of friendship. This symbol of liberty was then taken apart, crated in 214 boxes and shipped aboard the French ship, *Isere,* to New York, in May 1885.

The tall buildings of Wall Street glistened in the sun as we rounded the Southern tip of Manhattan Island and sailed into the East River under the many famous bridges and past the slim, glass-walled skyscraper of the United Nations Secretariat.

Peter started to look very sleepy but woke up when we found that hamburgers and Coke could be bought on board the ferry. When we got back to the hotel there was a message from Athol to say our flight had been delayed and we wouldn't be going out to Kennedy Airport until 3.15. We collected our luggage and sat quietly in the lounge until the crew car arrived. Athol told us on the way out to the airport that he'd checked the load. 'You needn't worry. It's a light load and there'll be plenty of room.' They dropped us at the departure terminal and with a cheery 'See you on board' drove off to do their briefing.

I stood feeling relaxed in the queue with the luggage and tickets ready. The young attractive girl at the desk looked as if she had just left school. But her manner was abrupt and the lady in front of me as we came to the desk looked really annoyed. I handed over my tickets. They seemed to confuse her. She kept running her finger down the list in front of her.

' You're not on the passenger list to Honolulu, Mrs Pascoe. And if you're a staff passenger, you're late checking in. You should have been here an hour ago.'

I explained that I had come out with the captain and that he knew all about me. She wasn't impressed.

' Well, if you do get on, there won't be any food for you on board as you aren't on this manifest. You'd better go upstairs and buy some sandwiches to take with you. Come back in ten minutes.'

Her curt manner did nothing for my morale. I know we were only staff passengers but that didn't excuse her rude manner. If we didn't get on this service it meant another three days in New York and that would upset all our plans for meeting John and Bill in Tokyo.

I hovered anxiously. I certainly didn't feel like going and looking for sandwiches. I'd never been told to do that before. Nor had I heard of any staff having to take food on board.

My smile was rather forced when I went back to the desk after ten minutes. The young lady was busy chatting up one of the officers standing nearby and didn't bother to turn round. Finally she deigned to notice me. 'Oh, there you are. You can go on board,' she said condescendingly 'There's no room in first class. You'd better hurry and not keep the plane waiting.'

I took the tickets and beckoned to the boys. We sped up the stairs, as fast as we could with Peter's gammy leg. I muttered things under my breath about pert, inexperienced traffic girls. 'Silly little flibbertigibbet. I hope I never see her again.'

The steward who greeted us at the top of the stairs as we climbed on board had been on the flight from London. 'We were wondering what had happened to you, Mrs Pascoe. The captain was just inquiring if you'd come on board.' I apologized for our late arrival and said I was sorry if I'd caused any delay.

'The young lady at the ticket desk was very unhelpful and told me there wouldn't be any food for us on board.'

'What nonsense. We always have some extra. And anyway we were expecting you. Let me take your luggage.' He took us through to the first class compartment. 'With Captain Foster's compliments,' he said as he settled us into our comfortable seats.

I was happy to feel secure, lap up the luxury and accept a glass of champagne as we took off. It was a happy flight.

Honolulu was all that I remembered. As we flew over Diamond Head, I looked down to see if I could pick out the flat where we had spent so many wonderful days. We flew along the coastline near Waikiki Beach and past the Aloha Tower to the runway at the airport. It was hot as we came out of the airport building but there was a breeze blowing.

When we arrived at the Alamoana Hotel the boys couldn't wait. They found their swimming togs and dashed off down to the beach and into the soft warm water. I needed a little time to sort myself out but I soon joined them. I lay on my back in the water. The worries over the last few weeks and the anxiety of the flight melted away. This was bliss! How fortunate we were to have these experiences as part of John's job. I hoped the boys wouldn't take it for granted but realize the unique opportunities they had of 'going places and seeing things'. What a wonderful way to learn

223

geography and history. The sun dipped behind the horizon but it was still warm enough to sit on the sand and watch the heavens glow red and gold as the colours spread across the sky.

The next day was just as wonderful! I hardly saw Richard – except when he felt hungry. He was off like a flash first thing in the morning to see about hiring a surfboard. He spent the day paddling out to the reef and waiting for the right wave to speed him in. I had to watch Peter to make sure his leg wasn't exposed for too long in the sun. But he was very happy to dash in and out of the water, fling himself at the waves and dive under them. He hadn't forgotten the lessons he learnt from the Japanese swimming instructor.

As our flight didn't leave until midnight and we had to get out of the hotel room by 2 p.m. I phoned some old friends and they invited us for an evening-meal. Their garden was a riot of colour, full of exotic hibiscus – red, pinks and yellow, single and double – such a variety. Ron drove us to the airport at ten o'clock and we cheerfully waved him *aloha*. We were full of sun, sea and good food. But it was a bit of a blow when we found that the aircraft had been delayed and wouldn't be leaving until 2 a.m. But the airport building was cool and there weren't many people about. Richard, who had a dark complexion and had never been troubled with sunburn before found that his back was red and sore. And Peter's leg, even though we'd been careful, needed some cream rubbed on it. When I went to the reporting desk about midnight to find out about departure time and seat availability I met a very helpful girl – so different from the young up-start in New York.

'Sorry about this delay, Mrs Pascoe. As far as we can tell at present it looks good. We don't have many passengers for Tokyo. Most of them are getting off here. I'm sure we'll have room for you.'

Time drifted by. What else can it do when you're waiting for a plane? The boys had curled up on the chairs and gone to sleep. I wondered what I would do if John wasn't at the airport when we arrived in Tokyo. I didn't even know the name of the hotel where we would be staying. I tried to read but couldn't concentrate. My back was sunburnt and the tops of my legs were on fire. That Hawaiian sun was powerful.

224

I didn't know the plane had landed until the traffic girl came over to me with the tickets in her hand. 'Here you are, Mrs Pascoe. There is plenty of room and we've given you first class seats. Can I help you with your luggage? We're ready to board.'

I roused the boys. We walked through the garden fragrant with the scent of frangipani and out to the waiting Britannia aircraft. We settled down very quickly and I gladly accepted a delicious *Mai Tai* drink with a slice of pineapple on the side of the glass and a small purple orchid floating on top. The engines started and we moved slowly along the runway. I looked across the aisle at the only other passenger in the first class. There comfortably curled up asleep was the New York 'flibbitigibbet.' I felt like shaking her and asking her if she'd bought her sandwiches with her and how she'd managed to qualify for a first-class seat. But instead I sipped my *Mai Tai* and heaved a sigh of thankfulness at being safely on my way to see John and Bill.

It was a clear beautiful morning as we approached the coast of the Japanese Island of Honshu. The captain's voice woke me: 'Good morning, everyone. I hope you've all had a good night's rest. We are sorry about the late arrival in Japan and trust it won't inconvenience you too much. We are just approaching the island of Honshu and almost straight ahead you can see the famous mountain of Japan – Mount Fuji – rising out of the clouds. You're lucky to see it so clearly this morning. Visitors can often be weeks in Japan without catching a glimpse of this sacred mountain. We crossed the date-line during the night and so you've missed a day and it is still August the 2nd. We will be landing in twenty minutes – at six-thirty. I wish you a happy stay in Japan.'

Mount Fuji looked like all the pictures I'd seen of it – the snow-capped conical peak rising out of the faintly tinted wisps of cloud that floated around its sides.

An awkward bounce and bump brought us back to earth as the wheels made contact and settled on the runway. Not the best landing, I thought. Perhaps it was the first officer. Richard looked rather the worse for wear. His nose was red and he walked stiffly down the steps of the aircraft. I stood for a moment at the top wondering if a miracle could happen and in spite of all the different flights and delays, John and Bill would be there to meet us. And then I heard our whistle, those first three notes of the Fifth Symphony. Never did music have a sweeter sound. At first I couldn't see anyone. Then, as we walked towards the entrance to the arrival building I saw them leaning on a fence; John still in uniform and Bill waving madly. I could have cried with joy and relief. A miracle had happened. After thousands of miles and many flights, some going east and some west, at 6.30 a.m. at Haneda Airport in Japan the five members of the Pascoe clan were together again.

22

Japan

'How long have you and Bill been in Tokyo?' I asked John as we went into the airport building.

'We arrived about an hour ago. I was afraid you'd be here first and wondering what to do. But as we landed I heard on the radio that you'd been delayed. So that was a relief.'

The boys were chatting away catching up on what Bill had been doing in Tehran. 'They all drive like maniacs there,' I heard him say. 'You can never go out without seeing an accident. I don't think there's a car in the city that hasn't been bashed at some time. It was fun being with the Pearsons and James' father took us up into the hills. We were going to camp for the night but we were eaten by sandflies. They were terrible, so we packed up and drove back home again. I saw the wonderful jewels belonging to the Shah. You would have loved that, Mother.' Bill caught up with me as we stood waiting for the crew car. 'I could just see you with a tiara in your hair. Some of the rubies and diamonds were so big they didn't look real. The Pearsons gave me a great time but I wouldn't want to live there. Tehran is dirty and noisy.'

We drove away from the airport and headed for the city. Even at this early hour the traffic seemed mad and taxi-drivers zoomed past us on both sides of the lane we were driving on. It was quite scary and I had to get used to being driven on the left again after the few days in the States. I was surprised that the Americans, during their 12 years of occupation of Japan, hadn't changed the rule of the road. Perhaps they figured that there were enough accidents with Kamikaze drivers without complicating matters by trying to make them drive on the other side of the road.

'Where are we staying, John.' I asked as we narrowly missed bumping into a taxi that had swerved across the front of us.

'At the San Banchio Hotel. It's quite small, but fairly central and not far from the Imperial Palace. There's a swimming pool in the new wing across the road which has just been opened. The boys will enjoy that because it's hot here at present.'

Bill was sitting next to me and I noticed that his right ear was very red. Dear Bill! His ears had always stuck out. I turned to John. 'What's the matter with Bill's ear?'

'He complained about his ear being sore the day after he arrived in Hong Kong. I took him to the BOAC doctor who diagnosed what they call "Hong Kong ear." I think Bill must have picked it up while swimming in Tehran.'

' How can it be "Hong Kong ear" if he picked it up in Tehran?'

'You can pick it up anywhere. It's a type of fungus that comes from swimming in pools in a hot climate. It seems to develop when the ears are not dried properly. The doctor has given him some drops which have to be put in every three hours. It's important to keep the ears dry. I'm afraid this means Bill won't be able to swim for another four days.'

I had a horror of ear infections. In Eritrea Bill had had a threatened mastoid. It had happened so suddenly and I didn't want any trouble in a foreign country where we couldn't speak the language.

'Poor old Bill.' I patted his knee. 'I'm sorry, darling. It'll be miserable for you to have to watch Rich and Peter enjoying themselves in the pool. Is it very painful?'

He grinned at me. 'Oh it's not too bad. Just feels hot.'

'Whew. I'm hot even without a sore ear. I'm longing for a shower and a sleep. You must be tired too, John, after flying all night.'

The crew car drew up at the hotel. Little men hurried out to pick up the luggage and we were bowed into the hotel reception hall. The girls behind the counter bowed and I found my head automatically bending in return. It doesn't take many minutes to adopt the customs of the country. It really is a sensible idea. If your hands are full of handbags you don't need to drop them to shake hands. It's so much easier to bow your head and it's a good relaxing exercise if you do it properly and bend from the hips. It's difficult to bow politely if you feel annoyed or angry. It then becomes a jerk rather than a bow. It requires control to make a polite bow. I had my first lesson in 'controlled relaxation' a few minutes later. John was busy at the desk signing the register. We waited impatiently longing to get into our rooms. John came over to us. 'The rooms aren't ready yet. We'll just have to sit and wait.'

'Oh no. I'm so tired and there's nowhere to sit here.' I walked over to the receptionist. 'We're all very tired as we've been travelling for many hours. Haven't you got another room we could use until our rooms are ready?'

The girl bowed her head. ' Hai, hai. Vely solly, Madam, no loom leady.' She bowed again even more deeply.

And that was that!

'Come on, let's go for a walk.' John's cure for all ills is to go for a walk. What with Richard being irritable because of his sunburn, Bill suffering from a bad ear and Peter looking white and tired, it was hardly a great idea to walk the streets of Tokyo on a very hot morning. 'We'll go and buy some bread. I think I smelt a baker's shop somewhere near here.' This was another one of John's little foibles. He loved French bread and we'd walked many miles in many countries trying to find a crusty baguette.

We crossed the busy road outside the hotel and wandered round some of the strange little streets, so narrow there wasn't room for two cars to pass. All the shops and tiny houses had their doors opening right onto the road, but outside the door, most of them had flowers or a miniature tree growing in pots. The construction was so flimsy I wasn't surprised they collapsed when there was an earthquake. They looked as if a puff of wind would blow them away.

We saw food displayed on plates in the window of a small café. It looked quite appetizing. Large bowls of noodles with all kinds of vegetables, fish done in batter with chips and a small salad, tall glasses with ice cream topped with fruit and cream, and even a hamburger with chips and egg (shades of the Americans). The price in yen was beside each dish.

229

'They're all made of plastic,' John said. 'There's a huge factory with highly trained special chefs designing these dishes to make them look like the real thing. Plastic food display is a Japanese speciality. Traditionally at Buddhist funerals a symbolic offering of food was placed near the body. Made of wax they were so realistic that someone was inspired with the idea of making displays for shops and cafés.' I looked more closely and saw that the slightly shiny glazed look of the fried egg gave the show away. 'Apparently it's now a law that all cafés must display their food in the window. It's convenient for the customers – especially foreigners – to be able to go in and point to what they want and know what it will cost.'

'Where's this baker's shop, John? Are you sure it's in this street?' I was getting tired of wandering around. I'd read somewhere that as the Japanese ate so much rice, bread wasn't easy to find.

'It's here somewhere but perhaps we'd better go back and see if our room is ready.'

We trailed back to the hotel and went through the same procedure of bowing politely as we entered and then bowing at the receptionist.

'One loom alleady.' said the girl and beckoned to the porter. We squeezed into a tiny lift. The room was small with no view. It had one huge bed taking up most of the space. The boys took off their shoes and fell on it. I asked John where the eardrops were and put some in Bill's ear. Exhausted, they were asleep before we closed the door.

After another hour we were taken up to our room. There was no wardrobe, only wall-pegs to hang clothes on. At least it had a loo – western style – and a shower. It also had a very noisy air-conditioner. Better than nothing, I suppose, but it was a bit like being on board ship with the persistent drone of the engines in our ears.

John was full of plans. 'We must take a trip to Nikko and climb Fuji. I've made arrangements for you to go to the Sogetsu school for a lesson when I come back from my next trip. I can look after the boys. Perhaps you'd like to go down south to Kyoto...'

I interrupted him: 'At the moment I'm not interested in going anywhere or doing anything. I'm hot and tired. I just want to sleep.'

I pulled off my clothes, got under the shower and then thankfully lay on the bed and closed my eyes.

The next couple of days we didn't feel like doing very much – just absorbing the atmosphere of a very different culture, learning to eat 'plastic food' and falling in and out of the pool to cool off. Bill's ear was giving him trouble and the inflammation spread behind the ear. John made an appointment with the BOAC doctor who confirmed that it was 'Hong Kong ear'. He told us it was very infectious and we would need to watch the other boys in case they developed it. Some different drops were prescribed – this time to be put in every two hours. Swimming in pools was definitely off.

When John heard he was due to go out on service in three days' time, he decided we'd sat around long enough. It was time to make the trip to Fuji and climb the mountain.

Fuji-san is a very special mountain to the Japanese who consider the climb to the top a sacred pilgrimage. It is over 12,000 feet high and sudden mists sweep down the long symmetrical slopes making it dangerous to climb when covered with snow, so it's only open for climbers during the months of July and August. We had been told that 50,000 pilgrims climb to the top of the inactive volcano each year to watch the sunrise and pay homage to the gods. Obviously for all those people it was a good thing to do. But I wondered if it was really necessary for the Pascoe family to labour to the top.

John took the boys and went off to the Japan Tourist Bureau (JTB) to find out how to get to Mount Fuji. The tourist bureau wanted to book the whole trip for him and provide a Japanese guide. But John liked the challenge of finding his own way. Besides it was cheaper and he considered it more of an adventure for the boys. He did, however, get them to book us for one night at a Japanese inn in a small town at the foot of the mountain. He also got all the instructions for the journey written in Japanese so we could show them to the guards at a station or a taxi driver.

We left the hotel at 7 a.m. and made our way to the nearest subway station. It was seething with people. John had studied the map and the colours of the different lines of the subway trains. We couldn't see the information desk or a guard. A train arrived and before we knew what was happening we were all pushed into one carriage and stood jammed together. For once I was glad to be tall. At least I could look over the heads of the small Japanese and keep my eye on John. There was no way of telling if we were going in the right direction although we tried to read the names of the stations. But they were written in Japanese.

At each stop everyone pushed and shoved – the bowing and the politeness forgotten, in the haste to get off before the doors closed. We had several changes to make but with John waving his piece of paper with the Japanese instructions at various officials, we finally got on the train that would take us to our destination. This was full of schoolchildren: girls clad in their navy blue gym dresses – rather long and shapeless – and white blouses; boys in their military-type suits with high collars and peaked caps on their heads. The girls eyed the boys and giggled behind their hands. I was intrigued how the hands fluttered over their mouths as if they were carrying fans.

John struck up a conversation with some of the girls standing near him. 'Hullo,' he said. More giggles and then a braver one said: 'Ullo,'ow are you? We are vely well, thank you. It is a good day, yes?'

The ice was broken and they produced their English books and homework to show John. Soon we were all involved in helping them. As long as they stuck to the book text, they were fine, but when I asked them a question about what sport they played, they looked puzzled. I was to find that in so many cases, although a Japanese student could say the word 'understand' and write the word 'understand' they didn't understand what the word 'understand' really meant. At their school station they all piled out with much waving and goodbying.

We were the only people left in the carriage and after the excited chattering it was peaceful to be in the train running alongside a beautiful blue lake which looked cool and inviting. We caught a glimpse of the top of Mount Fuji, but clouds were all round it and it kept disappearing. There were few people about when we got off the train and John had a job to find someone to direct us to the inn which was at the top of a hill. The boys had their first lesson in taking off their shoes as they went into the *genkan* (the entrance hall). Slippers were provided and the shoes put neatly on shelves.

With great ceremony and much bowing the hostess in her kimono, took us along the wooden-floored corridor. She pointed to a sign saying *benji* which by now we knew to be toilet. Then she opened the *shoji* screens and bowed us into a large room devoid of any furniture except a small round table and some cushions on the floor. I walked across the room and opened the window. It looked out into a garden where small well trimmed pine trees nestled beside a pond with rocks in the middle and golden carp swimming around.

'I'm hungry,' said Peter.' What have we got to eat?'

'Nothing here, I'm afraid. We'll have to go out and explore.'

Bill, usually the first one to react at the mention of food, said he didn't feel like anything to eat and wanted to lie down. I opened a cupboard door and found a futon and laid it on the floor. Bill collapsed on it. He didn't give in easily and I knew he must be in pain. I gave him two aspirin and put the drops in his ears but I was worried. I didn't think he was in a fit state to climb a mountain and I didn't like leaving him alone in a strange place.

'Come on,' said John. 'He'll feel better after he's had a sleep.'

It was a dear little village – so clean and tidy. We seemed to be the only foreigners about. There were lots of touristy shops but no cafés. We found a type of grocery store and stocked up on things we needed the next day. Richard insisted on buying a hat with a Fuji badge to take back to school. We'd been told to buy walking-sticks and get them stamped at each stage of the climb. They were long sticks made of very light wood. We bought five and practised with them as we walked back to the station.

John wanted to inquire when the bus left in the morning to take us up the mountain to Stage Five where the climb started. We couldn't find anyone who spoke English. It was hilarious watching my staid English husband miming to a small elderly Japanese station attendant his wish to catch a bus to Mount Fuji. There were many *Hai, hai, hais* from the uniformed man as if he understood perfectly what John was talking about. The mountain couldn't be seen so it was no use pointing in that direction. John tapped his watch and the man peered at it and then pointed to 5. We didn't know if he meant five a.m. or p.m. We'd just have to get up early in the morning and come and wait.

The smell, when we walked into the inn made me feel queasy. It was the smell of cooking oil. Bill was still sound asleep and John suggested we left him alone and go to inquire about having a bath. More miming and giggles from the little maid who pointed to a sign down the end of the corridor. Then she handed me a cleanly starched *yakarta* – or housecoat – and beckoned me to follow her. We went down a long passage and into a steamy room where the maid pointed to a basket on a shelf and indicated that I was to leave my clothes in it. She waited until I'd undressed and then sliding back a door, handed me a piece of soap and a tiny soft white towel about 18 inches long. I felt extremely naked and embarrassed. There's a first time for everything! The maid pointed to a small wooden stool by a tap. There was a plastic bowl under the tap and through the steam I saw other female forms pouring water over themselves as they sat on the stools.

I bowed and walked to a vacant stool about six inches from the floor, and with difficulty lowered myself onto it. I'm sure the rear of my anatomy was twice the size of any of the other ladies in the room. I turned on the tap, filled the plastic basin and threw the water over my body. I swear it was melted snow and so cold it took my breath away. Then I soaped myself vigorously, threw more water over myself and thankfully got into the large hot pool. Perhaps that's the idea! You suffer all these hardships of cold sluicing beforehand in order to enjoy the delights of relaxing in a hot bath. I wondered how the boys were getting on and hoped that John, who'd experienced the etiquette of a Japanese bath before had given them the right instructions.

I watched carefully when the other ladies got out of the bath, but I couldn't solve the riddle of how one got dry with a pocket handkerchief for a towel. When I'd had enough heat I climbed out, dried what bits I could and returned to the outer room. My underclothes had been removed from the basket and a fresh *yarkata* laid ready for me to put on. I padded along the corridor in my slippers. There were screams of mirth coming from the room. Bill was well and truly awake and all my males were clad alike in these blue and white garments. They'd been giving Bill a blow by blow description of the Japanese bath. John was concerned because his underpants and trousers had been taken away. I must admit we all looked clean and refreshed.

Before we went to bed, John went to pay the bill as we wanted to leave early the next morning. He tried to find out what had happened to our clothes, but all he got was a giggle a *hai, hai* and a bow. He needn't have worried. When he came back to the room he found that while he'd been away all the clothes had been returned pressed, and beautifully folded.

The sun was just rising when we came out of the inn into the street the following morning. We lifted our eyes and there, in all its glory, was Fuji-san, glistening in the sunrise with the snow tipped peak piercing the blue heavens. A glorious sight! Bill had had a good night, the ear less inflamed and he was no longer in pain. All was well with the Pascoe world.

There were several buses at the station and a lot of people. As we had our climbing-sticks everyone seemed to know where we wanted to go. We were directed to a bus that was ready to leave. We passed through agricultural land where rice was being harvested. The women in their large hats were gathering the sheaves and making stocks of the golden rice straw. We stopped along the road to wait for a party of schoolboys all carrying sticks. A uniformed girl with a whistle in her mouth and waving a flag, shepherded them into the bus. The rice paddies gave way to rough grassland where a type of pampas grass was growing, their fluffy heads waving in the breeze. The bus stopped after half an hour and the boys got out and lined up at a stall to get their sticks stamped. We followed them but were a bit taken back when we found we had to pay 100 yen for every stamp on each stick.

'How many stages are there?' I asked John. 'It's going to be an expensive business if we have to have them stamped at each one.'

' I think there are at least ten stages,' John replied. 'I know we get off the bus at Stage Five. We'll have something to eat there and see if we can buy some bread but we don't want to carry more than we need.' We'd already stocked up with biscuits, raisins, nuts, cheese and chocolates and something to drink.

Stage Five was a tourist set-up with shops full of gimmicky looking bits and pieces. Outside there were stalls where all kinds

235

of goodies were being cooked. John found one selling sweetcorn that had been dipped in soya sauce. It was delicious – and filling.

The whole place was alive with climbers in heavy boots with rucksacks on their backs. I looked down at my shoes. They were strong and comfortable but hardly fit for mountain climbing.

We set off at a good pace, now with five stamps on our sticks and 2.500 yen poorer. At first the going was easy and through shaded bush, we caught glimpses of the lake below. The air was pure and smelt clean after the stale, hot stuffy polluted atmosphere of Tokyo. Up and up we went. The vegetation gave way to low scrub and then lava stones and rocks which slipped under our feet. Energetic young climbers with ankle-boots dashed by looking surprised to find an English family stumbling along.

After Stage Seven, which was only a stall for stamping Fuji sticks, I called a halt. 'Oh, not yet,' said John, 'we'll go on for another quarter of an hour. There's still a long way to go.' We plodded on. It wasn't much good my saying anything. John always wanted to go that bit further.

Bill, who was walking behind me saw me stumbling and called to his father. 'I'm hungry, Dad, and it's time my drops were put in. Let's stop here.' We sat on rocks and marvelled at the view – well the far view! I was horrified to find that this sacred mountain was littered with piles of rubbish – dirty rusty baked bean cans, coke and beer bottles and eggshells scattered around. The Japanese, so clean and tidy in their eating habits – hot towels always placed before your plate to wipe your hands – seemed to have taken a fiendish delight in ridding themselves of all inhibitions, throwing and scattering their unwanted trash over the mountainside. It was quite disgusting. But then, what do you do with your rubbish on a rocky mountain? Hardly carry it to the top and down again.

I made chocolate, cheese and raisin rolls and we divided two nashi – the Japanese fruit which is a cross between and apple and a pear – a crisp fruit with a brown skin. The boys buried the peelings under some stones.

'Come on, let's get going.' John chivvied everyone along. 'We'll go onto Stage Eight and see if we can spend the night in the hut there on the way back. It would be good if we can off-load some of our gear as well.'

The hut at Stage Eight was cut into the rocks with only a few yards of path in front. There was a steep drop into nothingness at the edge of the path. Mama-san and Papa-san dressed in their peasant kimonos sat on a seat outside the hut. They solemnly stood up and bowed as we approached. John mimed the sleeping for one night and they bowed us into the hut. The boys couldn't be bothered taking off their shoes so they stayed outside.

The sleeping accommodation consisted of one room with wooden bunks where you laid side by side. There were no mattresses and only light-weight futons. It was primitive but there wasn't much choice. We left as much as possible with our host and hostess and hurried on. It got steeper and steeper.

I was glad of the support of my stick as I balanced on some of the bigger rocks. My shoes didn't grip properly and as I stepped off one stone, my ankle twisted over. The male members of the party were forging ahead. Bill seemed to have forgotten about his ear and Peter – amazingly – was having no trouble at all with his leg. I was finding it hard to breathe. We'd no idea how far it was to the top. The next notice, pointing to a superior looking hut, said 8A and not 9 as we thought it should be. John waited for me to catch up. 'Goodness,' I said, 'there could be 8B and 8C before we get to Stage Nine. I wasn't going to tell him about my twisted ankle. If it got much rougher I knew I'd never make it.

'You carry on to the top with the boys. I'm going to have a bit of a rest. Maybe I'll meet you on your way down. Here's my stick. You might as well have it stamped at the last stage. I'll sit here and admire the view.'

I sat on a rock and watched them disappear up the zigzag path. I felt miserable. This was the first time I'd had to give in and not complete a family expedition. The air was cool and clouds drifted across the top of the mountain. Down below I could still see the lake glistening in the sunlight. And then suddenly I was enveloped in mist. It happened in a flash. One minute I could see for miles and the next minute the cloud had obliterated the view completely. I looked up the mountain, hoping to catch a sight of the boys, but there was nothing but swirling mist. It was eerie to be all alone. Now I didn't know if I should go up or down. I sat still, hoping the cloud would clear away as quickly as it had come.

I'll never catch the family now, I thought, and decided to try and find my way back to the Stage Eight hut. I was panicky and frightened and had never felt so alone before. It was terrible not being able to see. I stumbled on hoping that I was sticking to the path. I lost all sense of time. I wished I'd kept my stick because the pain in my ankle, when I stepped on a stone, made me feel quite sick. It became an endurance test – one foot down – another step … I had to keep going. The path twisted and turned. I couldn't remember it doing that on the way up. I went on and on praying that when I turned the next corner I would see the hut. The lines of a poem I'd read somewhere came into my head.

> There was no wind – just stillness – white cotton
>   wool all round me
> And then I hear voices
> I thought I heard voices – now I am imagining things.

But as I stumbled round a corner, two ghostly figures material-ized. They looked startled at coming on a lonely female. I suppose I must have looked like a ghost appearing out of the mist. They bowed. I bowed. I held up eight fingers and pointed down the mountain. They looked bewildered. Then I put my hands to my cheek as I closed my eyes and pointed to my watch. They under-stood. '*Hai, hai, hai,*' they both said nodding their heads. One held up five fingers and pointing to his watch showed me five minutes.

They stood aside to let me pass. I hated to leave them but felt I mustn't lose face and stepped out into the cloud again. But it wasn't long before I saw the small hut looming out of the mist. Thankfully I tapped at the door. Mama-san slid back the *shoji* door and bowed me inside. '*Domo arigato, domo arigato.*' That was the full extent of my Japanese. I was so glad to be safely inside that I would have gone on saying it over and over again.

She bowed me to a low table and poured a cup of tea from a thermos. She knelt easily and rested on the back of her legs. I tried to copy her position but after a few minutes my legs ached and I tried to get them under the table. I was grateful for the hot drink but it was thick and green and quite different from any tea I had tasted at the hotel. One mug was enough so when she unscrewed the thermos I put my hand over my mug and shook my head.

I had a long, long wait. There was nowhere to sit in the hut. I had nothing to read and conversation was impossible. In desperation I went into the dormitory and found John's jersey in the rucksack. I went outside and sat on the seat where we had first seen Mama-san. It was damp and cold. Looking at my watch I saw that it was after six o'clock and the sun – wherever it was – would soon be setting. Surely the boys couldn't be much longer. Two trampers came past and I longed to ask them if they'd seen my family. The inability to communicate except by sign is a terrible feeling. I was worried stiff. Was Bill's ear giving trouble? ... had Peter's leg twisted because it wasn't strong enough for such a climb? ... was John finding the rarefied atmosphere affecting his asthma? I wasn't as concerned about Richard as he was usually able to cope. But what if the mist meant they couldn't find their way up – or down and were lost on the mountain?

And then a strange calm came over me and out of the mist I thought I heard my father's voice saying: 'Now, Vivienne , it's no good crossing your bridges before you come to them. Have faith.' There weren't any bridges to be crossed around here but the same advice could be given for climbing or waiting on a mountain. I wrapped my arms more tightly around my chest to keep warm, and decided to walk a little way up the path. Then, – as dear father would say – 'Hallelujah!' I heard their voices ... a wonderful sound! They were singing: 'They'll be coming down the mountain, when she comes, they'll be coming down the mountain ...' I whistled and blocked the path. First Bill appeared, then Peter, Richard and John. I hugged them all.

'Oh, it's good to see you. What a time you've been. Did you have a bad time finding your way in the mist?'

'We're all right,' said John. 'We wondered what happened to you. I've never seen mist come down so quickly before although I'd been warned that Fuji-san could be treacherous in this way. We'd better get Richard into the warm. He was mountain sick when we got to the summit and is still feeling groggy. The top was much further than it looked, but we made it and the boys climbed down into the crater and marked our name out with some of the white stones.

239

He handed me my stick. 'Here you are. We've had all the sticks stamped at every stage.'

I looked at the ten stamps. 'I really don't deserve this,' I said, 'because I didn't get to the top.'

'Never mind, darling. You nearly did.'

There was much bowing and twittering when we all went into the tiny room and Mam-san set bowls of soup and rice on the table. That went down well although eating rice with chopsticks needs practice. We hadn't yet learnt to 'slurp' our soup or bring the rice bowls right up to our mouth. Richard was not enthusiastic about anything to eat and when the green tea was served he took one look at the thick green mixture and with a rush, disappeared outside.

We were all exhausted and thankfully climbed up on the top-bunk. It was more like a wooden platform than a bunk and the five Pascoes lay in a row. But the night was hardly a success. With only one futon each it was difficult to decide whether to lie on it to make the board softer, or have it on top to keep warm. And those pillows! They were filled with sand and after a few minutes it was like putting your head on a rock. There was no way to get your neck in a comfortable position. The boys fell asleep but John and I tossed and turned. I tried snuggling up to him to keep warm but he was so restless I moved away nearer the window. We dozed fitfully and I willed the night away.

While it was still dark I heard voices outside the window and looking out, saw two well-equipped young men sitting on the seat drinking from their bottle. Then more climbers arrived and there was a lot of noisy chatter.

'What on earth are these people doing out there at this time of the morning?' I whispered to John.

'I guess they're going to climb to the top to see the sunrise on Fuji-san. That's the proper way to make this pilgrimage.'

'Pity we didn't do that. We might just as well be doing that as lying on these hard boards. What's the time?'

'Nearly four o'clock.'

I clambered down from the bunk, got my towel, and went outside to find the way round to the lavatory. I washed my face at a cold tap. Dressing wasn't difficult as we'd all slept in our clothes. There was a faint light in the sky. I tapped on the window. 'Johnnie, come outside and watch the sunrise. It's going to be a beautiful clear morning.' We walked a little way up the path until we could see the peak which was jet-black against the tinted sky. A wreath of cloud wound round the sides of the mountain making it look as if it was cut off from the earth.

We stood watching the clouds turning pink and gold and rising further and further up the steep sides until only the very tip stood out against the blue sky. This was the heavenly mountain that was so sacred to the Japanese.

'I think we'll try a different way down,' said John. 'I was told that there's a steep scoria slope that's much quicker than the zigzag path we came up on. Let's wake the boys up now and start down. Then we'll be back at Stage Five before it's too hot.'

The boys grumbled a bit but were quite glad to get going again. With the usual bowing, waving, '*sayornaras*' and '*arigatos*' we left the two little grey figures of Mama-san and Papa-san and strode off.

Now the light was brilliant. Not a cloud in the vivid blue sky. In front of us was the steep red scoria slope.

'It's a bit like going down a ski slope,' John told us. 'Just relax. Stride out and use your stick to keep your balance.'

We left the path and stepped onto the scoria. It felt like small pieces of coke underfoot and was slithery to walk on. The boys set off. I followed more gingerly testing my ankle. I'd only gone a few steps when my shoes were full of lava pebbles and my feet felt heavy. I sat down and taking off my shoes emptied out the offending pebbles. I realized now why all the Japanese had been wearing ankle-boots.

'Come on, Viv, it's no good doing that. We'll never get down. You'll just have to get used to it. Once your shoes are full they can't get any fuller. Try and zigzag across the scoria instead of going straight down.'

My feet got heavier and heavier and it was difficult to control them at all. But I had to keep going. Already the boys were far ahead, striding down the slopes at great speed. Then I saw Peter, who'd been trying to keep up with the other two, plunge down and topple over. John got to him as quickly as he could but the skin on his bad leg was scratched and his knee was bleeding. John tied his

241

handkerchief around the knee as we didn't have any Band-aids with us. Peter looked white and shaken.

'Just take it slowly.' John helped him up onto his feet again. 'We haven't got much more to do now and we'll soon be able to get onto the bus.'

When we reached the path leading back to Stage Five, I thankfully sat down and emptied my shoes. Peter was limping a bit but his knee had stopped bleeding and he was his cheerful self again.

We found a little café and ordered ice cold drinks and hamburgers. Thank goodness for the Americans who introduced this food which had now become universal. At least we knew what we were eating – or hoped we knew.

It was a quiet, subdued family that boarded the bus to take us back to Kamaguchi station. 'We did it,' John said with a satisfied grin. 'I don't suppose there are too many English families who get to the top of Fuji. The boys did well, I'm proud of them.'

I looked at my Fuji stick with its ten stamps down the side. I felt guilty about that. After all, even though I tried I had to accept the fact that I hadn't made the top. Was it a sign of weakness – or merely encroaching old age?

23

Ikebana

Japan was a land of contradictions. The 12 years of American occupation had given many of the Japanese the taste for a different lifestyle. Now, there was conflict between the old traditions based on the Buddhist religion, and the easier materialistic ways of the Western World. The tremendous importance of 'loss of face' to the Japanese was still something Westerners didn't understand.

When I knew we were going to Tokyo I had bought a Japanese – English dictionary and thought I could at least learn a few important words. I found that '*Hai, hai,*' meant 'Yes,' and the word for 'No' was '*Iiei*'. After being in Japan for about three weeks I was puzzled, because although I kept hearing everyone say '*Hai*' I never heard the word '*Iiei*'. I thought this must be a very strange country if the ladies never said 'No'.

Travelling north to Sendai by train one day, I studied my Japanese books. Sitting next to me was a businessman who spoke good English and he asked me how I was getting on with learning the language.

'Not very well, I'm afraid. What you hear and what is written is so different when the ends of many words are cut off when speaking.'

'We have many different inflections for the same word,' he told me, 'and that makes it a very difficult language to learn.'

As he'd shown an interest in what I was doing, I plucked up courage and asked him: 'Why is it that, even though I've been in Japan for three weeks, I've never heard anyone use the word '*Iiei*?'

He smiled. 'Well,' he said, 'you must watch people carefully. If they say "*Hai*" and nod their head up and down they mean "Yes" but if they say "*Hai*" and shake their head from side to side they probably mean "No". Japanese people hate to commit themselves. If they say "*Iiei*" they could lose face as they would be admitting they didn't know the answer. "*Hai*" leaves the options open.'

I laughed. This really did explain the conflict of negative and affirmative. When asking a question the answer was often 'Yes, you can't do that,' or 'Yes, you don't go this way.'

When John returned from his trip to India he said: 'Come on now, this is your weekend off. I'll take you along to the Sogetsu School this morning for your lesson which I've already paid for. Then after the lesson you can go into the city to the BOAC office and meet Noriko, one of the hostesses. I talked to her at the airport yesterday and she's going to try and get you a rail ticket to Kyoto. She'll take you to Tokyo central station, and put you on the right train. I've arranged with the office to book you into a hotel in Kyoto for two nights. You'll need to take your passport and travellers cheques with you.'

He handed me a wad of notes and a map of the subways. 'Here's some yen which should be enough to pay for your ticket and other expenses. Take a subway to Hibyia station which is near the BOAC office. I've marked it on the map. Here's a card with the address written in Japanese.'

'Wouldn't it be easier if I took a taxi from the school to the BOAC office? I haven't been on a subway on my own before.'

'Oh, you'll manage. It's quite easy. You buy a hundred-yen ticket from one of the machines. Just keep the subway map in your hand and follow the colours of the line you want.'

It didn't seem all that simple getting to the right station for the Sogetsu School in Aoyama-dori, although John had been there before. Even in 1960 the Sogetsu School was an impressive building overlooking the park where the crown prince had his palace. In 1977 it was redesigned by the famous Japanese architect Kenzo Tange and became one of the finest buildings in Tokyo.

We went up the stairs to the office where John introduced me to a tiny little lady in western dress, Meiko Tanibayashi. She was in charge of the foreign office and spoke very good English. Many of the American military wives had studied at the various schools of Ikebana during their time in Japan. The Sogetsu School was one of the more modern ones and very popular.

'I'll take you up to the classroom and introduce you to Mrs Ono, the instructor. We have a group of ladies here this morning from England. Perhaps you know them?' said Mrs Tanibayashi. She smiled at John. 'Goodbye, Captain, we'll take good care of your wife.' I could see that John had turned on his considerable charm when arranging these lessons for me.

'Have a good time ,' he said as he turned to go down the stairs. I was reminded of the remark he made when I was going into the nursing home to produce Bill and hoped that this experience wouldn't be as painful.

I followed Mrs. Tanibayashi. and we went into a big room with long tables and a dais at one end. She showed me shelves full of containers all shapes and sizes. 'You can choose whichever one you like but as this is your first lesson you'll need a big flat one like this.' She handed me a round black container about three inches high. 'Then you'll need a *kenzan*.' I wondered what that was but didn't like to ask. She put a round metal disc with spikes in the container. 'This is a *kenzan* and you can buy many different sizes. I think they're called "pinholders" in England and in America, for some reason, they're known as "frogs". Have you any *hasami* with you?'

I felt more and more ignorant. 'No, I'm sorry. What is "*hasami*"?'

'Oh, they're Japanese scissors. You can buy a pair from the office. I'll lend you these ones for the morning. Now we'll go and have a look at the materials.'

Outside in the hallway there were buckets full of branches and flowers. 'When you pay for your lesson it includes two bunches of material but of course you can buy more if you want to. You choose now what you would like to use.'

As I didn't know yet what I was supposed to do, it was difficult to decide. There was so much to choose from. I loved the beautiful branches of Japanese maple, so I settled for those and a bunch of pink roses.

'Now come and I'll introduce you to Stella Coe who is Director of the Sogetsu School in England. She used to live in Japan before the war and has brought some of her students over here for a visit.'

She took me back into the room and over to a table near the front. 'Miss Coe, I'd like you to meet Vivienne Pascoe who is also from England. This is her first lesson.' I shook hands with a petite blonde lady smartly dressed in a lavender linen suit and a crisp white blouse.

'Come and sit here next to me,' she said, 'and perhaps I can help you if you don't understand something. It's a bit strange at first.'

Mrs Ono stood quietly on the dais ready to demonstrate. Her assistant handed her a branch of maple. Oh good, I thought, at least I've chosen the same branches. She looked at the rather full branch carefully, showed it to us against the white background and then began to snip side twigs off. She measured it against her low container and cut it a certain length before putting it into the *kenzan*. (*Kenzan*, I must remember that word.) It looked so easy and simple. I was anxious to start my arrangement and picked up my branch.

'Don't be in a hurry, Vivienne,' Stella whispered. 'Wait until Mrs Ono has finished doing her arrangement.'

Mrs Ono went on deftly inserting branches and flowers into the *kenzan* bending them forward towards the class.

'This is called a basic upright arrangement,' the interpreter said. She pointed to a drawing on the board. 'We have three placements of branches, *shin*, *soe* and *hikae*. They are at different angles from the central perpendicular, two on one side and one the other, forming an off-balance triangle. Please copy the design on the board into your notebook before you start doing your arrangement.' I felt confused. Mathematics had never been a strong point in my education, and the thought of having to consider degrees and triangles when I was making a floral arrangement was daunting – to say the least.

Mrs Ono finished her arrangement and stepped down from the dais.

'Miss Coe,' I began …

'Oh, please call me Stella,' she said quietly, 'Come up and have a closer look at the arrangement and I'll point out where to put the branches on the *kenzan*.'

Dear Stella! Meeting her that morning was to open up a new way of life to me. Looking back on our friendship over 30 years it's hard to pinpoint just how she influenced my thoughts and feelings. I learnt so much from her – not only how to arrange flowers, but to look at the way they grew, and to enjoy the individuality of each blossom. But above all she pointed me in the way of controlled relaxation – something that as a professional musician I had always found difficult. When she demonstrated she was unhurried, she caressed her material and if a branch fell down in an arrangement she was gentle in her movements to pick it up and replace it on the *kenzan*. She had a aura of calm about her – developed through her study of Buddhism. But although she looked frail and gentle she was a strong character and the rock on which the development of Ikebana in Europe was founded.

For the last few years she was in a little world of her own, suffering from Alzheimer's disease. The recent news of her death has saddened me and I feel a great loss.

I'm not sure what happened that morning in my first lesson at the Sogetsu School … but there was a 'happening'. I came away from the school wanting to know more, fascinated and intrigued by what could be achieved with so little material. Stella's voice rang in my ears: 'Don't clutter, leave space. In every arrangement we need a "pool of silence".'

A taxi was parked in the street when I came out of the building. I hailed it and handing the driver the card with the BOAC address on, I got in. After an exhilarating but exhausting morning I was in no mood to struggle with the subway trains – whatever John thought.

It was nearly one o'clock by the time I arrived at the office and I wondered if Noriko would have gone to lunch. But she was waiting for me.

'We'll go to the station straight away,' she said. 'We may have to queue some time to get your ticket. I wasn't able to get it through the tourist bureau because they only sell tickets for the bullet train seven days in advance.'

I'd read in the travel brochures about the comfort and delights of travelling by the fast super bullet train from Tokyo to Kyoto. It left Tokyo at four o'clock in the afternoon and arrived in Kyoto exactly three hours later – so the brochure said.

We took a subway from Hybiya Park Station to Tokyo Central which was huge and crowded – a labyrinth of underground passages and escalators. Noriko insisted on carrying my small suitcase. I stuck closely to her as we dodged this way and that. I didn't want to lose her in this mass of humanity.

There were long queues at all the ticket windows and no English signs to help a foreigner. As we worked our way up the queue Noriko turned to me and said: 'The notice at the desk says there are no more seats available on the bullet train. Are you willing to go by a slower train?'

'Please ask about the bullet train. It'll be disappointing not to travel on that but I'll take whatever you can get. This is my only chance to get to Kyoto. How much do you think it will cost? You'd better take all this.' I handed her my yen.

When we got to the window, after waiting nearly an hour, Noriko had an argument with the ticket-seller. She got quite agitated and raised her voice – unusual for a Japanese lady. The man behind the window kept shaking his head – not saying '*Iiei*' – just shaking his head. Finally he handed over a beige piece of paper with a ticket attached.

'We'll have to hurry,' Noriko said, 'and I'll explain as we go. I've only managed to get you a second-class ticket on a slow train that leaves in ten minutes. It takes nearly nine hours to get to Kyoto. I'm very sorry but that's the only possible train today.'

The train was waiting when we dashed down the stairs onto the platform. Noriko looked at the piece of paper and hurried along trying to find the right carriage. She found my seat number and put my suitcase on the overhead rack. 'I'm afraid it's not a window-seat,' she said, 'but perhaps you can change it when the guard comes through. I must go now. Have a pleasant trip.'

The whistle blew as I went with her to the door. 'Thank you for all your help. I'd never have managed this without you.'

I went back to my seat as the train began to move. The carriage was a long Pullman type with shiny black upright seats. These were in groups of four: two facing the engine and two the other way. Mine was an outside seat with its back to the engine. As I looked around I saw that I was the only female in the coach. The three men in my section took off their shoes, spread newspaper on the

248

floor and lit cigarettes. When the blue haze of smoke began to make me cough I asked the man next to me – by sign – if he would open the window. I made no impression whatsoever. He grunted and went on reading his cartoon book, but didn't attempt to open the window. I took down my suitcase to find my book and knitting. I found to my dismay, that in my hurry this morning, I had picked up a book I'd nearly finished, and had forgotten to put in a new ball of wool. I only had enough wool with me to knit about three rows. As there hadn't been time to buy anything to eat at the station before I left, I went to look for a restaurant car. I struggled through eight long cars without success and when I saw a guard I tried to ask him. All I got the shake of the head with the inevitable '*Hai, Hai, Hai*.

I went back to my seat. The men were now eating from their neat little wooden boxes of food and drinking cartons of green tea which they'd bought with them. Eggshells, apple-peel, mandarin skins were thrown, at random, under their seats – as well as the boxes and cartons. They flicked ash from their cigarettes onto the floor.

When the train stopped at Nagoya station the men piled out. I struggled, without success, to open the window. A little peasant woman dressed in grey kimono with her hair tied up in a scarf came into the carriage with a large broom and started to sweep the rubbish from under the seats. I stepped down onto the platform to get a breath of fresh air, hoping that I might see a stall selling fruit or some chocolate. But I didn't want to move far away as I'd no idea how long the train was stopping.

It was a journey I shall never forget. For nine hours I was absolutely and utterly ignored. No one spoke to me. I might as well have been a doormat and all my female hackles rose at being treated as if I didn't exist. If this was the treatment Japanese wives were given, I felt sorry for them. I decided I didn't care for Japanese men and by the time the train arrived in Kyoto I was very, very angry.

I spent what was left of the night in the hotel John had booked for me. It was next to the railway station. Trains clattered by continuously and blew their whistles, making sleep impossible. In the morning when I went downstairs to find some breakfast, I felt as if my eyes were a couple of dried prunes on burnt toast. But I was determined that I was going to see everything in Kyoto – all in one day. I booked a bus-tour for the morning and one in the afternoon. I was in and out of temples – shoes off, shoes on – keeping my eye on the uniformed guide's flag as she weaved us in and out of other tour groups.

I went to see the famous rock garden at the Ryoan-ji Temple. I looked over the sea of white sand which rippled round the fifteen dark rocks. I read the brochure. It quoted a Zen riddle,

> The sand moves because it is still
> The rocks speak because they are silent
> A man does not arrive until he has stopped travelling
> At a place – which is no place
> In a time which is no time.

It was beyond me in my present state of mind. I bought a sandwich for lunch and was ready, waiting at two o'clock for the next tour. More temples, more steps to climb to see the statues of Lord Buddha in all his positions. I tried to understand this different culture, this different religion. With the sheer effort of striving I began to feel as if I had a steel band around my head.

Just as the sun was setting, we stopped outside a red tori gate. 'We go through this gate into the garden of the golden Kinkakuji Temple,' the guide said as she stepped off the bus. 'Follow me.'

It was cool under the trees. As we walked along I kept looking for flowers, colourful flowers – my idea of a garden. Instead there were deep carpets of emerald green moss and beautifully shaped trees. The paths twisted and turned. We walked on large flat stones with moss growing in between. As we came round a corner I looked through the pine trees – and – there was my 'pool of silence'. The golden temple was reflected in the water and glowed in the setting sun. I felt the peace and calm flow over me and the tight band around my head melt away.

I became aware of silence, deep silence. This was for me, the real beginning of my Ikebana – the nowness and awareness of that moment can never be recaptured. But out of it was born an awareness of the beauty of nature and the awareness of the futility of striving without understanding.

I slept well that night. The train left at ten o'clock but I wanted to see the flower market. Noriko had told me it was a wonderful sight. I wished she'd written down the address because I had difficulty in making the hotel receptionist understand where I wanted to go. I kept on repeating '*Hana*' the word for flower – learnt at my lesson the previous day. I paid my bill and she wrote something in Japanese on a piece of paper to give the taxi-driver and gave me a hotel card so I could get back. We set off at great speed and I kept an eye on my watch so I would know how long it would take for the return journey. I hadn't a clue how far it was or how much it was going to cost. After about 20 minutes of turning into sidestreets and around corners into more sidestreets, the taxi-driver stopped outside a large open area. '*Hana?*' I asked.

'*Hai, hai,*' he said.

I got out of the car and looked around. There were stalls of meat and large displays of all kinds of fish. I couldn't see a flower anywhere. I walked over to one of the fish tables. '*Dozo, hana*' The seller seemed surprised to see a foreign lady so early in the morning. '*Hai, hai,*' he said and pointed to a building in the distance. I hurried along between the stalls thinking the smell of fish was very different from the fragrance of flowers. When I got to the building it was full of vegetable stalls. Again I tried my question, sniffing this time as if I was smelling flowers. '*Hana, hana.*' The stall-owner, bowed and indicated that I was to follow him. We walked along an alley and he stopped at another stall. Picking up a huge cauliflower he bowed and said proudly: '*Hana, hana.*' I gave up.

Looking at my watch I realized I'd have to hurry if I was going to get back and catch the train. I retraced my steps through the meat and fish and was glad to find a taxi waiting outside. The journey back was hair-raising and I thought that although this driver may have been anxious to become a kamikaze hero I still had a lot to live for. We arrived with a jerk outside the hotel. I paid the driver. I'm sure it was far too much. There was no time for argument.

I picked up my suitcase from the foyer and hurried over to the station. The guard at the gate onto the platform, looked at my ticket and bowed politely. 'Tokyo?' I said. He pointed to the train coming into the station and held up five fingers. He looked again at my ticket and taking my suitcase, beckoned me to follow him. We stood on the platform between two yellow lines. The guard pointed to the restaurant car as it went past and when the train stopped the door of my carriage was exactly between the lines. I stepped aboard.

It was a different type of train, with small compartments and I had a seat by the large window. I was happy to settle down, relax, watch the changing countryside and think of all the things that had happened in the last 48 hours.

24

Hong Kong and The Beatles

We returned to England from Japan in time for the boys to go back to school. This was the last Japan posting as the company decided it would be cheaper for the crews to be based in Hong Kong. Japan was an expensive place to live – even in those days. Because of English tax regulations the postings abroad were for 90 days only. Families were given a free standby trip so they could have a holiday together but allowances were the same whether you were single, married or had your family with you. To cover accommodation costs and feed a family of five on this allowance was quite difficult – especially if they had good appetites – like our boys. With the help of an electric plunger to boil water, I became an expert in providing breakfast in our hotel room, and making sandwiches to take with us if we were going on an excursion. We usually went exploring for our evening-meal, making sure we knew the price of the food before we ordered.

Peter, at the age of nine, got a scholarship to Vernon Holme in Canterbury so the three boys were at boarding-school. This meant that when John got a posting to Hong Kong in 1963, I was free to go with him and arrangements were made for the boys to fly out and join us for their holidays.

Hong Kong Island and Kowloon Peninsula across the harbour are fascinating places – especially for the tourist. If you scratched beneath the surface you found many problems. Although the borders between the Northern Territories and Communist China were officially closed, there was a constant stream of immigrants wanting to escape from communism, entering Hong Kong illegally. The population increased dramatically. Although the land area of Hong Kong was only 400 square miles it was estimated that over 5 million people lived there. Housing became a priority. Not only housing, but water. We arrived just after a new reservoir had been constructed on the island of Lantau and the water was piped under the sea to Hong Kong Island. It was thought that this would relieve the water shortage, but that year the 'little rains' that were expected in April – May, didn't come to fill the new reservoir. The situation became desperate.

We rented a Cathay Pacific pilot's flat in Kowloon for the three months but it wasn't a happy period. The Chinese servants resented our arrival as they had understood they were going to have three months' holiday while the Cathay Pacific family was away. Water was so restricted we only had two hours' supply every fourth morning. During that period, the bath and every bucket and holder of water had to be filled. We had a pitcher of water for washing and a cup of boiled water to clean our teeth. It reminded me of the water shortages I suffered in Eritrea. I wished we had been living in a hotel instead of the flat. At least the loos could be flushed there – with sea water.

A water-pipeline was laid between China and Hong Kong. The Hong Kong government had a contract with China for so many millions of gallons of water every year. Because of the acute shortage this year the amount was dwindling rapidly. The paper every morning gave a warning that just so many more gallons were available, and it quoted the day's figure. China could at any time – if it wished – hold Hong Kong to ransom by cutting off the supply of water in the pipeline.

John returned from his trip to India with a grandmother-of-all attacks of dysentery. He only had to smell India and he got tummy upsets but this was the worst attack he'd ever had. I was worried about the cleanliness of the kitchen and whether food was being washed properly. John could eat very little. I decided I had better prepare the meals myself and went into the kitchen. There I found not only the cookboy and the maid, but five other relations sitting around. I said I would get lunch and went to the cupboard to find some rice. It was an uncomfortable exercise. I was made to feel very quickly that I was not wanted in 'their' kitchen. They stood

254

in my way and were generally unpleasant – almost threatening. We ate our lunch but I vowed I wouldn't try and do any more cooking. We'd eat at the YMCA in Kowloon or the Mariner's Club.

A week later it rained. Oh, the joy of that sound on the roof! I rushed outside and bent back my head to feel the rain on my face. Then I hurried to the kitchen to ask the servants to bring as many receptacles as possible outside to collect the rainwater. They were sitting round the table drinking tea and were reluctant to move. It made me mad and I shoved a jug or a bucket into their hands and told them to bring them outside immediately. It was such a relief to feel we had some water again.

I had found an excellent Sogetsu teacher, a delightful half-French, half-Chinese lady who was willing to give me a concentrated course in Ikebana. I'd carried on with lessons in England, going up to London to Stella Coe's studio in Dorchester Square. I was becoming more and more fascinated with the art. There was so much to learn. I was glad to escape every morning from the unpleasant atmosphere of the flat and spend time with Laine in her apartment on the Peak on Hong Kong Island. I worked hard, loving every minute of it. It was Laine who decided that having already passed my four grades she would recommend me for the Teacher's Certificate of the Sogetsu School.

The BOAC office phoned one morning. 'Please would you ask Captain Pascoe to come into the office this afternoon. He will be taking the flight down to Australia tomorrow evening. We need to brief him on special arrangements at Kai Tak Airport for getting some VIPs on board.

We'd known of the possibility of a flight to Sydney and John had bought my ticket and arranged for me to go with him. 'That sounds intriguing.' I said when I told him about the phone call. 'I wonder who the important people are? Must be a governor general or it could be a royal.'

We went to the office that afternoon and John was called in to see the manager. 'Well who is it?' I said excitedly when he came out looking a little bewildered.

'It's The Beatles. Who are The Beatles? Why all this fuss? I have to board all the other passengers first and then taxi to another gate to take on board four young men.'

'The Beatles are a very popular singing-group. Surely you've heard about them? I saw something in the Hong Kong paper this week about them giving a performance and how they were mobbed by screaming teenagers before they got to the theatre. Police had to be called in to get them inside. I don't know much about them – not my type of music – but there's been a lot of publicity about their long hair and the clothes they wear. I think this is their first trip to the East and a big fuss is being made of them. Did the manager give you their names? I know one of them's called John Lennon but I don't know the other names.'

'No, he just said The Beatles expecting me to know all about them.'

'Let's go to a music shop and look at one of their records. We're sure to be able to find their names there.' Their photos and names were on the cover – John Lennon, George Harrison, Paul McCartney and Ringo Starr. I asked the shop assistant to play the record to us. I was pleasantly surprised. The group produced a good sound and in the song 'Yesterday' an understanding and pathos came through in voices that blended well together. I bought the record.

There were crowds of girls and boys everywhere when we arrived at the airport the next evening. I noticed also a number of policemen standing around patiently. There was no sign of The Beatles. I went through the formalities, waited in the departure lounge and when the time came, followed the other passengers out to the aircraft. The hostess greeted me at the top of the stairs leading to the first-class cabin and said: 'The Captain wonders if you'd like to sit up in the cockpit for take-off. We're nearly ready to depart so I'll take you there straight away.'

I didn't like to say No because I hated to admit that the take-off from Kai Tak airport on a runway built out into the sea, scared me stiff. I'm always nervous too, when John has the responsibility of being captain. I went with her and sat, rather anxiously behind John and the first officer. The two pilots started to go through their departure checklist. The doors were closed and we were towed to a specified gate. When we stopped and the door opened again we could hear a roar of screaming voices. I looked out the cockpit window to watch the loaders hurriedly pushing the steps in place.

256

A black limousine drew up beside the aircraft. Four figures dressed in black emerged. The roar of the crowd became more frenzied as the young men dashed up the stairs.

'All aboard. Ready for take-off, captain.' a voice behind me said calmly.

We turned onto the runway. Water was everywhere – on either side of the runway and straight ahead. The engines roared, our speed increased. I said a little prayer as the seconds ticked by. The first officer said quietly, 'V one, V two,' and then immediately, 'Rotate.' I watched John pull the control column back as we lifted off the runway. Not before time. I thought as we skimmed over the water. The aircraft swayed and bounced as the wind caught it. There was a whir as the wheels came up and with the lights of Hong Kong twinkling on our right, we flew out through the gap between the island and the mainland and climbed away into the black night.

I let out a big breath. I hadn't realized how tense I had been.

John turned round and smiled at me. 'OK, Viv. I'm afraid we've got typhoon weather ahead and strong head winds. We couldn't take on enough fuel in Hong Kong to fly straight through to Darwin. So we'll be landing in Manilla. I'm just going to inform the passengers about the change of plan.' And he switched on the RT.

I waited until he'd finished and then said: 'I think I'll go back now and have a look at these famous young men. I guess there are lots of those hysterical females who'd love to be on this flight with them. I guess I might as well make the most of it.'

'Oh,' said John as I got out of my seat. 'Would you mind asking Jane, the hostess, to give the group an invitation to come up on the flight-deck if they want to? By the way I heard before we left that the drummer, Ringo Starr is not with them. He developed tonsillitis before they left England and had to stay behind. There's another drummer with them but I don't know his name. We've also got John Lennon's aunt on board. She's going through to New Zealand.'

As I walked through the cabin to my seat I had a good look at the young men to see if I could recognize them from the photo on the cover. One of them was sitting with an elderly lady so I decided he must be John Lennon. George Harrison and Paul McCartney

257

were in front on the other side and were busy looking at some music. I felt quite sorry for the drummer who was sitting on his own behind them. He didn't seem to be part of the group.

All my life I'd been a stuffy old classical musician. I didn't know anything about rock and roll – or whatever they called it – and I couldn't stand loud-beat music. To me they were just another pop group who'd made the top of the charts. I wasn't prepared to be at all impressed by these young men. But – although their hair was long – by the standard of that day – it was clean, shiny and well cut. They looked smart and well-groomed in their black suits, polo-neck shirts and twinkle-toe shoes. And there was a boyishness and freshness about them as they relaxed and clowned with each other.

It wasn't a very comfortable trip as the weather and winds made the plane dance in an erratic style. But the boys didn't seem to mind. They'd taken off their jackets and shoes and were relaxing in their seats. I noticed that John Lennon was very solicitous towards his aunt and was making her laugh.

When we landed at Manilla the passengers were requested to stay on board as this was an unscheduled fuelling stop due to the adverse weather conditions caused by the typhoon. It was raining heavily when we taxied to a stop near the airport buildings. When the door was opened a wave of sound engulfed us. 'We want the Beatles. We want The Beatles'. Screams and more screams filled the air. The boys looked surprised.

'Oh damn,' I heard Paul say to John Lennon. 'We weren't supposed to be landing here. How did all this crowd get to know we'd be here at this time of night. What a bore.'

When John came into the cabin with the Manilla traffic officer, they stopped to speak to the four boys. I couldn't hear what was said but the boys at first shook their heads. The man sitting next to me, who turned out to be one of their press agents, went over to join in the discussion. Paul shrugged his shoulders and turning to the others said: 'Come on, you guys. Put your shoes on.' They went to the top of the aircraft steps and stood waving to the crowds packed into the observation deck of the airport building. Through the windows, I saw armed police holding back more youngsters outside the building. The noise was deafening. After a few minutes the traffic officer brought them back into the cabin. 'Thank you for doing that,' he said. 'Your fans would have been very disappointed not to see you'.

'I still don't know how they knew we'd be here,' Paul said.

The traffic officer replied: 'As soon as Hong Kong told us your aircraft was coming into Manilla to refuel the news was broadcast on all stations. You're very popular in this country.'

'Does this sort of thing happen all the time?' I asked the pressman when he returned to his seat.

'It's been the same everywhere we've been: India, Pakistan, Singapore – ever since we left England. Wonderful publicity but I wonder how long the boys will stand it. They couldn't even go out of their hotel in Hong Kong because of the crowds. The mob, when they tried to get to the theatre, was quite terrifying.'

John came into the cabin briefly after take off. 'It's going to be a fairly rough flight, Viv, so keep your seat-belt fastened. I'll go and tell The Beatles about arrangements in Darwin.'

He said goodnight and went to speak to the boys. He told them we would be arriving in Darwin about 3 a.m. He hoped they wouldn't have to cope with crowds at that time of the morning. They should be able to have a peaceful breakfast at the restaurant at the airport before going on to Sydney.

There wasn't much chance of sleep that night. I put on my eye shade and tried to settle but there was too much movement both inside and out of the cabin.

When we came in to land at Darwin just after three o'clock the whole airport was a blaze of light. There were crowds everywhere. So much for John's hope that The Beatles would have a quiet time!

The chief steward made an announcement. 'As Darwin is a port of entry into Australia, all passengers must disembark and go through immigration. Please take your passports and other documents with you. It is a health regulation here for the whole aircraft to be inspected on arrival and sprayed against insects. This takes several minutes. Please remain seated until this has been completed and clearance is given.'

The white coated healthmen came aboard as soon as the steps were in place and proceeded to carry out their duties. They were followed by the Darwin station manager. He went into the cockpit to talk to John and then came through to greet The Beatles.

He seemed a bit agitated. 'The whole place has gone mad,' he said. 'I would think half the people in the Northern Territories have arrived at the airport. I've never known anything like it and there aren't enough police available at this time of the morning to control the crowds. The only transport I've got is a jeep or a tractor. Would you be willing to drive around the area in the open jeep? The fans can see you then but won't be able to get anywhere near you. The other passengers will disembark and have breakfast. I've arranged for you to come back on board while we are refuelling and have your breakfast here. Is that OK?'

I was standing just behind John Lennon. 'Come on let's go for a ride in a jeep.' He turned to speak to his aunt 'I'm sorry, Auntie. We'll have to leave you. Will you be all right?'

'Would you like her to come with me?' I said. 'I'll look after her.'

He gave me a big grin. 'OK. That's great. See you.' They disappeared through the door and the crowd of excited overwrought 'bobbysockers' let out a howl of delight. The boys piled into the open jeep and drove slowly away.

I took the aunt's arm as we went down the steps. It had been a rough flight and when we reached the firm ground, she was a little unsteady on her feet.

'Poor lads,' she said, 'they never get any rest.'

Over breakfast she chatted away. 'John's mother left him when he was a little boy and I've looked after him for years. I think he looks on me as his mother. John, Paul, George and Ringo have been pals for years. They were always in and out of my home. The boys had guitars and spent hours singing and making up songs.' She smiled. 'John is quite special to me and a very clever boy. I hope all this nonsense doesn't spoil them. They're full of fun and high spirited but they're very young to have all this fuss made of them.'

My John had been busy with briefing and weather forecasts all the time we were having breakfast. I went to see him as soon as I returned on board. George Harrison was in the cockpit chatting away and asking all kinds of technical questions about the aeroplane. He said he enjoyed making model aeroplanes as a lad. John introduced me and I plucked up courage to ask if I could have their autographs for my sons. I'm not an autograph collector but

260

this seemed too good an opportunity to miss. George was very pleasant and said he'd give me a signed card before we arrived in Sydney.

We saw a most amazing sunrise as we flew south over Australia. It started as a pinprick of light and then spread in glowing reds and golds along the distant horizon. It looked as if the whole area was on fire. I dozed, but we were still being buffeted violently about. The plane was demented, tossed around the sky like a cork. As we flew on into New South Wales the sky darkened and we were enveloped in menacing clouds.

John's voice came over the RT. 'Good morning to you all. But I'm afraid it isn't a very good morning in Sydney. The weathermen have reported that there are severe thunderstorms about and it's pouring with rain. Please keep your seat-belts fastened as in a few minutes we'll be going through some severe turbulence.'

It became dark as night outside. Jagged flashes of lightning exploded nearby. The plane ducked about and fell with sickening bumps. It seemed out of control. The passengers looked tense and all was quiet inside the cabin – except for The Beatles. They tore pages out of their notebooks and made paper darts which they threw at one another. They were like excited school boys and made whooping noises every time the plane took a dive. John Lennon was sitting with his aunt patting her hand reassuringly. I didn't like it at all and wondered if I was going to hang onto my breakfast. I looked in the seat-pocket for the bag – just in case.

I heard the rumble of the wheels going down but couldn't see anything but mist and rain. There was a bump. I held my breath. The wheels made contact with the runway. The reverse thrust roared as we slithered along the wet tarmac as the pilots applied the brakes to bring the great bird under control. The Beatles shouted and clapped and the applause echoed throughout the aircraft. Everyone was mighty glad to be brought safely back to earth.

The chief steward came into the cabin and began talking to the boys. They started to gather up their things. John's voice came over the cabin radio again. 'This is your captain speaking again. Welcome to Sydney where the sun, I'm afraid, is not shining to greet us. As I'm sure you are all now aware, we have had a very popular and special group of people on this flight. For security's sake I have been advised to stop at one of the gates away from the main building and let these passengers alight first. Then we will proceed to the usual gate for disembarking. I wish you all a happy time in Australia – in spite of the weather.'

Outside a gale was blowing and the rain was bucketing down. As we taxied to a stop a black car drove up. An official came on board and handed each of The Beatles a black umbrella. As the boys walked down the steps in their black clothes and black umbrellas, the elements took hold. It was pouring. As they stepped onto Australian soil a tremendous gust of wind turned the umbrellas inside out. Before they could get to the car they were soaked.

That was my last glimpse of The Beatles – a group of four young men who made music that survived many years. Rock bands come and go but it seems that The Beatles will go on for ever.

At least, in the future, I could tell my grandchildren that 'I spent the night with The Beatles!'

25

Family Holiday

We were gluttons for punishment! Every time we returned safely to England after uncertain flights, I vowed that was the last time I would travel under standby conditions. The anxiety and frustrations just weren't worth it. And yet, after 50 years of marriage to an airline pilot, I'm still doing it.

John's comings and goings were part of our life. He sometimes talked so casually about his trip to some exotic place, it sounded as if he'd just been down the road on a bus. A friend in Chipping Norton once said to me: 'You know, Vivienne, you go off to the other ends of the world with less fuss than I make when I visit London for a couple of days.' It made me think. I hoped the boys didn't sound blasé to their chums at school when they recounted their experiences abroad.

After a certain number of years service with BOAC, staff were eligible for a free family trip to anywhere in the world. We had qualified for this a few years before but John had banked it because there had never been a convenient time for the family to take it.

The boys were growing up. Richard won an RAF scholarship when he was 17 and did his training at Oxford airport for his Private Pilot's Licence. Now he had been accepted for a two year course at Hamble Flying School, which was run jointly by British Overseas Airways and British European Airways. We had hoped he would go to university and take a course in engineering. The world market for pilots was so fickle – one year there was a shortage of trained men and the next, the airlines couldn't find enough. Richard had never wanted to do anything else but fly. He was happy to be doing his training at Hamble with the prospect of a job with the airlines when he qualified.

Bill, now in the sixth form at Kent College, was planning to go to New Zealand and complete his schooling at an agricultural college in Feilding. This would give him an entrance into a New Zealand university where he could study for an agricultural degree.

Peter was at the senior school with Bill in Canterbury. He had a few years before he had to decide what to do.

John came home one day after having his sixth-monthly medical check at the airport. A pilot's career depends on him being medically fit. The tests are very thorough, – quite rightly so – and no pilot ever takes this examination lightly. Secretly I always dreaded this check, both for John and for Richard and worried until they came home with their licence cleared for another six months.

There was a smile on John's face when he came into the house so I knew that all was well this time.

'I think we'll have to take our family trip pretty soon,' he said after giving me a hug and taking off his uniform. 'There's a rumour going round that if you don't take the trip within a certain time it'll be cancelled. So I've put in for summer leave in August and we'll hear in a few days if I've got my bid.'

'With school holidays in August, surely that's not a very good month for trying to get anywhere as a family. Everyone else wants to go away at that time.'

'Ah, but with our free trip we are entitled to a firm booking, so we shouldn't have any trouble.'

'Oh, that's different. Where shall we go?'

'Let's go to South Africa. I'd like to see all our friends down there and show Richard where he was born. We could hire a car, do a trip through the Kruger National Park and motor down through Swaziland to Durban.'

Confirmation of leave came through in June so we had plenty of time to plan our trip. I was very excited at the thought of a family holiday with John away from flying duties. Postings had been fun but they weren't holidays for John. I wrote to our friends in Africa. I booked accommodation at Skukusa, one of the camps in Kruger National Park and a cottage for a week at Umhlanga Rocks up the coast from Durban. John's sister, Nonie, and his brother-in-law,

Colin, lived in Kenya so we decided to make Nairobi the first stop and spend a few days with them.

Our doctor-friend in Johannesburg, Paul Gauss, and his New Zealand wife, Paddy, delighted that we were coming to see them, replied, offering to lend us a car for two weeks. Paul said he'd meet us at Jan Smuts Airport in Johannesburg if we let him know the date and flight number. I couldn't believe it. Fancy having a firm booking and being able to warn friends ahead when we would be arriving.

The plan for departure was worked out. On the second Monday in August, I would take Bill and Peter to Nairobi to stay with Nonie and Colin. John was due back from a USA trip on Tuesday and would catch a service to Kenya that night. We'd have several days there and fly on to Johannesburg on Saturday. Richard was trying to arrange a supernumerary flight to Johannesburg as part of his flying training. With luck we would all arrive in Johannesburg together, have the weekend with our friends, and take off for Kruger National Park on Monday. Super planning!

John flew away to Baltimore and I was left with the final preparations. If there's one job I hate before I go away, it's clearing out the food in the Frigidaire. The last couple of days it's either a feast or a famine.

Ted, who sometimes did odd jobs for us, offered to take us to the airport, bring the car back and make sure it was safely garaged. We set off at four in the afternoon in high spirits, excited about going to Africa after all these years.

When we arrived at Terminal 3, Bill went to get a trolley and we quickly loaded our luggage onto it. 'Thank you very much for driving us down, Ted – and for getting us here in such good time.'

'Do you want me to wait and make sure you're on the flight?' Ted had a brother who worked for BOAC as a porter and knew all about standby travel.

'No there's no need this time. I phoned just before we left home and our seats are confirmed.'

There was a long queue at the BOAC desk when we went into the departure hall but this time I didn't worry or hate all the other passengers standing there with their luggage. John had told me to book in as ordinary passengers at the ticket desk, instead of going to the staff travel office in the other building.

265

'Looks as if we'll be some time here, Bill. Do you want to go with Peter and buy some chewing gum?' Bill still had trouble with his ears when flying, especially if the plane descended quickly. We'd found that chewing hard on gum helped.

When I finally got to the counter, the girl said: 'How many of you travelling Mrs Pascoe?'

'Three,' I replied.

She took the tickets and went to consult the traffic officer who came over to speak to me. 'Mrs Pascoe, we're having a bit of trouble. Due to engine failure and a delayed aircraft we have to accommodate a large party on this flight. At the moment things don't look too good for you getting away on the service tonight.'

'But,' I said. 'we've got confirmed seats.'

'I know, but we have to give priority to full-fare paying passengers. This flight is being delayed for two hours because the party hasn't arrived yet from America. Please come back at eight-thirty and we'll see what we can do.'

I just couldn't believe it. This time I'd been so confident. I hadn't even had the usual butterflies as we drove through the tunnel into Heathrow.

The boys came back with their chewing-gum. They were quite distressed when I told them the news. 'But, Mother,' said Bill, 'our seats are confirmed. You said they were after telephoning. What's gone wrong?'

I explained that engine failures, and large parties of full-fare paying passengers from delayed flights made our confirmed seats invalid. 'Come on, let's find a seat. I'll look after the luggage and you can both wander around. We'll have something to eat in an hour's time.'

I returned to the desk at eight-thirty to find a line of harassed passengers with piles of luggage. The traffic officer saw me and came over. 'There's a further delay as these passengers have only just arrived. I don't think there's a hope of you getting away tonight. Why don't you let me book you on the service tomorrow night?'

'Thank you, but I'll wait just in case.' I suppose in a way I was just putting off the decision as to where we would have to stay if we didn't get on. Ted had gone with the car so we couldn't go back

266

to Chipping Norton. I didn't want to leave the airport until I knew the service had departed.

We hovered as the queue moved slowly forward. The ticket girl was very patient with the passengers who were obviously tired, bad-tempered and fed up with all the delays. My tickets were still at the desk so I had to wait to collect them.

There was a lull as the last passenger disappeared up the staircase. I went forward and stood near the desk. The girl was busy counting tickets. She looked up. 'I'm sorry, Mrs Pascoe. Better luck tomorrow night. Here are your tickets.'

As she handed me the three tickets the traffic officer came over quickly, 'Look there are two seats after all. If you want them you'll have to decide straight away. The aircraft's ready to depart.'

My mind, which had been in limbo for the past three hours, sprang into action. 'OK. Let the two boys go.' I handed back two tickets and the traffic officer helped me fill in the departure forms.

'Hurry now,' he said to Bill. 'Do you think you can find Gate Eleven?'

I gave Bill and Peter their overnight bags and raced up the stairs with them. 'Oh, goodness, passports.' I was still holding the tickets and passports. 'Here, Bill, hang on to these very carefully. As soon as you get on board put them away in your bag. Auntie Nonie will meet you in Nairobi and you'll have to explain why I'm not with you.' I fumbled in my purse and took out a £5 note. 'Here take this. Put it with your tickets. Bill you're responsible. Look after Peter. It's Gate Eleven. Bye, darlings.' I gave them a quick hug and they disappeared behind the immigration barrier. I was left standing.

Whew! Had I done the right thing in letting them go on their own? What would Nonie think? I hoped to goodness she'd be there to meet them. I hadn't even given them her address or telephone number.

Slowly and miserably I walked down the stairs to collect my baggage. Seeing the traffic officer I asked him the name of the hotel where the crews stayed and if there was any transport available.

John wasn't due until four o'clock the following afternoon. At least the hotel had a swimming pool and I spent a lazy morning swimming, reading and trying not to feel guilty about sending two small boys off to Africa by themselves. There'd been no time to think! Perhaps after all these years, I was conditioned to accept any seats available.

I wasn't sure how I was going to contact John. The crews didn't come through the normal arrival channels and he wouldn't be expecting me. In the afternoon I went into the airport office to leave a message for him. As I was talking to one of the staff he came bustling in with his crew, to hand in his voyage report and collect his mail. He looked very surprised when he saw me standing by the counter. 'Good gracious Viv, what on earth are you doing here? I thought you'd left last night. Where are the boys?'

'There wasn't room for all of us – only two seats. The boys have gone and I hope they'll be in Nairobi by now. I feel terrible about letting them go by themselves.'

'Never mind, dear. Now we can go together tonight. Did you alter your booking? As soon as I've finished here we'll go over to the departure terminal and make sure we're on the flight. I confirmed my seat before I left the USA this morning.'

John didn't seem to worry that the boys had gone off on their own. But then he always expected them – and me – to cope with any situation connected with travel without blinking an eyelid.

The same girl was on duty at the departure desk. John always looked very handsome in his uniform and had a way of charming all the office girls and stewardesses. I don't mind admitting that I often suffered pangs of jealousy when he was away, thinking of all those attractive hostesses and the socializing on stop-overs. I suppose all pilots' wives feel the same.

But now I stood back thankfully while he took charge and handled the tickets. 'Captain Pascoe, we still have a backlog of passengers. The flight is overbooked. I'm sorry but you'll have to come back at seven o'clock when the flight is closed. We'll do our best for you.'

I could see by his face as he walked towards me that something had happened. When he told me that we were only on standby and way down the list I exploded. 'So much for this precious "firm" booking. It's ridiculous!'

'Come on. Cheer up. There's nothing we can do about it just now. I'm going to change out of this uniform and then we'll go into the restaurant and have a leisurely drink and something to eat.'

I needed that drink. I began to calm down. John has a way of making light of all difficulties.

' Stop worrying, darling. Be thankful that we're together and on holiday – even if we do have to spend part of it messing about at Heathrow airport. I'll find out who the captain is taking the flight, and maybe he'll let one of us have the jump seat on the flight-deck.'

As we walked back to the counter John saw an old friend of his, Captain Paddy Sheppard who'd been a skipper on the flying boats. They were soon deep in conversation, oblivious of the urgency of finding out whether we were on the flight or not.

'Captain Pascoe,' I heard the girl call.

'Johnnie, our name has been called, better hurry.'

He collected the tickets and as we walked away he called. 'Hope you'll make it, Paddy. See you on board.'

After a 24 hours of anxiety, it was such a relief to get on board, be shown a seat by a caring hostess, fasten my seat-belt and accept a drink. I let out a big sigh and clutched John's hand. 'We've made it. Where does this flight stop and what time are we due to arrive in Nairobi?'

We saw Paddy come on board and go up to the flight-deck. 'He must have got the jump seat after all. He'll enjoy being up there with the crew. Oh, I didn't check the route but I think we call at Rome to refuel. We should be landing in Kenya about seven a.m.'

Several hours later the aircraft glided in over Rome. We went into the transit lounge and I drooled over the beautiful soft leather handbags and Florentine tooled leather. John bought me a lovely blue scarf similar to the brown one he'd bought in Italy years ago when he had his first trip back to England after the war.

We heard the departure call and strolled leisurely back to the barrier. Paddy, who was an Irishman with a shock of red hair and known to have a hot temper, was standing there gesticulating wildly to the Italian traffic officer. He looked as if he was about to explode. As soon as he caught sight of John he called him over. 'God damn it, Johnnie. This is ridiculous. This young traffic officer,' and he pointed a finger menacingly at the man beside him, 'has just taken me off the flight. He says they're overbooked. I must get back to Durban tomorrow. Sheila's expecting me and I have a very important business engagement. Tell him I must go.'

The officer shrugged his shoulders and threw up his hands. '*Scusi, Capitano*. Impossible. *Niente* seats. Too many passengers. Aircraft must leave pronto.'

John had always had a soft spot for Paddy. He'd enjoyed flying with him as a first officer when he was seconded to BOAC in Durban. Paddy was a great character with a fund of stories which he told in an engaging Irish brogue. He'd been retired for some years and although entitled to a rebated fare didn't have a high priority for seat allocation.

Turning to the traffic officer John said: 'If my wife and I are willing to give up our seats and let Captain Sheppard continue on this flight will you authorize our accommodation and allowance for a nightstop in Rome?'

'*Si, si, bene.*' A smile broke out on his face. Anything to get rid of this troublesome passenger.

'But Johnnie this will mean we won't arrive in Nairobi until Thursday morning. We'll have no time with Nonie who must be wondering …'

'Shush, Viv. Never mind. I'll go on board and collect our stuff.' And he was off like a flash before I could protest any more. Paddy hurried along beside him patting him on the shoulder and thanking him profusely.

I was very quiet as we drove through the streets of Rome to the Quirinalli Hotel where we had stayed some years before when John was doing chartered flights, taking scouts down to Nairobi for their special jamboree. When we got into our spacious room I was still feeling mad with him for giving up our seats. He put his arms around me and gave me a hug. 'Just think, darling. We're going to have a night and a day in Rome. You didn't expect that, did you?'

'No, I certainly didn't. And I'm not at all happy about it. I'm worried about the boys and Nonie. She'll think I'm quite irresponsible.'

'Oh forget your conscience – and the boys. Make up your mind to enjoy yourself.'

It's hard to be cross with John for long. It was a fun stay. We walked down the Spanish steps and John bought me a red, red rose from the flower sellers sitting on the steps. We threw coins in the Trevi Fountain just to make sure, according to the legend, that we would return. On the Via Venete we sat under umbrellas and drank cappuccino with cream and flaked chocolate floating on the top. Even the language sounded familiar and phrases kept coming back. We'd spoken Italian in Eritrea all those years ago. I became happy and carefree.

In the afternoon we walked to the Vatican City. St Peter's Square was crowded with tourists walking on the uneven cobblestones and gazing up at the window where the Pope stands to address the crowds on special occasions.

Nothing can prepare you for the immensity of the cathedral. It's the world's largest Christian church. To walk down the aisle and stand under the dome is to be made to feel like a tiny midget. I was sorry mattresses were not provided so you could lie down on the floor and look up and enjoy the wondrous scenes. I marvelled at the way the painters of the sixteenth and seventeenth centuries had painted their masterpieces on ceilings.

My neck swivelled backwards and forwards, down and up, until I felt quite dizzy. It sure was a 'think-big' project. Without the aid of computers that we in this century are so proud of, how did they conceive and build a dome of this magnitude – and what's more make it stand up for hundreds of years. St. Peter's Cathedral was a sixteenth-century Sydney Opera House in its conception.

The day wasn't long enough for all we wanted to see. John phoned BOAC when we returned to the hotel to see if the flight was on time. We tossed up whether we would have a meal before we went out to the airport but thought it was wiser to go out and make sure our names were listed. Having given up our seats the previous night we'd lost our so-called 'confirmed' priority.

Mario, the same traffic officer was on duty. He greeted us like old friends, but then began to apologize most profusely. 'I'm sorry, Captain Pascoe, the flight is delayed and won't be here until eleven o'clock. Please accept these meal vouchers and go to the restaurant. The latest news from London is that the flight is overbooked, but I will do my best for you.' His English was very good when he wasn't excited.

We climbed the stairs to the restaurant and ordered a bottle of Chianti. It had been such a lovely day. The dinner was excellent and we spun it out as we watched planes land and take off. When we went back to the counter Mario was shouting excitedly, throwing his hands up in the air in that despairing gesture so typical of the Italians. John walked over to him. That caused even more agitation.

'Is no use, Capitano. Too many passengers. Why do they do this to me? I cannot find seats that aren't there. No room for you or your wife.' He was almost crying. John took his arm. 'Wait here,' he said firmly to me. 'Come on Mario. We'll go and find the captain.' They both marched off. The passengers were filing past and handing in their tickets at the barrier. I stood by helplessly.

Even John looked a bit agitated when they came back. 'Listen carefully, Viv, because there's not much time. The captain has agreed for me to have the jump seat to Nairobi, so I'll go and collect the boys. You must wait here until the next flight comes through at four a.m. But that one goes to Entebbe in Uganda – not Nairobi. It flies on to Salisbury (Rhodesia that was) and should arrive in Johannesburg on Thursday afternoon. I'm sorry you'll miss seeing Nonie and Colin but it can't be helped. We'll fly down to South Africa on Saturday afternoon and, maybe, on the same plane as Richard. If this works out we'll have the weekend together before setting out for Kruger Park. I've got the two suitcases so you won't have to bother with those. I'll have to go now. Bye, darling. Have a nice time.'

Another 'nice time'! I bit back the tears as I watched him disappear down the stairs and then cross the tarmac to the waiting aeroplane. He stood at the top of the steps and waved, went inside and the door was shut immediately.

I looked around for Mario. I wanted to ask him if there was BOAC lounge where I could wait. He'd disappeared. Everyone had disappeared. There was no one about. The whole place was deserted. One minute all was bustle and hurry and now the place was like a morgue. Even the lights were dimmed and I couldn't find a seat where I could see to read. Such stupid seats anyway – no ends – no place to put your head. The restaurant was closed. I walked around and gazed at the lovely things in the little shops, now firmly closed. It was very strange and frightening to be all

272

alone in a large airport building. I lay down on one of the awkward bench seats, made my coat into a pillow and shut my eyes.

About 3 a.m. there were stirrings around me. I sat up and watched the cleaners at work emptying ashtrays and washing floors. As yet there was no one manning the BOAC desk. I found the ladies' room, washed my face, cleaned my teeth and put on some make-up. It's amazing how a bit of lipstick boosts the morale. There were no other passengers around. I wondered if this plane was really coming or if it was a figment of some demented Italian's imagination.

When I returned to the desk a sleepy looking traffic officer took my ticket and made out a boarding pass. 'The flight is early and will be landing in a few minutes. There are no other joining passengers. Here's your boarding-pass, Mrs Pascoe.'

When I got on board I asked the hostess for a timetable so I could work out when John and the boys would be likely to leave Nairobi. I found that if I got off the plane at Salisbury, I could stay a couple of nights with my cousin, Pat Munn, and join the Saturday flight they would be taking from Nairobi. Then we would all arrive in Johannesburg together.

Just before landing at Entebbe the captain's voice came on the RT, 'Good morning. I hope you have had a peaceful night. Unfortunately I've just received news on the radio that it's not as peaceful here in Entebbe. There has been an uprising and trouble at the airport. I'm afraid all passengers, except those disembarking must remain on board. We leave you here and another crew takes over. I wish you a pleasant onward flight.'

The plane landed, taxied along the runway and parked some distance from the airport building. We could see soldiers with rifles stationed behind a barrier of sandbags in front of the building. There was tension in the air.

As soon as the steps were in position two armed soldiers took up their posts at the bottom. When the crew were ready, they and the disembarking passengers were escorted across the tarmac to the building. I longed to have my feet on African soil and smell again the peculiar African scent. There had just been a shower of rain and everything looked fresh in the brilliant sunshine and blue, blue sky. But we were relieved when the new crew arrived – under escort. They settled in quickly and we flew off again down through the centre of Africa.

My cousin, Pat, was delighted and surprised to hear my voice when I phoned from Salisbury Airport. I asked if I could come and stay until Saturday. 'Of course,' she said, 'I'd love to see you. I'll be out to collect you as soon as possible.'

It was hot and dry outside but I sat on a seat and took deep breaths of African smells. The jacaranda trees were in full bloom and the strange rock formations all around looked as if giants had been having a game throwing stones at each other.

Pat was Irish but had lived in what was then called Rhodesia for many years. She'd never lost her soft Irish brogue and was a great character. Her husband had died recently and she was finding it hard to adjust to her new situation. Her home was spacious and cool. We sat out on the patio where bougainvillaea of all shades climbed up the poles. It was a riot of colour. But the lawn was completely brown because there'd been no rain for months. We sat and chatted and drank long glasses of fresh lime juice with ice cubes and a cherry and a slice of lemon floating on the top.

Lunch was served by Betsy, the Rhodesian maid, in the dining room where a ceiling fan kept the air moving. Betsy was a well-covered African girl dressed in green and white gingham with a white cap and apron. She'd been with Pat since the children were babies. She was part of the family.

After all the ups and downs of the last three days I was very happy to lie down on my bed after lunch and relax. I didn't even have to offer to wash the dishes. Betsy was there to do that. I slept the sleep of the drugged and had a job to pull myself off the bed to take a shower before joining Pat again on the patio in the cool of the evening. This was a very pleasant way of living!

When we drove to the airport early on Saturday morning I was excited at the thought of seeing my family. I watched with anticipation as the big plane landed, turned, taxied along the runway and came to a halt just opposite where Pat and I were standing. The steps were in place, the door opened and I thought, Any minute now I'll see three or maybe four Pascoes walking down the steps. I imagined John's surprise at seeing me in Salisbury instead of Johannesburg – another surprise for him – a pleasant one I hoped. Not like the one all those years ago when I flew in the flying boat with Richard to meet him in Lourenço Marques.

One by one the passengers came out and walked down the aircraft steps. I waited patiently expecting any minute that John or one of the boys would appear. But there wasn't a Pascoe to be seen. 'Maybe they're still on board,' I said to Pat. 'I'd better go through immigration now and be ready as soon as the departure is called. Thanks for looking after me so well. It was a wonderful break and lovely to see you again.'

I kissed her goodbye, went through the formalities and waited impatiently until the departure call came. As soon as I climbed aboard the aeroplane I spoke to the hostess at the door. 'Good morning. I'm Mrs Pascoe. I'm looking for my husband, Captain Pascoe. Can you tell me where he is sitting? I'd like to sit with him if possible.'

'I'm sorry, Mrs Pascoe, Captain Pascoe isn't on this flight, I've flown with him before so I'm sure I would have noticed him if he was flying as a passenger. He's certainly not air crew.'

'But he was supposed to join this flight in Nairobi this morning with our two boys. Did you see him at the airport?'

'No. No staff passengers got on at Nairobi.'

I staggered to my seat. I simply couldn't believe it. I'd been so sure they'd be on this plane. It wasn't easy telephoning from Salisbury but I'd eventually got through to Paul in Johannesburg and explained about our delays. I'd given him this flight number and time of arrival.

When I came through customs at Jan Smuts airport he was there to meet me and greeted me warmly. I knew he had a soft spot for me and I hugged him thankfully.

'Where are John and the boys? I thought you said you'd all be arriving this morning.'

'Well I don't understand it. I expected them to be on this flight. Has John telephoned from Nairobi?'

'No, we haven't had a word. We didn't know what was happening until you called from Salisbury. We'd better go and inquire when the next service gets in.'

Paul took me over to the information desk and spoke to the girl in Afrikaans. It had been a long time since I'd heard that language. 'Vivienne, this young lady says there's no other BOAC service from Nairobi until Monday. Let's go home. We can't do anything else here.'

The family seemed to have disappeared completely. It was a miserable feeling not knowing where they were or when they were going to arrive. I asked Paul what I should do about the bookings at the camp in Kruger National Park but he said to leave it in the meantime. Paul was an Afrikaner doctor and an honorary warden of the Kruger Park where he and his wife, Paddy often went for their holidays. He was very knowledgeable about the various camps and how to look for the animals. 'I'll lend you my binoculars. You'll need these to find the lions. They're not easy to see. They lie on the rocks which are the same colour as themselves so they're well camouflaged. It's best to go out early in the morning especially if you want to see elephants.'

During the war, when I first met Paul, he'd been very outspoken against the British which I found hard to accept. But he and Paddy had been very kind and taken me into their home when I first arrived in Africa in 1941. Unlike so many Afrikaners who are rather dour, Paul had a very good sense of humour. Both he and Paddy tried to ease my anxiety over the family by showing me around the sights of Johannesburg. It's an amazing city, full of modern skyscrapers but still dominated by the huge tips created by the waste from the Rand goldmines.

On Sunday afternoon we visited Johannesburg Tower where there was a wonderful panorama of the city and area. The phone was ringing as we got back home. Paul answered it. 'It's for you, Viv. It's John.'

I grabbed the phone. 'Darling, where are you?' The line was bad and I could hardly hear.

'We're in Bulawayo. I managed to get seats on Central African Airways and we've been on a milkrun to Dar-es-Salaam and Blantyre. We left Nairobi early this morning. We'll be arriving in Jo'burg about four ...' The phone crackled and John's voice faded.

'What time did you say?' I shouted. But the phone was dead. 'I'll have to call the airport now to see if I can find out when this flight is due. It doesn't sound as if it's a scheduled flight.'

'Never mind,' Paul said. 'It should take about an hour and a half to fly from Bulawayo. We'll drive out to the airport to meet them. At least now you know they're on their way.'

We'd hardly got up to the observation deck at the airport when we saw a Viscount aeroplane trundling along the runway. It stopped opposite us, the steps went out and the door opened. Bill bounced out and looked around followed by Peter who moved slowly and even from this distance looked white and unsteady. I thought he'd probably been very sick. He wasn't a good traveller at the best of times and an all day flight with ups and downs among the pockets of the afternoon African air, wouldn't have been his idea of fun.

John came down the steps chatting to the captain. No doubt he'd thoroughly enjoyed the flight and the chance of revisiting some of his old ports of call from flying-boat days.

It was a great reunion! But we were still not a complete family. There was one more to come. We'd not heard a word from Richard.

John, the eternal optimist said: 'Don't worry, I'm sure he'll be on tomorrow's BOAC flight.'

'How can you be sure of anything after all this mess-up?'

But John was right. On Monday we drove the car Paul lent us out to the airport and at 1 p.m. – right on time – we watched Richard in his uniform walk jauntily down the steps of the Boeing 707 and wave to us.

After seven days the five Pascoes were assembled in Johannesburg and ready for their holiday!

26

African Adventure

Travelling in Africa! What were the boys expecting to see? Had they got a vision in their minds of 'darkest Africa' with massive areas of thick jungle and wild animals hiding behind every tree? Were they going to be disappointed to find that much of the country we were going to motor through was brown, dusty and uninteresting with stunted thorn trees struggling to give a little shade to tired, hot humped-backed cattle? After the confined organized spaces of England would they be able to accept the hugeness of this land – going on and on without a glimpse of the sea? Would they understand the tremendous drawing power the Voortrekers must have felt as they encouraged their oxen to climb yet another small koppie to see what was on the other side? For those Boers it was a harsh land full of diseases and disappointments. They laboured to produce food from the dry red earth for their families and animals. It was a country of survival for the fittest.

But when the rains came, this parched earth was transformed overnight and produced not only the necessary grain but a wondrous carpet of wild flowers. The Boers made it *their* land. They loved it fiercely and were willing to fight for every inch of it.

Africa's a fascinating country – so full of changes. It has glorious colourful trees – the purple jacaranda, the red flamboyant poinsettia and golden shower creeper. The Africans in their kraals with their shining blackness look picturesque dressed in native costume, but in the city, incongruous in Western dress. In Natal the Indian women, clad in their colourful saris, walk with grace and dignity.

278

This all gives relief to the eye from the brilliant sunshine and hard brown earth, and the contrasts are fascinating. It was going to be interesting to watch the boys' reactions to all the different things they would see.

Knowing Paul's political views, I had been a little nervous about how Paul – the Afrikaner – would meet John, very British and an RAF officer. But I needn't have worried. If an Afrikaner takes you to his heart there is nothing he won't do for you. Paul accepted our family immediately, in spite of all the inconvenience we had caused. To lend us a station wagon for two weeks so the boys could enjoy the wonders of the Kruger National Park was a generous gesture.

Gaily we waved goodbye and sped along the highway towards Pretoria. In the early nineteenth century the Voortrekers blazed the trail, taking months – years – to travel rugged distances which now can be driven comfortably in a few hours, along good tar-sealed roads. Everyone was in high spirits and the boys chatted happily in the back.

Soon we turned off the main road and headed east for Witbank. The country got flatter and dustier. There were signs of coalmines in the area. It was hot in the car.

'When are we going to see some trees or a big river?' Peter asked. 'There doesn't seem to be water anywhere.'

We stopped when we saw an African by the side of the road selling oranges, and bought a whole sack of the juiciest, biggest oranges for two shillings. They were navel ones with thick skins and easy to peel. That kept the boys quiet for a bit. They were intrigued when we passed through small villages made up of rondavels – round mud huts like beehives with thatched roofs. Women with babies tied on their backs sat in the doorways chatting and pounding mealie meal. Chickens fussed around scratching the bare earth in search of titbits. There was little shelter from the fierce sun, no trees and nothing in the way of a garden, except for a few straggling mealies growing near the thorn protection hedge that surrounded the village. There was no sign of any men around – just women, children and chickens.

Paul had warned us to fill up with petrol and water at Nelspruit before we entered the park. The rangers were not keen on rescuing tourists who ran out of petrol in the middle of the park. He had also provided us with a large bottle for extra water as he said the car had a tendency to stall if it got hot.

As we drove along I read the boys the story of the development of the park. It was due to the foresight and determination of a sixth generation of Voortreker stock, Paul Kruger, that this area of land was set aside, for nature to preserve wildlife – a tract of land as a sanctuary for game animals.

At the end of last century Kruger struggled against the prejudices of his fellow Afrikaners. To them, the land was a means of livelihood to be tended and cared for, not to be allowed to go back to nature where wild, carnivorous animals roamed at will. But he persisted, and the first area of several hundred kilometres, the Sabi Game Reserve was declared a protected area in 1898. Unfenced, unguarded and riddled with malaria-carrying mosquitoes, as well as the dreaded bilharzia disease which sapped a man's strength and will, it had little to recommend it. Then the bitter Anglo-Boer war in 1901 wiped out any niceties of the rules of a game reserve as both Boer and Briton shot what they could to supplement their meagre rations.

But although Kruger, when he was President, fought to preserve the idea of an animal sanctuary, it was another man, Lieutenant Colonel Stevenson-Hamilton – a colourful character – who really re-established the game reserves. After the Boer War ended, the Government entrusted him to develop the original Sabi Reserve.

'Isn't there a camp at Sabi?' Richard asked. 'Is that where we are going to stay?'

'No, we're booked in at Skukuza, a camp in the southern part of the reserve. It's named after Colonel Stevenson-Hamilton. The Africans called him Skukuza. It means "he who turns things upside down" and that's just what he did.'

For over 40 years this man fought tooth and nail against agriculturalists, industrialists and mineral seekers with vested interests, in order to expand his sanctuary, until a territory of fertile, well-watered low veldt, no bigger than Wales, was set aside exclusively for the conservation of wildlife. The park now is actually about 350 kilometres long and 60 kilometres wide.

'Why is it so popular and so well-known?' Bill asked 'Even the boys at school had heard of the Kruger National Park.'

'I suppose the turning point came when the South African railways in the 1920s included a trip to the game reserve in one of their much publicized tours. Passengers returned home with memories of nights spent under African skies, of the roar of lions and the mysterious sounds of the bush veldt. They raved about it and it gripped the imagination of the public. Then a grand-nephew of Kruger, Piet Grober, became Minister of Lands and introduced the National Parks Act in Parliament. It was announced that the game reserve would be renamed "Kruger National Park" after the man who first had the idea and fought for the ideal of setting aside land where animals were protected. General Jan Smuts, as Leader of the Opposition seconded the motion which was carried unanimously. So you see, boys, it's taken over fifty years for the Government to develop and maintain this large area which has now become a tourists' paradise.'

It was about four o'clock when we drove up to the gates of the Pretoriuskop entrance to the National Park. A smiling African ranger in his smart uniform came forward to meet us. We paid him our entrance fee for the few days and he put a sticker on our car. 'Here are maps of the area with all the camps marked.' He pointed to a large notice-board in front of the gate. 'Please read the instructions on that board very carefully. It is for your own safety.'

We all got out of the car while John took a photograph of us reading the notice. 'Gates into the camps will be closed at dusk. Visitors are warned not to get out of their cars in the park. The speed limit is 15 miles per hour. Please keep to the marked dirt roads. Do not to wander off into the *bundu*.'

'What's *bundu*?' Bill asked.

'That's an Afrikaans word for going off into the blue or as the Australians say, "go walk about" – not a good idea when man-eating lions are at large?' John explained.

I'd visited the park during the war with Paul and his wife when a great part of the park was closed and only two camps were open to visitors. It had been my first real taste of Africa and I was excited. When we left the park I bought two sets of table-mats made of real lion skin from the tourist shop at the gate. One set I sent to my

281

parents and the other has been a conversation piece at many a dinner party in our home. They are still being used every day and don't show any signs of wear after 50 years. It must have been a tough old lion.

The boys wanted to go into the shop and look around but John had other ideas. 'Come on, you chaps, let's get going. I'll buy you an ice cream but we've still got a way to go to find the camp.'

There was a bit of a scrap when the boys got back into the car licking their ice creams. They all wanted to sit by the windows to get the best view of the lions that sprang out at us. Bill kept the peace by offering to sit in the middle.

'That's enough,' I said. 'You'll take it in turns. I don't suppose we'll see lions tonight. Paul says they're quite difficult to find.'

We crawled along looking intently from right to left. Suddenly right in front of us, three springbok leapt high across the road and vanished into the bushes. John stopped the car but they'd disappeared completely. On the other side of the road we saw a number of impala nibbling away peacefully at the low scrub. With their shaven half body and legs, they looked as if a barber had been at work. Of course the boys were all keyed up for the big stuff: lions, giraffe and elephant, and took it in turns, thank goodness, to look through the binoculars that Paul had lent us. It was all very exciting because you never knew what might appear. It became a game as to who would see something first.

I spied a black wart-hog with two babies trotting along a path with their tails erect. The boys hadn't seen these before.

'Aren't they ugly animals?' Peter said. 'They're all out of proportion – all front and no back. I wonder why their tails stick up like that?'

'Oh, look,' said Richard, 'over there – a whole herd of zebra and what are the black animals with the curved horns? They look like oxen.'

'No those are wildebeest – very cumbersome looking creatures – rather like an oxen with a ruffle round its neck.'

The boys wanted to stay and watch but John drove on until we saw a notice to Skukusa camp. There was a wonderful red-gold sunset and everything seemed to glow. As we neared the camp the landscape changed. Great koppies thrust themselves up from the plains in the most amazing shapes and sizes. Huge stones, balanced precariously on top of smaller ones like giant hats on granite statues. One couldn't believe they'd stayed that way for thousands of years and felt that at any minute they'd come crashing down.

We wanted to get settled in the camp before dusk. The boss boy, Klaas, immaculately dressed in white shorts and bushshirt met us as we drove through the gate of Skukuza camp. He showed us to our rondavels and told us that we were welcome to join the other guests for a *braaivleis* (barbecue) at seven o'clock . The smell of the meat being barbequed wafted across and made us feel very hungry. There was just time for a shower before we walked over to enjoy the meal and chat to the other guests, some of whom had been in the camp for several days.

Skukuza camp is the largest camp in the Kruger Park. A thorn fence surrounds the area. One of the men told us that when we came back from our early morning expedition we should climb one of the highest koppies in the camp and look down on the Sabi river. There hippos grunt and bellow and crocodiles bask on flat rocks and sandbanks. When we went to bed we lay and listened to the sounds all round us, African sounds and smells. Just as I was feeling comfortably settled and drowsy, the sudden roar of a lion that sounded as if it was just behind the rondavel, made me sit up with a start. My heart fluttered. I looked at the half stable-door of the rondavel to make sure it was securely fastened. John was sound asleep and his snores added to the noises. There was a strange scratching and snuffling outside. I lay down but it took me some time to settle.

At five o'clock the next morning the three boys, fully dressed, knocked on our door. 'Wake up,' they said, 'We want to go and look for elephants.'

Although it was still dark, there were stirrings around the camp. The dawn was just breaking as we drove out of the camp and followed the map towards Letaba where Paul had suggested we might see elephants. The new light softened the tips of the giant rocks and the shadows played and danced a ballet between them. North of Skukuza the scenery changed and gave way to grassy plains, broken up by patches of the knob thorn tree with its curious knobbly prickly trunk. Near the Olifants River the character of the

283

park changes again. Here in unbroken stands, grows the tree which the elephants enjoy most – the mopane tree. They stump around with their trunks ever busy as they strip great mouthfuls of the nutritious mopane leaves. Like animal bulldozers they push the trees down that get in their way. A bull elephant can eat up to 300 kilograms a day.

We were all keyed up, sitting on the edge of our seats and looking all round. Bill, who was sitting on the left-hand side suddenly exclaimed: 'Stop, Daddy, quickly. Look behind those trees.' And there they were, a whole family of them, pulling at the trees and enjoying their breakfast. One elephant bent her trunk down to the baby and fed it a special gourmet mouthful. They were so close. I wondered what it would be like if they suddenly got wind of us and charged the car. Those great big hoofs! They looked enormous. We watched them absolutely spellbound. John leaned out the window with the cine-camera.

'Careful,' I said, 'You're not supposed to have the window open.'

And then the elephants turned and ambled sedately across the road about 20 yards in front of us, stirring the sand with their ponderous feet. There was huge papa-elephant, middle-sized mama-elephant and two dear little baby elephants They took no notice of us. We waited hoping they might return but after quarter of an hour John decided to move on. We circled around but saw no more big game that morning. We went back to the camp for breakfast.

That afternoon in the distance we saw some lions sleeping on a sand-coloured rock. Richard, to his delight, spotted them first. It was difficult to make out which was lion and which was rock; they were so well-camouflaged. We took turns with the binoculars to look at them. But there was lots of game to see. More zebra, all different kinds of antelope and in the distance we saw three giraffe. A couple of ungainly hyenas were grazing near the road but scuttled away quickly as we came near.

'I hate those creatures,' I said. 'Mean scavengers and so ugly. I think God must have run out of ideas when he made them. Did you hear them snuffling around last night – probably looking for rubbish.' My eyes began to feel tired as I peered through the thorn bushes.

'We'll have to leave tomorrow morning,' John said as we turned to go back to the camp.'

'Oh can't we stay another night?' Richard pleaded. ' We're having such fun and there's so much to see. We must stay until we've seen lions after they've made their kill.'

'No, I'm afraid not.' John said firmly. Richard could be very persuasive. 'Paul warned us that you could be here a whole week without seeing lions at close quarters. We've still got a long way to go, down through Swaziland to see the Hluhluwe Game Reserve in Zululand. We're supposed to be at the cottage at Umhlanga Rocks near Durban on Friday.'

Suddenly as we turned a corner just about a mile from the camp, John stopped the car and said 'Sshush!' I gasped, because there, walking towards us along the road was a lion, a lioness and two cubs. The lion moved with the incomparable grace which tells of latent strength, great muscles relaxed, with a stride long and purposeful and his tufted tail dangling almost to the ground. The lioness followed demurely behind.

There was an awed silence in the car, I don't think any of us could have spoken if we'd tried. The lions came up one by one to examine the car, sniffing it, as if it was some kind of strange animal. Then the lioness went to the front of the car and looked at the number plate. I imagined her saying to herself, 'Ummm, visitors from Jo'burg – better do my stuff.' My window was open. I was too scared to close it. She came and stood by the running board looking up at us. I froze. She was within patting distance. It was the queerest sensation looking down into those light amber eyes. They hypnotized me. I couldn't look anywhere else. My heart thumped and funny little shivers went up and down my spine . Time stood still. That noble face with its pride and indifference humbled me.

And then she broke the spell. With a disdainful look and an almost shrug of the shoulders, she turned and padded along the road after her family giving the cubs a playful nudge with her powerful leg as she passed them to join her husband – the Lord of the Jungle.

'Wow!' The boys let out a sigh as if they'd been holding their breath. 'Oh boy, that really was something,' Peter said 'Did you see her eyes and those great big paws? Wait till I tell the boys at school about that.'

'You really should have put your window up, Mother,' Bill reprimanded me. 'She could easily have jumped up at you.'

Richard was bubbling with excitement but mad with himself because although he had the camera he had been too mesmerized to take a photo.

John started the car and we returned to the camp absolutely thrilled that we'd seen our lions. 'There'll be another early start tomorrow morning,' John warned the boys. ' See that you do all your packing before you go to bed tonight.'

The next day we motored back to the entrance gate and then headed south for Swaziland, a small landlocked kingdom ruled by a monarch. It was a British protectorate but later gained its independence. We drove along the low veldt plains with the Lebombo mountains which divide Swaziland from Mozambique towering above us.

We made for Big Bend – we liked the name and found a delightful motel nestling in the bend of the river. The rooms were fresh and clean and the dinner we ate that night was a feast. There was so much choice. It was hard to make up our minds but Bill was in his element and ready to try everything. John was even more delighted when he went to pay the bill the next morning to find how reasonable it was.

It was quite late in the afternoon when we turned off the main road and made for the Hluhluwe Game Reserve in Zululand. This was a small reserve mainly given over to protecting the white rhino which had been almost hunted to extinction.

I looked at the map when we drove through the entrance gate. 'Let's take the direct road to the camp, John, because I haven't made a booking here. I hope they'll have room for us.' The camp was on the top of a hill – a much smaller camp with limited accommodation. When we went into the office the ranger in charge said he wasn't sure if we could stay the night. There were several guests still to arrive but he would do his best. He suggested we go for a drive and come back in an hour.

'Can you tell us the best road to take to find the rhino.' I asked him. 'We've just been in the Kruger Park but the boys haven't seen a rhino yet – black or white.'

'Take the left-hand road out of here,' he said. 'I saw a white rhino under some trees early this afternoon. He may still be there so look carefully.'

We travelled along slowly. The terrain was quite different from the Kruger – more grassland and quite steep hills. We stopped to watch some giraffe stretching their necks and pulling at the branches. We disturbed them and they took off and lolloped away with a curious lopsided gait. As we came down a slight rise Bill exclaimed: 'Over there. Isn't that a rhino under those trees?' As John pulled up rather quickly the engine stalled but we were too interested in looking for the rhino to worry about it.

'I thought they were supposed to be white. That one's a dirty grey,' said Peter. ' What's the difference between a white and a black rhino?'

'I read somewhere that it had to do with a misinterpretation of an Afrikaans word.' I said. 'Somehow "wide" which was describing the rhino's bottom lip got interpreted as "white".'

'They're certainly not white,' John explained. 'But the white rhino is bigger and has a square bottom lip. Because of this he can eat grass. The black ones have a prehensile upper lip. You can look that word up in the dictionary. They are browsers. Because of their pointed upper lip they can nibble leaves and pluck twigs from the branches. But it's the horn that makes them so vulnerable.'

'Why is that?' asked Bill

'They've been hunted and almost wiped out because their horn is valuable both as a medicine and for carving the handles of daggers used in the Middle East, specially in the Yemen. The daggers are worth hundreds of dollars.' John went on: ' A famous Chinese pharmacist in the sixteenth century believed that rhino horn could cure all ills: snake-bites, fevers, carbuncles, hallucinations. And if the horn was burnt and mixed with water it would cure vomiting and food-poisoning. In the little chemist shops in Hong Kong you can still find rhino horn for sale. Like the velvet from the deer's horns it's supposed to act as an aphrodisiac. So men buy it even though it's very expensive.'

'What's an aphrodisiac?' asked Peter. Before John could answer that the rhino raised his head, stirred himself, clumsily got to his feet and started walking towards us. He was huge, with mighty shoulders and great tucks in his skin around his middle and backside. He came lumbering on with his ears erect and head down as if it couldn't support the heavy pointed horn in the middle of his face.

John decided it was time to leave and pressed the starter. Nothing happened! He pressed it again. Not a sound – not even a wheeze. We remembered Paul's warning about the car stalling but it hadn't given us any trouble while we were in the Kruger Park.

The rhino was increasing his pace and getting closer looking even more menacing. 'Quick, boys, out you get and give us a push.' The three boys without a thought got out of the car and went behind to push. I held my breath. The car rolled along gently and started sweetly as soon as John let out the clutch. The boys raced behind. I leant back and opened the car door so they could climb in quickly. I turned round to see the rhino, looking rather puzzled, come to a stop by the roadside.

'That was a bit unwise, Johnnie, to tell the boys to get out of the car. What would we have done if the rhino had charged?'

'Well, he didn't did he? And I forgot to tell you that the white rhino is supposed to be a gentle tame animal compared to the black ones who can be fierce and bad tempered when disturbed.' John as usual had an answer to everything.

'Well my nerves can't take too many more frights like that. Be sure and keep that engine going if we have to stop again. It's time we went back to the camp to find out if they've got some accommodation for us. What will we do if we can't stay there? There's no other camp or motel near here marked on the map.'

'Let's not worry about that until we have to. We can always sleep in the car.'

As we climbed up a hill near the camp we suddenly saw a great enormous giraffe standing like the Eiffel Tower in the middle of the road. I swear we could have easily driven the car between his legs. He blocked the road and stretched his long neck to pick a tasty twig from a tall tree nearby. John stopped the car a few yards away and put on the brake. Fortunately it didn't stall this time.

'Put your windows up,' I said urgently. The giraffes we'd seen in the Kruger Park had looked quite dainty compared to this fellow. He was the grandfather of all giraffes with a dark tawny coat and huge black spots the size of a card-table. Having munched his titbit, he unwound his neck and gazed down at us with beady eyes. He came towards the car, stopped and rubbed himself against it. The car rocked gently as if it was a baby's cradle. But we certainly weren't falling asleep in the car. We were very wide awake wondering what was going to happen next. He stretched his neck down until he could look in the windows. and slobbered over the glass thinking it was something tasty to eat. Bill had the camera and was trying to get the whole of the giraffe in the picture.

After a few minutes – I suppose it was minutes although it seemed like hours – he decided there was nothing interesting to eat and with one last rock he moved away slowly and ambled down the road with his neck stretched and his ears cocked.

I broke the silence.'That's enough for one day. I'm exhausted. Back to the camp.'

It was a tremendous relief to find that one party of guests hadn't arrived and there was room for us to stay in the motel after all.

'We've just seen an enormous giraffe with very dark spots – quite near here,' Peter told the ranger.

'Oh that must be Rufus,' the Ranger said. 'He's quite a character and very old. He hangs about near this camp. He's quite harmless but likes to sniff cars. I think he gets 'high' on petrol fumes.'

We had a pleasant drive the next day; no great excitements, just motoring along through Zululand where great areas of tall sugar-cane blotted out our view. It was hot and the boys were longing to get to the sea. The cottage we had booked for the week had a strip of garden leading down to the beach. A lovely stretch of yellow sand with huge breakers rolling in and pounding the beach. It wasn't an ideal place for swimming because the waves were too strong and there was a fierce undercurrent. But there was a pool at the hotel and in front, a section of the sea which was netted against sharks – a real threat on this Natal coast. There were fishing-rods in the cottage and the boys spent hours trying to catch their tea – without success – but they had fun and the joy of anticipation of making a catch. They made friends with other fishermen with more experience and knowledge in the art of throwing lines into the sea, who generously shared their catches with us.

It was my idea of a holiday: sun, sea, books, easy-eating and being together as a family. There was a good built-in barbecue or *braaivleis* in the garden so Richard was appointed chief cook. He soon organized the other two as helpers. He cooked the traditional South African sausage – *boerewors*, tender steaks and mealies or sweetcorn on the fire. We bought succulent oysters, crayfish and the small delicious langoustines. Chewing *biltong* (sun-dried lean meat) went well with our evening drink. It was spicy and salty and a good appetizer. And then there was every kind of fruit. Remembering my craving for fresh pineapple when Bill was knocking his way into the world, I indulged myself. It was a glorious gastronomic experience.

John had to fly from Durban at the end of the week as he was due back on duty in the UK. We had our last swim, cleaned the cottage and left the key at the hotel before driving into Durban. Then we had fun showing the boys the broadcasting house where I played in the orchestra, the church where we were married, the nursing home where Richard was born and the flat where we lived on the Berea. Happy memories! I felt we had completed a full circle.

It was strange not to turn off for Congella where the flying boats had landed all those years ago. We drove straight out to the airport – a small airport where little planes of all sizes and shapes fussed around importantly.

'I'll ask them to confirm your return flight from Johannesburg before I leave,' John said as he went to book in at the desk. I refrained from passing any remark about confirmed seats! He returned after a few minutes and said cheerfully: 'Well that seems to be OK but check the flight when you arrive in Jo'burg.' He was booked straight through to London without any difficulty. He hugged me cheerfully and said to the boys: 'Now look after your mother, you chaps, she's very precious. Have a good journey back to Jo'burg. Drive carefully, Richard, and thank Paul for lending us the car.' We all stood by the fence and watched until the plane took off, until it disappeared among the afternoon clouds.

'Now, we'll drive back to Durban and up into the Valley of the Thousand Hills,' I said as we walked back to the car. 'We're staying the night with our old friends, Lester and Margaret Hall. They came to see us in England. Do you remember the two daughters, Caroline and Penny? I know they've got a tennis court so maybe you'll be able to have a game.'

We sped along through well-kept suburbs with large homes and immaculate gardens – no shortage of manpower here – and then started to climb into the foothills of the Drakensberg Mountains. The Halls' home was in Kloof, a large friendly house with a spacious garden where beds of vivid red and purple petunias splashed over onto the green grass. Steps from the patio led down to a splendid tennis court and the boys wanted a game before it got dark. Lester and Margaret welcomed us but were sorry not to see John as he and Lester had been very close friends. They couldn't get over the likeness between John and Richard who was about the same age as John was when they first met him.

We were off early the next morning because it's a long drive to Johannesburg and we wanted to do it in the one day. The dawn sun was just splashing the wisps of cloud that daintily clung to the craggy hills as we drove back onto the highway and on towards Pietermaritzberg. Shadows danced around between the deep valleys, and the hills turned blue as the sun burst forth with all its strength.

Richard and I shared the driving – there were miles and miles of road to be covered. Our only excitement was due to my not watching the petrol gauge while Richard was driving and forgetting what great distances there were between fuel stations. We had a few miles of anxiety when the gauge was showing empty and were very glad when we saw the sign for a turn-off into Harrismith and found a petrol pump. Margaret's maid had packed a lunch for us with lots of fruit and orange drink. There hadn't been many shady spots along the road to stop, so we found a small park in the town and sat at a table under a jacaranda tree and enjoyed our picnic. We left Harrismith refuelled and refreshed.

There was lots of chatter that night over dinner as we babbled on to Paul and Paddy about our adventures. I was happy to hand the car back to Paul in good order and condition.

'I don't know what we'd have done without it, Paul. It just made all the difference to our holiday. John sends a special thank you. I hope it wasn't too inconvenient for you both to only have one car for these two weeks.'

Before leaving the house the following evening I turned to Paddy and said: 'Please don't take the sheets off our beds until you know we've really departed.' I'm superstitious about this. If my hostess removes the sheets I have this awful feeling that I'll be back and the bed will have to be remade with clean sheets.

But when we went out to the airport and checked in we were given our boarding-cards straight away. To a standby passenger that's a precious piece of paper.

I sent up a prayer of thankfulness when we were settled in our seats. I watched the brown earth hurry by and the great bird lifted its wings and began its homeward flight back to England. It had been a holiday of a lifetime – a real family adventure.

27

Retirement Party

January 15th 1972. John's fifty-fifth birthday – an important but sad day for him. This was the British Airways Corporation's retirement age for pilots. RETIREMENT. John wasn't prepared to accept that he wouldn't fly again and was already making inquiries with other airlines whose retirement age was less rigid. We had been reading library books about the change in our lifestyle that would come as a result of retirement. Friends sent John encouraging cards for his birthday about all the things he could do now that he no longer had to fly for a living.

For years I had moaned about the uncertainties of life as a pilot's wife and the difficulties of having to deal with emergencies when he was away. But was I ready to accept having a husband around for breakfast, lunch and dinner for 365 days a year? It was a daunting thought.

John's birthday was a good excuse to throw a party at Anakiwa. I'm not sure if it was a celebration, or merely to mark the event of retirement. In case the weather was bad, as it was the middle of winter, we had decided to have a curry luncheon-party. We were expecting about 40 of our friends. All was hustle and bustle around the house that morning. I was doing all the catering and tried to prepare as much as possible ahead of time. The day before, while I thought of it, I had put a tin of salmon, one of pineapple and another of Nestlés cream from the larder on the kitchen bench ready for making a special dip to have with our drinks. When I came down to get the breakfast the morning of the party they had disappeared.

'Have you seen my tins'? I said to John. ' I put them on the bench yesterday.'

'Oh, I put them away. I thought they were just lying around.'

I shrugged my shoulders and got the tins from the larder again and put them back on the bench. I did the flowers – special celebration Ikebana arrangements – saw that everything was put out of sight that shouldn't be showing, cleaned the bathrooms and was just going to get changed when I remembered I hadn't made the dip. I rushed to the kitchen. My tins were nowhere to be seen! I yelled at John who was carrying chairs into the lounge. 'What have you done with my tins?'

' They were messing up the bench when I was washing up so I put them back on the shelf.'

I exploded. ' Hell's teeth, John Pascoe! You leave things alone in my kitchen. If I put tins on this bench I want them left there because I'm going to use them. If you must put things away why don't you start on your workshop. It's a wonder you can find anything there. You're always complaining about "those boys" taking your tools and not putting them back.'

I continued shouting at him. 'Come on, get cracking. They'll be here any minute. Have you got the ice out? What about the drinks? Is there enough tonic water and ginger ale in the fridge? And beer – did you get the beer? Isn't it time to light the fire?' I was as ruffled as an agitated hedgehog and all my prickles were out.

It would have been lovely to have had all the boys home for the party. Since our family trip to South Africa many things had happened. The family circle had grown. Richard had fallen in love with a delightful stewardess, Tina, and they'd been married in Lincolnshire on October 30th 1970. Bill had flown over from New Zealand to be Best Man at the wedding – a very happy occasion for us all. He was continuing his education 'down under' and studying agricultural science at Massey University, Palmerston North. We missed him. It had been hard to let him go so far away. He always had a calming influence and I could have done with his shining face around me while I was preparing for this party.

It had come as quite a surprise when Bill wrote to us in April 1971 to tell us he wanted to marry an English girl, Elizabeth, and asked us if we could come to New Zealand for the wedding in May.

294

It would have been pleasant to have got to know Elizabeth before they were married – but then who were we to say anything? John and I had done the same thing in South Africa and only met our 'in-laws' some years after we were married. Bill hadn't made up his mind what he wanted to do when he'd finished his degree, but had great faith in the Lord and was certain he would be guided in the right direction. We had flown out for the wedding and Bill had plenty of support from my side of the family. It was sad for Elizabeth that none of her English relations could be with her. Now she was working while Bill was studying to complete his degree.

Peter was very happy as he'd been accepted at Liverpool University to do a degree in veterinary science. This was a hard course to get into. It seemed that since the books by James Herriot had been published, veterinary science was the 'in' thing and every student hoped to follow in his footsteps. Peter had driven down from Liverpool especially for the party.

Tina was a joy to us all and we were excited because she was now a lady in waiting – our first grandchild was due in June. This was really something to celebrate – more so than retirement. It was a relief when they arrived early and Richard took charge of the drinks. As my dear John seldom drank anything alcoholic himself, he knew little about mixing drinks. He once handed a very fussy lady who enjoyed her whisky with just a touch of soda water, a large glass of whisky mixed with tonic water. Her face was a picture when she took her first sip!

At midday all was ready. Just as we were greeting the first guest the telephone rang. Richard answered it. 'It's for you, Dad.' John went to the phone which was in the hall. Strange how our lives have been changed over the years by a phonecall. The guests continued to arrive and there was laughter, greetings and plenty of noise as they walked through the hall into the lounge, bright with a warm fire burning cheerfully.

The boys poured drinks and Tina served the canapés. I was busy in the kitchen and thought John was in the lounge entertaining our friends. But when I went through into the dining room 20 minutes later he was still talking.

I hissed at him: 'Johnnie, for goodness sake get off that phone and see to your guests. This is your party.' He waved me away and went on talking. I glared at him every time I passed by, carrying dishes into the dining-room.

Finally he got the message and put the phone down. He came out to the kitchen and said cheerfully: 'That was Ernie Brown. You remember him. He was with us in Honolulu. He's asked me to go to Lisbon to fly for TAP. How would you like two years in sunny Portugal? I have to let him know my decision tonight.'

I'd had enough. 'You can't be serious. This is your retirement party Johnnie – not a get another flying-job party.'

'We'll talk about it later,' he said and went off to chat to his pilot-friends.

It was five o'clock before the last guest went home. It had been a great party, everyone said they'd enjoyed it. But I had a job to appear unruffled and keep my mind on being a good hostess.

Ken, the New Zealand pilot who had taken me on my first flying-boat trip, gave me a hug as he left and said: 'I'm sure you'll enjoy Portugal, Viv. I've heard all about it from Johnnie.'

More than I have, I thought. When they'd all gone, John took my arm and sat me by the fire. I was tired and didn't want to be involved in lengthy discussions about moving to another airline.

'This is a great chance, Viv, TAP ...'

I interrupted: 'And what's TAP. when it's at home?'

'It's the Portuguese airline, *Transportos Aeros Portuguese*. They've just taken delivery of some 707 Boeing aircraft and don't have enough pilots to fly them. Ernie has been asked to find seven retired pilots to go over immediately. It's a two-year contract and the pay is good.'

'But I thought you were keen to fly for Singapore Airlines and that we were going to have a holiday first.'

'We can have a holiday in Portugal instead – and a paid one at that. I have to fly out next week to have an interview and a medical examination. You can come too and we'll look for some accommodation.'

'So you've more or less accepted the offer.'

'Well, yes. I told Ernie I'd go if you were willing. We have to be prepared to start flying by the end of January.'

And so we didn't retire but went to Portugal.

28

Portugal

It turned out to be a bonus two years. John was very happy to be flying some of his old African flying-boat routes. I suspected he enjoyed the greetings he received from the TAP stewardesses when he went on board before a flight. It was the custom for these dark attractive girls to kiss their captain three times – one cheek, the other cheek and then again on the first cheek in the Portuguese way. This was John's cream on his coffee! I couldn't imagine the British hostesses doing that – not in public anyway.

The other British Airways pilots had found furnished apartments in the suburbs that nestled along the Tagus Estuary. We looked at a few flats in the morning when I flew over with John but didn't see anything we liked. The estate agent, Tom Skinner, drove us past Estoril with its famous casino and on to Cascais, a small fishing village at the entrance to the estuary. We left the car and walked up the hill to a little square behind the Catholic cathedral.

'This is Passos Vella Square', the agent told us. It was quiet and peaceful. The sunlight filtered through the trees making patterns on the mosaic pavements. We walked past a statue of an imposing looking man gazing down on the flower-beds.

'Who's that?' I asked.

'That's Doutor Manoel Passos Vella, a physician who rescued and helped many people at the time of the bad earthquake in Lisbon in 1775.'

'Do they often have earthquakes in Portugal, Tom?' Having lived in New Zealand and experienced earthquakes at first hand I wasn't keen to be in another country where they had frequent shakes.

He assured me that he'd never felt one although he'd lived in Portugal for many years. 'This square was named after the doctor and as a reward for his bravery he was given that big house over there.' He pointed to a large forbidding stone mansion on one side of the square. 'I believe members of his family still live in the house. At present it's occupied by three unmarried sisters. The little attached cottage on the right-hand side is on my books for rent, but as it's unfurnished it wouldn't be any good for you.'

We walked on past the statue and the two men went ahead. I turned and looked back at the little house. It seemed to be beckoning. The whole square had an atmosphere of tranquillity. I felt I had stepped into another world.

I called to John: 'Why don't we just have a look inside the cottage now we're here. I'd like to see it. It's rather attractive.' It was the sort of tiny house you draw as a child. A front door and a window downstairs, and two windows upstairs. The only thing missing was the chimney.

Tom found the key on his ring and we went inside. It was carpeted throughout in a soft mossy shade of green. The small lounge downstairs and the upstairs bedroom looked out over the square. There was no back door. The minute kitchen had a gas stove and plenty of cupboards. It was a doll's house with a happy atmosphere.

John and Tom stood impatiently in the little hall while I looked around like an excited child. 'Come on, Viv, we've got one more apartment to see in Cascais. We haven't much time if you want to catch the plane back to London tonight. Without furniture this house is quite unpractical.'

We walked further up the hill to look at the apartment. I didn't like it at all. It was in on the third floor in a big brick building. And there was no lift. John would have hated it.

'Let's walk back through that square again' I said to Tom. 'I want to have another look at that little house.' I wandered along and sat on the stone wall surrounding the little garden. The doctor looked down on me. I wondered who planted the flowers. On the other side of the square a small fountain was playing. I watched a peacock strutting about with its tail at full sail. Three rugged looking fishermen in their sea-faring garb were sitting on the ground behind the cathedral mending their nets. It was an intriguing and interesting scene.

'Johnnie, if you bought a bed while I'm back in the UK you could move in and camp here until I come over at the end of the month. Then we can look for some suitable furniture. We wouldn't need much.'

John looked at me pityingly. 'Portuguese furniture is very heavy and large. We'd never find anything that would fit in that tiny house. And we don't need any more furniture. We've got enough in England.'

'Well I'm not coming to Portugal if we have to live in a flat. You could make some furniture when you're not flying – or design it and have it made.' I looked up at the window of the big house. The curtains twitched and three faces peered down at us. I turned to Tom who was fussing about wanting to return to the car.

'Would you mind going and asking the ladies if the cottage is available and what the rent would be, please?'

He walked over and banged the large brass knocker on the solid door. It was some time before the door opened and then a lively conversation in Portuguese went on between Tom and the lady.

John came and sat on the wall beside me. 'We'll have to decide on something before you leave as I'm going out on service tomorrow. What about that last apartment we saw? It had plenty of room and was well-equipped. One of the other captains, Lew Carey, has already moved into a top-floor flat in that building. You know him and he'd look after you while I'm away.'

Tom came back. 'Yes the cottage is available and the rent's very reasonable. Apparently it's been vacant for some time. It used to be the chauffeur's house. Are you interested?'

John looked at me. I looked at John. And then I said determinedly: 'Come on, darling. Let's be mad and romantic and make it our dream cottage.'

'As long as it doesn't turn out to be a nightmare,' John said rather tersely. He turned to the agent. 'I'll let you know our decision before I fly off tomorrow.'

Tom went back to Lisbon and over a good fishy meal in a local restaurant we decided to take the cottage. I flew back to England that evening with all kinds of plans racing around my head. I was going to make that doll's house into a really feminine cottage. For years I'd lived in a male household and never indulged in fluffiness as far as furnishing went.

When John returned to Lisbon from his trip, he phoned to say our luggage had arrived from England. He'd bought a bed, moved in and was using a packing case as a table. He gave me the measurements of the windows. There were only three that needed curtains: the sitting-room, the bedroom and the small window at the top of the stairs. I bought a Sanderson's curtain material – a cotton fabric with lovely colourful sprays of flowers on a white background. I felt it would look just right with the soft green carpet. I went to Witney and bought two light-weight satin-trimmed blankets, a pink and a green. And I found a white nylon bedcover with lots of frills and pale pink roses all over it. I'd never been a 'pink' person but this time our bedroom was going to be the quintessence of femininity.

The boys were living their own lives and I was free to come and go as I liked. John sent me a ticket for the flight to Lisbon. I was excited when I landed and found him waiting for me. When I'd left Heathrow it was cold and foggy but when I stepped out of the plane here, the air was fresh, but warm. White fluffy clouds fluttered across the blue sky as we drove from the airport through the ancient city of Lisbõa down the Avenido da Libertade and along the water front to Cascais. So much had happened since we'd last seen each other. I was full of questions and babbled away. John said he was thoroughly enjoying his flying. He'd just returned from his first trip to Rio de Janeiro. 'You can come with me the next time I'm on that service. They've got the most wonderful jewellery shops. You'll be very tempted.'

'What about the language problem? Doesn't that make things difficult when you are flying? How much Portuguese have you learnt? It's such a "hissy" language and what's written down doesn't seem to bear any relation to the spoken word.'

'English is the universal language for traffic control and we always fly with a Portuguese first officer. They get a bit excited if anything goes wrong and forget their English. But so far I've had no problems.'

We stopped at a traffic-light. The car was making such a noise I could hardly hear John speak.

300

'Why is this car making such a din? It sounds like a tractor? Where did you get it from? You haven't bought it, I hope?'

'Yes I have. I bought it from one of the Portuguese aircraft engineers. It's a German car, a DKW. It's noisy because it's only got three cylinders and a two-stroke engine but it goes well.

'He must have seen you coming. It sounds as if it's suffering from acute bronchitis and the fumes from the petrol are terrible. I thought you'd decided to buy a new Fiat.'

'Maybe later on. This will do us in the meantime.'

I was impatient to see the cottage again. I liked the address in Portuguese 'Numero Nove Passos Vella.' I didn't like the car but – the sun was shining, the sky was blue and all was right with our world.

We stopped outside our little green front door. The curtains on the upper window next door fluttered. With my arms full of parcels I walked into the sitting room. John had been busy in between his trips and had constructed a tiny folding table between the two seats either side of the window. The stone walls of the cottage were about two feet thick. He'd also lined an alcove in the room and made it into a *tokonoma* where I could put a flower arrangement. As a special welcome he'd arranged some lovely red roses in one of my Japanese containers. I was absolutely delighted.

And then I ran upstairs. I was anxious to see the bedroom. It was going to look so light and pretty with all my floral furnishings. I stood at the door and gasped in horror. I couldn't believe my eyes. The high bedhead John had chosen – with great care no doubt – was covered in dark brown leather with thick straps and heavy metal buckles at each side – the most masculine, ugliest bedhead I'd ever seen. The tears rolled uncontrollably down my face and I flung myself down on the bed. 'How could he?' I sobbed. 'How could he think of buying such a terrible monster.'

John came in to see where I was and was astonished to find me prostrate on the bed. 'Darling, what on earth's the matter? I thought you were happy to be here in this cottage.'

I didn't want to speak to him. I turned away and buried my head in the pillow. He sat down beside me 'Come on, Viv, what have I done? Tell me what's the matter.'

301

'Matter!' I gulped. 'It's this bedhead. Where did you find such an atrocity?'

'What's the matter with it? The bed's very comfortable.'

'The bed may be all right but the bedhead! It's beyond all description. Dark leather with buckles! It's like something out of a medieval castle – or a sordid brothel. My lovely bedcover will look horrible against such a monstrosity.'

'Well you said "buy a bed". You didn't say what kind of a bed. I don't know why you're so upset. There's nothing wrong with the bed. It's big and comfortable and good for sleeping on. You don't have to look at the bedhead if you don't like it. You'll have your back to it most of the time.'

Men! How could I explain that all my dreams had crashed and that nothing would look right in that bedroom with such an overpowering leather bedhead.

'Come on, Viv, Cheer up. Let's go downstairs. I've got another surprise for you.'

I didn't know if I wanted another surprise after this one. Reluctantly I got off the bed and went into the bathroom to wash the tears away. John had put a gift-wrapped parcel on the little table. When I opened it I found a china Portuguese figurine of a bull fighter – a matador in his full regalia with red cloak swirling and twisting around him – very lifelike.

'I thought this would look well in the '*tokonoma*' with your Ikebana.'

Bulls and bedheads!   I just stopped myself from saying ungraciously, 'Goes well with the bedhead.' I kissed John and thanked him rather subduedly for my present and all he'd done to welcome me to our new home.

Disappointments don't last for ever. At least when we were in bed the beastly bedhead was behind us and I could feast my eyes on my pretty curtains.

We had a wonderful stay in Portugal. I think it's the only time in my life that I've been content to sit at a window and enjoy watching the world go by.

Every morning – at breakfast time – two old ladies dressed in black from top to toe passed by the window. On their heads they balanced red plastic buckets. Gracefully they walked across the square to the tap near the fountain. Holding their full buckets on their heads they returned and walked down the little cobbled lane between the houses.

At sunset we often walked down to the little Cascais beach when the sturdy colourful fishing fleet returned with their day's catch. The village folk came to help pull in the boats and children of all ages screamed happily and scampered about on the sand. It's quite an experience to watch a fish auction. The fish were graded and put into heaps according to type by the fishermen ready to be auctioned. The auctioneer stands by each heap chanting in a high voice. This is a curious chant – just a string of numbers. The auctioneer begins high and works low in a long singsong. The pile of fish goes to the first buyer who stops him in his song.

Now when I think of Portugal my nose recalls a particular smell – the smell of sardines grilling on a small charcoal grill outside the tiny cafés or *tavernas*. At lunch-time we'd wander along the road and join the locals sitting at tables in the sunshine. The grilled sardines were a far distant relation to the tiny fish in tins. These were large, fat and delicious – very moreish. Served with bulky crusty bread and the rough Portuguese wine, *vino verde* – which isn't green at all – they made a tasty meal.

Fishermen came regularly and squatted on the pavement behind the cathedral, laughing and chatting in guttural Portuguese as they mended their nets and swapped stories about their catches. The bells of the cathedral rang out on Sundays and fiestas. The women, swathed in black with shawls over their heads, looked like black crows. But the children were delightful, dressed in their colourful Sunday-best, with white socks and brilliantly clean shoes, their black hair immaculately plaited and their faces rosy with scrubbing. There seemed to be a goodly number of festivals to celebrate. The most colourful one was the fishermens' fiesta, when everyone dressed in their Portuguese costumes and paraded from the seashore to the cathedral, carrying banners of saints and fish, to give thanks to God for all his bounty.

And then there were the characters who lived in the square! I watched them come and go and wove romantic stories about them. The three curtain-twitching sisters next door saw everything. Their upstairs window was never vacant. They kept a check on all our visitors. Lew Carey often appeared at breakfast-time even when John was away. I could almost hear them 'tut-tutting' – or whatever you say in Portuguese – through the wall.

A frail austere, elderly aristocratic lady lived next door and would emerge every afternoon about four o'clock for her walk round the square. She leaned heavily on a walking-stick. Maria, her devoted maid, walked beside her. I felt sorry for her as she never seemed to have any visitors – yes, I kept check just like the three sisters! One afternoon I met her when I was returning from a swim. I plucked up courage and invited her in for a cup of tea. That was the beginning of an interesting friendship with Madame Wertheimer.

She came from what was then Czechoslovakia where her wealthy family owned large shoe factories. But when the Germans invaded her country in 1939 the family lost everything and she fled to Portugal. All her life she'd been waited on hand and foot. Now a sad, lonely soul, she was dependent on her loyal Portuguese maid to help and care for her.

One morning there was a tap on our door and Maria stood there with a note from Madame Wertheimer inviting me to tea at four o'clock that afternoon. It was a very formal occasion. Maria in her black dress, white apron with cap perched precariously on her head brought in the tray with the Georgian silver service and delicate Meissen teacups. We 'took' tea – a choice of Indian or China. Once started, Madam Wertheimer couldn't stop talking.

She picked up a photograph from the piano of a distinguished looking man. Ah, I thought, this must be her husband, Herr Wertheimer.

But no! 'This is my famous brother, Sir Rudolph Bing,' she said. 'I'm very proud of him. He's a fine musician, was manager of the Glyndebourne Opera Company in England for several years and organized the first Edinburgh Festival.' She knew I was interested in music. 'Did you ever go to Glyndebourne? It's such a beautiful setting for opera.'

' No, I'm afraid not. I always wanted to but when I was a music student at the Royal College of Music I couldn't afford it.'

She put the photo back on the piano. 'Rudolph is now director of the Metropolitan Opera House in New York. He's so busy he never has time to visit me here. Now I'm too old to travel on my own. She picked up another photograph. 'This is my son and his wife. He lives in Paris and writes regularly but I don't see him very often. His wife doesn't like him to come down to visit me.'

After that day she always waved and stopped for a chat. I never heard her mention her husband. Herr Wertheimer remained a mystery. But she didn't miss much and loved to gossip, especially about the larger-than-life couple who had moved into the house at the other end of the square.

Pamela – the wife – well, we weren't quite sure of the relationship – was a tall ample lady with unruly auburn hair. She floated around the square in long flowing garments and a large straw hat. James, her thin, nautical looking husband – or ex-husband – was trim and tidy. He came from Scotland where his family – we thought – were in shipping. He loved sailing and owned a very smart trimaran which was moored in Cascais Bay. They quite openly said they had divorced for tax convenience and that it was cheaper to live in Portugal than England. Their two very polite and well-mannered sons appeared at holiday-time from their school, Eton in England. They certainly added flavour to the square.

Family and friends came and visited us. We were happy proud grandparents when Tina and Richard brought Sophie, a gurgling smiling baby for a holiday. Then Bill arrived from New Zealand. He came on his own as Elizabeth had flown straight to England to see her mother. Bill, a farmer, had become more New Zealand than a true New Zealander. He was intrigued by the very English sophisticated Pamela. It was a glimpse into another world.

One morning Pamela banged on our door and shouted: 'Do you all want to come for a sail up the river to the Salazar Bridge and watch the celebrations?'

Bill went to the door. 'What celebrations?' I heard him say.

' It's the anniversary of the Treaty of Friendship Portugal signed with Britain hundreds of years ago. The RAF has sent over their team of Red Arrows to give a flying display near the bridge at two o'clock this afternoon. We'll meet you at the wharf in half an hour. Don't bring anything. We'll have lunch on board.'

Bill was delighted. He'd been dying to have a sail in the trimaran. We got ready quickly. There was no sign of anyone when we went down to the Cascais wharf. Pam had no idea of time. An hour and a half later they arrived in their sleek black Riley. Picnic baskets, thermoses, bottles of booze and passengers were transferred to the dinghy and rowed out to where the yacht rocked gently in the breeze. We stepped gingerly onto the trimaran with James shouting orders to Pam about letting go and casting off. General commotion, conflicting instructions, while a torrent of colourful nautical language flowed freely. I was glad to settle down quietly on the deck out of the way. The sails were set. With James at the helm we sailed past Estoril into the main stream. Skilful manoeuvring was needed as every other sailor along the coast had the same idea – to go and watch the flying-display.

I loved the spray on my face as we dipped and bounced over the water with the sails fluttering in the stiff breeze. We anchored near the monument for Henry the Navigator – a huge boat-like structure that juts out over the river. Gin and tonics were dispensed freely as we waited for the show to begin. A family of helicopters danced overhead. Then we heard the roar of engines as the team of Red Arrows tore across the sky like angry bees and swooped down near the suspension bridge. Red, white and blue smoke belched out behind making patterns in the sky as they criss-crossed, manoeuvring their planes within feet of one another. A startling performance to watch lying on your back on a gently moving yacht.

It was a holiday time – relaxed and leisurely. Meals and time were not important. Which was just as well because the gas stove in the cottage was nearly as temperamental as the old Eritrean black range. The oven only had two heat levels – hot or cold. I remember trying to make a pavlova dessert one night hoping to impress Sheila, one of our English friends who was a cordon-bleu cook. By hand, I beat and beat the eggs and sugar until it was stiff and glisteningly white. Lovingly I placed it in the oven. I watched carefully through the glass oven door as the meringue rose beautifully. Never before had I achieved such height in a pavlova. It looked like a ballerina ready to take off at any minute. Just then the doorbell rang. It was Maria with a message from Madame Wertheimer. As I stood talking in my halting Portuguese I suddenly smelt burning. I rushed back to the kitchen. The meringue had turned a dark brown. I quickly switched the oven off. I watched through the glass as my beautiful ballerina pavlova sank to the ground like the dying swan. I served it for dinner filled in with egg custard smothered with cream and decorated with strawberries. I called it VDD which could stand for Vivienne's delicious – or disaster – dessert. My friend didn't ask me for the recipe!

And then the blow fell. In 1974 there was a revolution. The president, Marcello Caetano was unseated and escaped. The military took control. A few weeks before there had been rumours in the airline when some of the senior Brazilian pilots were given notice. The contracts of all foreign pilots were terminated immediately. There was nothing for it. We had to pack up and go. John would retire once again.

29

Abu Dhabi

But it didn't happen that way! John wasn't ready to give up flying. He'd heard on the grapevine about a job with an airline in what was then the Persian Gulf, Gulf Air. He applied, flew to London for an interview, came back to Lisbon and told me he'd got the job.

I was flabbergasted. So much for retirement! 'And where are we going to live? In Bahrain?' This was the only place I knew in the Persian Gulf.

'No, although the Gulf Air has its headquarters in Bahrain I'll be operating out of Abu Dhabi in the United Arab Emirates. By the way, its no longer the "Persian Gulf". Its now called the "Arabian Gulf".'

'Arabian or Persian, I've never heard of the United Arab Emirates – or Abu Dhabi. What sort of a place is it?'

'Abu Dhabi's a town on the coast of the Arabian Peninsula. It's about eighty miles south of Dubai where I used to land and refuel in the flying boat days. The whole area is rich in oil – black gold! The Abu Dhabi Emirates – or State – is the centre of the desert and off-shore oilfields. With the Arabs holding the world to ransom over oil prices, it's a very important place.'

'What sort of climate is it to live in? If it's desert it must be unbearably hot.'

'Yes, very hot for four months of the year, but I believe it's quite pleasant for the rest of the time.'

Here we go! I thought. It was Eritrea all over again. Hunting in an atlas to find the place we're going to live. Hot sandy desert in an Arab country! It didn't sound my sort of place at all.

'At least in the United Arab Emirates you'll be able to drive,' John said.

'What do you mean – drive? There's nothing wrong with my driving. Or isn't a British licence valid there?'

'I think so – in Abu Dhabi. If we were going to Saudi Arabia, as a female you wouldn't be able to hold a driving licence.'

'And I suppose that's why you haven't taken a job with Saudi Arabian Airlines,' I said scathingly. 'What aircraft will you be flying with Gulf Air, – and where will you be going?'

'I'll be operating round the desert oilfields. They're mostly short day-trips so I'll be home at night. The aircraft's a small, two-engine, single-crew plane – an "Islander", – only carries nine passengers.'

'That'll be a change for you after a Boeing 707 with a hundred and fifty passengers. You'll miss all those glamorous hosties.'

'It'll be different. But at least I'll have a job – and doing what I love – flying.'

'And when does all this happen? When do we have to leave Portugal?'

'My contract finishes here at the end of the month.' There was a pause and John looked a bit uncomfortable. 'There's only one snag –' He paused.

'Only one?' I asked tersely.

'They want me out in the Gulf for training as soon as I finish with TAP. The snag is that you can't join me until accommodation is available. Because of the fantastic oil development, Abu Dhabi just hasn't enough houses or apartments. The company won't pay for wives to live in a hotel indefinitely. But never mind! One of the Abu Dhabi pilots is being transferred to Bahrain soon and we can have his house when he leaves.'

'And when is that likely to be?'

'Oh, I don't think it'll be very long. Maybe a month.'

'Well I must say it's all gloriously vague. What do I do in the meantime?'

'You could have a holiday in New Zealand – or Japan. Why not go to Tokyo and have some more lessons at the Sogetsu School. You'd enjoy that. I'm sure you'll find plenty to do.'

As usual John was the supreme optimist. He didn't anticipate any difficulties – expecting me to cope and keep fully occupied.

He changed the subject. 'Now we'd better think about packing. It's furnished accommodation so we won't need to take very much with us. Gulf Air has agreed to fly our luggage from Lisbon to Abu Dhabi. We'll send a suitcase of clothes and a tea chest with the linen, china and kitchen things. The furniture we've had made here – the Portuguese painted bedroom chests, the gold lounge suite and walnut desk, table and chairs, we'll ship out to New Zealand ready for our retirement.'

I gave a hoot of laughter. 'Retirement! For the first, second, third or fourth time? You don't know the meaning of that word. At least there's some consolation, we won't be packing the leather bedhead.'

Packing! How I hate that word. I suppose most people move house at least once in a lifetime. But we seemed to have been doing it all our married life. It's not so much the trauma of moving – that's bad enough – but the endless decisions about where to put things in a new house. And that inevitable, unenviable business of rehanging curtains – shortening, lengthening, joining and matching patterns. I dream of going into a house and having all new curtains – made by a professional.

William Shakespeare may have written 'Parting is such sweet sorrow,' but I don't think he can have moved house very often. Parting is always sorrowful and 'departing' is hell. Saying goodbye to friends, sorting precious belongings – books that are too heavy to pack, pictures, photographs, – and – all John's odd pieces of wood that 'just might come in handy one day'.

The most dreary thing is running down a kitchen. The bench gets covered with a conglomeration of half-bottles of tomato, worcester and soya sauce, essence bottles with only a few drops used, chicken and beef cubes, part-packets of cornflower, custard, baking powder – tea, sugar and coffee – a motley collection.

As John had been assured by Gulf Air that our luggage would be flown out to Abu Dhabi without delay, I decided that this time I'd pack all my grocery bits and pieces in the tea chest with the linen. At least when we arrived we'd have the basic household things.

What a mistake!

John went to Abu Dhabi. The luggage went to Abu Dhabi. I didn't go to Abu Dhabi! There were endless difficulties – visa, accommodation, medical (the shadow on my lung again) to be sorted out before I could join him. It was six months later – in August – the hottest month of the year – when I finally got to unpack that tea chest. In the meantime it had been stored in a damp warehouse where rats had special accommodation. Soft towels, sheets and tablecloths made very comfortable nests. Cornflower, sugar and spices were just the things that rats like best. The cork mat on the teasmade machine was particularly tasty, and tea bags – quite delicious. You never saw such a mess! It was tea leaves with everything!

My departure from Heathrow was not exactly a thrilling experience. After so many delays, it was the last straw to find I was – as usual – on standby, especially as the London office of Gulf Air had assured me that I had a firm booking. After an anxious couple of hours' wait, I was given a boarding-pass, welcomed on board and shown to a first-class seat. I took my shoes off, got out my book and settled down to relax. Time passed! Nothing happened.

Then the captain's voice came over the intercom. 'Good afternoon everyone. This is Captain Bailey speaking. I apologize for the delay due to a technical fault. We hope this will soon be fixed and we'll keep you informed.'

We sat – and sat. Three quarters of an hour later the captain came on air again.

'Thank you for your patience and again we apologize. The engineers are still working on an electrical fault.'

A few minutes later the chief steward announced: 'I'm sorry but as there is to be an indefinite delay we will have to ask you to disembark and wait in the lounge. Please take all your hand luggage with you. Our traffic officers will take care of you.'

We sat in the lounge. Drinks, coffee and sandwiches were served. No one seemed to know what was happening. At about six o'clock when the aircraft was still unserviceable, we were all herded together, put on buses and taken to the airport hotel for the night. Our departure was set for seven the next morning which meant a wake-up call of five a.m. I had a restless night and when we finally took off, I was too tired to read, eat or sleep. The eight-hour flight was endless.

When we landed at Abu Dhabi the heat struck me like a wave of fire. Dark, sinister looking men in long white robes and carrying guns lolled about the tarmac. As I stumbled down the steps feeling like an inebriated sea lion, I didn't recognize John in his dark green Gulf Air uniform standing at the bottom.

He held out his hand to steady me, took my bag and hugged me tightly. 'Darling, welcome to the United Arab Emirates. Thank God you've arrived. I'm so glad to see you. When you didn't come yesterday I wondered what had happened. We didn't know about the delay and I came out to the airport in the morning to meet you. Never mind, sweetheart, everything's all right now. You're here! It's hot, I know, but you'll soon get used to it.' (Like hell I would!)

The airport building was dingy and dirty and the air inside blue with cigarette smoke. The two immigration officials sitting at a desk, thumbed through every page of my passport and eyed me suspiciously. Unsmilingly and reluctantly they stamped it. They made me feel, because I was a female, I wasn't worth bothering about. The customs men painstakingly opened all my cases. John was patient and very polite. 'Looking for guns or drugs I suppose,' I muttered to him under my breath. I wondered why John had come to meet me in uniform and not in civvies. I knew soon enough.

'Viv, darling, if the plane had been any later arriving I wouldn't have been here to meet you. I'm terribly sorry but I have to fly to Asab – one of the oilfields. I leave in half an hour. I'll be back this evening.'

'Oh no, Johnnie. You can't leave me here alone. It's all so strange.' I struggled as I felt tears coming. 'What about the house? Have you moved in yet?'

'I'm afraid not. The Taylors haven't gone yet so I've arranged for us to stay at the Al Ain Hotel for a few days. You'll be quite comfortable. We've an air-conditioned room and there's a swimming pool. The Gulf Air bus will take you to the hotel. I've bought a car –a Nissan Bluebird –with air-conditioning. You'll find it in the hotel carpark. Here are the keys. As it's Sunday, I suggest that after you've had a rest, you drive along the Corniche and go to the six o'clock evening service at the little Anglican church.'

'Oh, you do, do you! What and where is the Corniche?'

'It's the main road running along the sea front. Look I really must go now. Here's the bus. The driver knows where to take you.'

As I climbed into the bus I heard John call out: 'By the way, don't forget you drive on the right hand side of the road here, not the left. Be careful!'

The hotel receptionist greeted me pleasantly. 'Good afternoon, Mrs Pascoe, I'm Janet. We've been expecting you. Sorry you were delayed. Here's your key – Room Twenty-eight. Let me know if there's anything I can do for you.' At that moment I could think of lots of things that could be done for me.

The room looked across the road to the sea. I opened the window to get a better view. A blast of hot air rushed in. I hastily shut it and flung myself on the bed feeling miserable and utterly exhausted. As I lay, the drone of the air-conditioning unit throbbed through my head. 'I'll never get used to living with this noise!' I thought. Then I decided as I couldn't rest I might as well have a swim in the pool. In my befuddled state I couldn't remember where I'd packed my swimsuit and scrummaged in two cases before I found it.

The indoor pool looked inviting and there was no one around. When I slipped into the water it was like getting into a bath of warm milk. I swam a few strokes, turned on my back and lay on top of the water and tried to relax. But it was hopeless. I got out and sat on the side dangling my feet in the water. But even the tiles were hot. So – I went back to my room. Something seemed different. The room got hotter and hotter and I realized the air-conditioning wasn't going. It became quite unbearable. I picked up the phone and rang down to reception.

'Janet, this is Room Twenty-eight. There must be something wrong with my air-conditioning unit. It was OK when I arrived but now it doesn't seem to be working. Please will you send someone up to fix it?'

'Oh, I'm sorry, Mrs Pascoe. There's a power cut and we don't know how long it'll last. It often happens here on a Sunday afternoon.'

I looked at my watch. It was half past-five. I didn't fancy the idea of driving a strange car on the wrong side of the road in a city I didn't know. But if the car was air-conditioned I could park it

313

somewhere, leave the engine running and keep cool. I changed into a cotton dress and went down to the carpark. I knew Nissan was a Japanese make but I didn't know what they looked like. Although John had given me the key he hadn't told me the number of the car – or the colour. I found two cars in the park with 'Nissan' on the front – a blue and a grey one. I tried the key in the door of the grey one. It didn't fit. I walked over to the blue car and opened the driver's door. Johnnie hadn't bothered to lock it. As the car had been standing in the sun it was so hot I couldn't touch the steering-wheel. When I put the key in the ignition the car started easily, but I had to fiddle around with the switches until I found the blower to cool the car down. I tried several gears before I found the reverse. I backed gingerly and drove slowly out of the carpark turning left onto what I hoped was the Corniche.

There was a sudden screech of brakes and blast of horn. The Arab driver of the car coming straight for me made a rude gesture as he swerved out into the middle of the road and flew past on my right side. I was completely unnerved as I realized with horror that I was on the left instead of the right. With my heart thumping like a pile driver, I eased across and drove along very slowly, keeping the sea on my right. Large cars roared by – all driven by men. I was to find that very few Arab ladies drove their own cars. They preferred to sit in the back and be driven. Draped from forehead to feet in the black *abba*, or cloak, with only their eyes showing through the hideous *burka*, (a mask made of coarse black iridescent silk with a central rib resting on the nose like a beak), they liked to see without being seen. It gave them a sense of security.

I looked for somewhere to park. And then I saw the little Anglican church with a cross on the side of the building facing the sea. Perhaps John was right. It was Sunday and nearly six o'clock. I drove into the carpark and went inside the church.

Even though the power was off, the church was cool compared to the fiery furnace outside. It was quiet and peaceful. I sank to my knees to give thanks for my safe arrival in this Arab town and my escape from a near car accident. As I knelt in that place of worship and felt the soothing hand of our Lord, the iron band across my forehead was released. I had found a haven. I don't think I could ever become an Evangelist and sincerely take part in the charismatic religions of today. I find drum-beating and guitar-playing for songs with words repeated three times and tunes with little musical inspiration, disturbing. When I enter a church I long to be quiet and still – to be reassured of the Lord's love and forgiveness through peace and tranquillity. For a Christian there is only one road to God and it's well signposted. But there's a great variety of transport along that road. How you travel – be it by car, bus, bicycle, horse, camel, or with a Catholic, Protestant or Evangelist driver, is your personal responsibility and decision.

I wasn't aware then what an amazing thing it was that, years ago, the ruling sheikh – a Muslim – had gifted a prime site on the sea front for a Christian church to be built. In fact he gave two sites – one to the Roman Catholics and the other to the Anglicans. Some years later – maybe under pressure from the King of Saudi Arabia when on an official visit to the Emirates, the ruler changed his mind. The land was taken back and the two churches moved inland to a less conspicuous site.

We spent ten days in the hotel and then moved temporarily to a dreary apartment in a large concrete block, where there were long cracks in some of the walls, especially in the bedroom. After a couple of days I had a sack full of rubbish to get rid of. 'John, would you ask our neighbours what day the garbage is collected?'

He came back laughing. 'Apparently, as yet, the Government hasn't organized regular rubbish collection in this part of the town.' He went to the window and looked out into the street.' Jim says I take the sack downstairs and empty it on that pile over there. It'll be removed sometime.'

I shuddered. 'That's horrible! The place must be teeming with rats getting fat on all that filth. I won't go across that street at night until it's all been cleared.'

And SAND! There was sand everywhere. A few roads were sealed but there were no footpaths. It was uncomfortable walking around the streets in sandals. I was puzzled by the constant stream of lorries full of sand driving past.

'John, why do all these lorries full of sand keep coming into town? Surely there's plenty of sand on the beach.'

Johnnie carefully explained. 'The salt, rounded Abu Dhabi sand is not suitable for making concrete. Sharp sand is needed and has to be brought in from the interior. This block of flats we're in was one of the first to be built. They must have used the wrong type of sand to mix the concrete. That's why cracks are appearing all over the place. The building's been condemned and will, eventually be pulled down.'

'Now you tell me.' My imagination brought the whole building tumbling around my head. 'The Koran obviously doesn't warn people about "building your house upon the sand." John, how much longer are we going to have to stay in this rabbit-warren?'

'Don't worry. The Taylors are going to Bahrain at the end of the week. We should be able to move into the house at the weekend.'

What a relief! It was a small semi-detached house in a quiet street near the Corniche, where we could walk down to the beach for an early-morning swim in the cool blue water.

At the side of the house there was space to make a small garden. I had been told by an enthusiastic gardener in Abu Dhabi that I would have to dig a sack of sweet sand and camel's dung into the sand already there, if I wanted to grow anything. I love herbs and brought mint and parsley seed from England. But even though I watered it regularly, everything was very slow in growing. One night it rained – the first rain since my arrival. I lay listening to this wonderful sound thinking how much my parsley was going to enjoy it. When I went into the garden the next morning I found, to my horror, that the parsley had a white ring around it and looked very droopy. The rain, instead of helping the plants, had merely brought the salt to the surface and almost killed them.

The ruler, Sheikh Zayed, declared he was going to transform his desert city, Abu Dhabi into a colourful green oasis. Grass was imported, horticulturists were contracted from Cairo to establish nurseries and an expensive water sewerage irrigation plant was developed. The cost was enormous! Every blade of grass was an achievement and every flower a miracle. No matter, there was plenty of oil to pay for it.

The city planners – if there were such people – had a thing about roundabouts. One day, for fun, I went for a drive and counted 37 within the city boundaries. Abu Dhabians, themselves, did little manual work. The labour force was imported from other countries

316

– India, Pakistan, Kerala and from the hills of Northern India – Baluchistan. They came on a two-year contract and no visas were given to wives.

The Baluchis wore wide baggy trousers with a long shirt in all kinds of colours: blue, pink and even purple. On their heads they had massive black turbans with a tail hanging down one side. They did manual work and some were employed to water the grass and shrubs planted in the middle of the roundabouts.

Now when I remember Abu Dhabi a very vivid picture comes to mind. One afternoon, driving home from the studio, I was caught in a sudden storm. The sky was black and the rain so heavy the windscreen wipers couldn't cope. As I cautiously approached a roundabout I saw a Baluchi in vivid, baggy trousers with his long shirt hanging out, standing in the middle of the roundabout. He stood patiently holding a hose sprinkling the plants with the treated sewerage water. The rain tumbled down, soaking him to the skin. His clothes clung to him and his turban flapped drearily round his face. He continued to hold the hose. He'd been told to water the plants and no matter what – rain or shine – he would do his job.

The British Club was the hub of the ex-patriot life. We swam, ate, drank, played tennis and sailed. Abu Dhabi was a boom city where gas, electricity, desalination plants needed to be developed quickly. Enterprising firms from all over the world sent their most talented young men out as their representatives. The men working in oil fields for periods of four or five days, were flown backwards and forwards by Gulf Air, while Marine Company helicopters flew to the oil rigs in the shallow waters of the Arabian Gulf.

For a few weeks I enjoyed being lazy, but it wasn't long before I felt I needed something to do. I was lying on the beach at the club one day when Penny, who had married an Arab from an important Abu Dhabi family said: 'Vivienne, Abdulla tells me that the Abu Dhabi radio station is starting an English programme and are looking for announcers. You've done a lot of radio work. Why don't you apply?'

I thought about it and rather nervously phoned the radio station to make an appointment. The news editor, Hassan, a red-haired Palestinian interviewed me. He said they were looking for someone to produce a half-hour classical music programme each week. I got the job. With few reference books, no library and a very limited number of records, it was a challenge.

Fortunately the radio station received programmes from the BBC and I was able to use John Amis's records, 'Talking about Music.' That's what I did – just chatted about music – using the experiences I'd had as a student at the Royal College of Music in London, and playing in orchestras under many famous conductors.

Then a travel programme was added to my job. I enjoyed that because I'd always loved going places and seeing things. It was fun to talk about the countries I'd been to and give information about what airlines to use, and the cost involved. I visited travel agencies regularly and made full use of the wonderful geographical magazines. I produced those two programmes every week for nearly five years.

It took some time to learn to work with the Arab technicians. The announcer sat in one studio and the record turntables were controlled in another room by the technical staff. Some were helpful – others didn't understand English.

My favourite was Hassain, a tall overweight young man who was polite and patient when recording my programmes. In spite of his protruding tummy he looked quite a dandy in his freshly ironed *dishdasha* – the shirt-like garment with a Chairman Mao collar. He wore his kaffia headdress at a rakish angle – the fine white cotton cloth thrown back on one side and held in place by the *aghal*, a single or double, black silk camel cord, hanging down his back with two tassels. He was a 'mummy's boy' in more ways than one, I suspected. He wanted to travel and get a job as a steward but 'Mummy doesn't want me to be away from home,' he confided to me. When I'd finished the afternoon session I'd wave to Hassain and call, 'Goodbye. See you tomorrow.'

His reply would always be '*Inshaa-aalah*' meaning 'if God wills'. One day I admired an ornate silver bracelet he was wearing. Immediately he took it off and, in spite of my protests, insisted on giving it to me. Another lesson learnt! If you admire something, an Arab feels obliged to make you a present.

I didn't enjoy working with Abdullah. He was a small dark arrogant character who made it plain, in a typical male Arab way, that females were second-class citizens and it was beneath his dignity to have to work with me. He was an ardent Muslim and during Ramadhan would often sit at his turntable with his head in his hands – exhausted no doubt from the fasting during the day and the revelry by night.

Having lived in Erirtrea I knew about the restrictions of the Holy Festival of Ramadan. In Arabic this means 'a time of burning pain'. Throughout this ninth month of the Islamic calendar all except travelers, pregnant women and soldiers on duty, are required to abstain between sunrise and sunset from food, drink, tobacco and sexual indulgence. (So the guide book on life in an Arab community told me. The book didn't give any information about what went on between dusk and dawn!) I found it difficult to work with the Arabs during this fasting time. Nothing got done. Working hours were erratic, concentration lacking and tempers short.

My duties at the radio station were increased. I became a newsreader and announcer. During one afternoon's session, I suddenly heard the horrible noise of a record stuck in a groove. I looked through the glass into the studio and Abdullah, who was on duty, was nowhere to be seen. Frantically I pressed my buzzer. The record droned on and on. I kept my finger on the buzzer but nothing happened. In desperation I pushed open the heavy padded door into the corridor and flew into the control room. Abdullah wasn't at the desk. I moved the needle back into the groove and Beethoven's Fifth Symphony continued. As I turned I saw Abdullah in the far corner of the studio on his knees with his forehead on the ground, saying his prayers. He was quite oblivious of the fact that the needle had stuck. It was no use reporting him. Prayer was sacred.

Everywhere you went in Abu Dhabi – in an important bank or in the smallest shop in the market – a photograph of Sheikh Zayed gazed down on the customers. But nowhere, anywhere, or at any time, was the face of the First Lady of the land – Sheikha Fatima – seen, except by members of her family. Although unseen she commanded great respect. She was known for her social enlightenment and her concern for the welfare and education of the women and girls of the land. According to her strict upbringing and within the structure of her religion she believed in Women's Rights.

Sheikh Zayed bought one of Queen Elizabeth's planes –a VC10. Part of the contract was that British Airways crews should fly it. There was competition among the VC10 Pilots for the three months posting to Abu Dhabi – a good holiday job. Richard applied and we were absolutely thrilled when he wrote and told us he and the family would be coming out – house, car, everything provided by the Sheikh. It was great to think we'd have our grandchildren, Sophie, five and Nicholas two, near us.

They arrived in Abu Dhabi a few weeks before the start of the month of Ramadan.

In the Muslim world there are special yearly holidays celebrated according to the Islamic calendar. The most important one, *Id*, comes after the holy month of Ramadan. It was the custom in Abu Dhabi, for Sheikh Zayed and his wife, Sheikha Fatima, to hold receptions *a majllis,* at the palace, when foreigners would call and pay their respects.

While Tina was with us we decided the *Id* holiday was a good opportunity to visit the palace and meet this unseen lady. When we presented ourselves at the gate the guards peered into the car and opened the boot – 'probably to see if we were harbouring any males,' Tina murmured. We parked the car, walked through a lovely garden with oleander trees in full bloom, and climbed the palace steps into a large courtyard. Four ladies were sitting on a bench under a brilliant poinsettia tree. Two were wearing beautiful silk saris but the others had their faces covered with the Arab mask. They came forward as we entered and politely showed us into a vast *majllis* room. Huge crystal chandeliers hung from an elaborate ceiling intricately painted in green and gold. Very formal red velvet chairs and high – backed couches hugged the walls round the room and the floor was covered with an enormous Persian carpet.

Dotted around the room were huge crystal vases stuffed full of heavy gladioli. 'No sign of any Ikebana here,' I whispered to Tina. In the far corner the biggest coloured TV set I'd ever seen blared forth, showing an American western with Arab subtitles.

No one else had arrived although it was nearly half-past ten. We sat and chatted to the two Pakistani ladies. One was a very charming doctor and the other, her sister, a nurse at Sheikha Fatima's hospital for women. They interpreted for us when we tried to talk to the two Arab ladies who didn't speak English. The one I was sitting next to wore a full-length accordion pleated dress in a lurid Reckitts-blue, with an intricate gold belt at the waist and three heavy gold necklaces round her neck. The other woman had on a garish multicoloured shiny silk dress and her arms were weighed down by thick gold bangles – from wrist to elbow.

Other foreigners and embassy staff filtered in. We sat around waiting – as I thought – for the arrival of Sheikha Fatima. Two little women, completely enveloped in their black *abbas* and wearing the burka mask over their faces, trotted in and squatted on the carpet. They were – explained the doctor – two elderly aunts of Sheikh Zayed.

Tina gave me a nudge and passed me a little bronze container. A pleasant smell of incense floated from it. I sniffed, wondered what I was supposed to do with it and decided the best thing was to pass it on. It continued to be handed round the room until it was passed down to one of the old aunts. Here there was no hesitation … she knew exactly what to do. With a flourish she waved the incense under each armpit, and then with a sweep, she lifted up her skirts and let the smoke waft between her legs. She passed it on to her companion who went through the same routine.

Coffee was served in exquisite gold-leaf bone-china cups and the guests began to move around. Catching sight of one of my friends from the British Embassy, I crossed over to her and asked if she had any idea what time Sheikha Fatima would arrive. I had to be on duty at the radio station and was worried I would have to leave before she came.

'But she's here already,' said my friend. 'She's sitting over there – in the blue dress.'

'What!' I exclaimed. 'You mean to say I've been sitting beside the first lady for twenty minutes or so without knowing who she was.'

Suddenly there was a flutter and a flurry round the room and the lady in blue rose and walked back into the courtyard. Others followed, and Tina and I tailed along. There was no difficulty in recognizing the man who was greeting Sheikha Fatima. It was Sheikh Zayed – a tall dignified man with a neatly trimmed beard and very piercing eyes. His gleaming white *dishdasha* was covered by a finely woven woollen beige cloak edged with gold. Sheikha Fatima stood beside him. One by one he greeted us with a firm handshake.

Tina and I left the palace on cloud nine. Sure, we'd met and chatted to Sheikha Fatima without knowing who she was ... but we'd shaken hands with the most powerful man in the United Arab Emirates, His Excellency, Sheikh Zayed. bin Sultan Al Narhyan.

30

At Last – A VIP

From camels to Cadillacs in ten short years! And all through OIL – oil that comes out of the sand and the sea. Its production and profits dominated life in Abu Dhabi. During the 70s the shortage and distribution of oil was the concern of all nations – particularly those with limited natural resources.

One morning I was in the garden watering my precious parsley when I heard the phone ring. I rushed inside. The telephones here had a habit of ringing a few times and stopping just as you lifted the receiver.

I grabbed it. 'Hello, Viv Pascoe speaking.'

'Good morning, Vivienne. David here. Is John around?'

David and his wife, Liz, lived next door and were very good friends. He was manager of the oilfield at Asab and away quite a lot. 'No, I'm sorry David, John left yesterday for Bahrain. He's taken an aeroplane there for a service and won't be back until tomorrow.'

'Oh good, because I want to ask you some questions without John hearing. What's John's favourite menu for lunch? What does he enjoy most? I'll tell you the reason I want to know in a minute.'

'Goodness, let me think. He's pretty conservative over food. I suppose it's a traditional English meal – tomato soup, roast beef and Yorkshire pudding with horseradish sauce, roast vegetables, fruit salad and cream – or apple pie with cheese.'

'Apple pie with cheese! That sounds like a Yorkshire dish. You know of course, that it's John's birthday in a week's time – on January fifteenth.'

'Yes, he'll be sixty-three. Time to stop flying. We'll be sad to leave Abu Dhabi. I know he hates the idea of having to retire.'

'I've just discovered that John's last trip on that day will be to Asab and we'd like to give him a surprise luncheon party. That's why I want to know his favourite menu. He's very popular with all the men in the field. And as a real surprise, we want you to come along too. You'll be our VIP for the day. John mustn't know anything about it until you get on the aeroplane. I've fixed it with Gulf Air. The return flight will be delayed until after lunch so can you spend the morning with us and see over the oilfield.'

'Oh, David, what a wonderful idea. Ever since you did that interview with me on oil for my radio programme, I've wanted to visit Asab. It'll be great fun – something to look forward to. And I'll make sure it's kept a secret.'

'Good. It'll mean an early-morning start. We'll let John leave at the usual time. I'll pick you up half an hour later and drive you to the airport. OK? See you about six a.m. on January fifteenth.'

I sat out in the garden feeling very excited. This time I'd make sure it really was a surprise – not like the fiasco in Lourenço Marques all those years ago. What a lot had happened since then.

On January 15th I got out of bed, put on my housecoat and made John a cup of tea. As he left I gave him a big hug and borrowing his saying when Bill was about to be born said: 'HAVE A NICE TIME, DARLING. It's sad to think this'll be your last trip with Gulf Air. Enjoy yourself!' I stood at the door and waved him goodbye.

I dressed hurriedly and waited impatiently for David to arrive. It was still dark and quite foggy as we drove to the airport. I hoped bad weather wouldn't cancel the trip. The little Islander was sitting on the tarmac ready to take the men back to Asab after their time at home with their families. David parked the car and we walked towards the aircraft where John was standing, making his last-minute checks. 'You stay here, Vivienne, until I make sure everything's ready. I'll wait until the other passengers are on board, and John is in his seat before I call you.'

I stood behind the Islander, out of sight, and heard David say to John, 'You'd better move that dilapidated old brief-case off this seat beside you. I've got a VIP coming.'

John's brief-case was almost a legend. The ground engineers called it 'John's dog'. It had been with him ever since he started flying – a total of nearly 25 thousand hours. One Christmas I gave him a present of beautiful pigskin case but he never used it. He stuck to his 'dog'.

After a few minutes David beckoned to me and got in the aircraft himself. I walked to the front and climbed in. John had moved his brief-case from the seat and had his headset on listening to the take-off instructions from the control tower. As I pulled myself into the seat, he turned his head. With a gasp and a look of absolute amazement he said: 'Viv, what on earth are you doing here?' There was a burst of applause from the men at the back.

'Oh, just coming along for the ride. I'm David's VIP – not a standby passenger this time. Happy birthday, Johnnie dear.'

'Well I'm jiggered! [John's favourite expression when he is bewildered.] What a surprise! I never expected to see you again this morning.'

After so much jet-flying it was exciting to be in a tiny aircraft. When the engines started, the propellers began to turn slowly and then whirr faster and faster until the blades couldn't be seen. We taxied onto the runway. John revved the engines and took off just as the sun was peeping over the horizon. As we turned and headed south-west, I looked down and saw the intricate patterns of the sea and sand flats underneath. In the early-morning light they were all shades of grey and looked like a child's finger-painting. When we climbed above the clouds it was like sitting on white cushions. Then, as the sun rose above the horizon they were tinted in all the colours of the rainbow.

John turned to me with a grin, 'You could have knocked me down with a feather. Who planned all this?'

'Oh, David thought it would be a birthday treat if I came on your last trip. It's all right. He cleared it with Gulf Air.'

'Well now you're here, I guess I'd better radio ahead to the mess at Asab for TWO toasted bacon and egg sandwiches. They're the best in the world. I always enjoy one when I land.'

I kept quiet, knowing that we were going to get more than a bacon sandwich on arrival.

When we landed on the sandy airstrip at Asab, John switched off the engines and David and the boys got off. He sat waiting for a few minutes. 'I wonder what's happened to our sandwiches? They're usually so prompt in bringing them out to the plane.'

David came back and stood beside the window. 'Come on, John, we want you and Viv to come into the mess and have breakfast. In fact you won't be taking off again until after lunch.'

Soon we were sitting in the pleasant dining-room eating a magnificent breakfast – bacon, eggs, kidneys, mushrooms, tomatoes ... You only had to name it – they had it!

The rooms were built around a small courtyard where a fountain splashed water over blue tiles. There were oleander and hibiscus shrubs growing beside a neat green lawn. After the intense glare of the sun outside and the harsh, red-yellow of the desert, it was like coming into another world, a psychedelic world of dreams.

What an amazing engineering feat it was to build these oilfields. Just getting all the heavy equipment there in the first place seemed impossible. It meant moving incredible weights over difficult terrain. The machinery used – and in particular the gigantic Kenworth machine-made normal motors look insignificant. Tyres were eight feet tall and a ladder was needed to look into the 350-horsepower engine. There had been many adventures getting the equipment to the right place. Once a truck with some special flanges got lost on the drive out from the UK. John had been involved in the air search to look for it. Eventually it was found with its nose dug into a sandhill. The mighty Kenworth came to the rescue – the flanges were delivered and installed. Now there is a tar-sealed road for part of the way from Abu Dhabi to Asab but between there and another oilfield, lies a natural barrier of sand-dunes and *subkha* – treacherous quicksands.

The men in the mess were all dressed in lightweight pale-coloured boiler suits – pale blues, greens, and pinks. They didn't look very practical to me when they were working with oil. As we sat at breakfast, I asked David about them.

'We try to avoid bright, harsh colours as much as possible. Did you notice the colour of the oil tanks as we flew in?'

'Yes I did. I wondered why they were painted blue instead of the usual silver?'

David explained. 'Some years ago at a management meeting in Bahrain, there was a disagreement about the colour for the tanks. Silver was thought to be hard on the eyes in the fierce sun. The argument went on. Then one of the team said: "Look, I'm wearing a turquoise-blue tie. Why don't we use this colour?" He took his tie off and threw it on the table. The tie was carefully wrapped up, sent to a paint manufacturer in the UK with a request that they produce that colour. It was called "Abu Dhabi blue" and to this day it is a British Standard colour in England paint shops.'

I laughed. ' So there is Cambridge, Oxford – and – Abu Dhabi blue. What about the tiles around the fountain in the courtyard? They're also blue.'

'Yes that's true. In the old days when a well was cleaned after drilling, the mud, acids and general debris were blown into a pit through an open-ended pipe, and burnt. When the flame was really hot the silica melted and fused with the sand to form a bank of a solid, glasslike substance, rather like the black obsidian found through volcanic eruptions. The glass we found here is very heavy and solid – and almost the Abu Dhabi blue – just right to use around the fountain.'

After breakfast we went on a tour. Outside it was like hell on earth – the heat and roar of the burning-off gases is absolutely terrifying but fascinating to watch. Some of the waste gas is used to generate power and fuels the enormous jet engines which drive the generators. But inside the control rooms full of computers, it was cool, calm, and clinical and the men's pale boiler suits looked just right. John was fascinated but it was far too technical for me to understand.

Then we set off in a Range Rover to see the water installation plant which surrounds the field. Our driver, Bob, was the water engineer – a softly spoken Canadian. I hadn't realized the significant part water played in the surfacing of the oil. 'In this particular field,' Bob said, 'an area of fifteen by four miles, large quantities of electrical power are required to drive down one and a half barrels of extremely corrosive saline water for every barrel of oil extracted. This whole operation is run by about thirty-five British engineers with the help of Indian and local Arab staff.'

'Don't you get bored having to spend so much of your life in the desert?' I asked him as we rolled over the sand hills in the four-wheeled-drive vehicle.

'Well, I suppose it's a tough life but I don't find it boring. The desert has a fascination all of its own, It's like the sea – always changing – always on the move.'

He was quite right. I was enthralled to be bumping over the sand-dunes because everywhere you looked there was something different – ripples, waves, swirls making colourful patterns that seemed to be designed by some divine artist.

A little way to the left I saw what looked like Arab tents and asked Bob if it would be possible to go and have a look at them. It was a real Bedouin camp – two black and white woven camel-hair tents – one for the men and one for the ladies. I wasn't sure if we'd be welcome but as I got out of the Rover, a young Arab beckoned me round behind the tent and there – lying on the ground was the dearest little coal-black woolly baby camel. 'Why black?' I wondered. '*Etnane*' the boy said holding up one finger. I gathered he meant it was one day old. With help the baby got to his rather wobbly feet and staggered around for a few minutes before collapsing in the sand again and rolling over.

Meanwhile the mother camel, tethered to a stake, was making a huge fuss, baring her teeth and belching forth very rude noises. She objected to anyone coming near her baby. The men had disappeared so I walked round to the front of the second tent. A young lady with her black *abba* wrapped round her, pulled aside the tent flap and invited me inside. '*Asalem Alehcum,*' she said.

I went inside responding with the traditional reply, '*Alehcum Salem.*' Two tiny girls in long dresses clung to their mother's skirts and peeped round to look at this strange white female. '*TeFadell.*' I sat down awkwardly on the lovely carpet laid on top of the sand. In one corner of the tent an elderly lady squatted on the ground with her legs crossed. She looked up, nodded, and went on with her knitting. Conversation was difficult. I felt in my pocket and found some barley sugar which I held out to the little girls. Shyly they came forward and were puzzled by the paper round the sweets. I showed them how to unwrap them. There was a strong smell of coffee in the tent. The mother handed me a small cup and filled it from a gleaming copper Arab coffee-pot. It was very black, very strong and full of cardamom spice. I drank it slowly, but when she came back to refill it, I held the cup in my right hand and wiggled it, indicating that I didn't want a second cup. (I had learnt that Arabic custom early on.) My foot began to go to sleep. I stood up and bowing slightly said, 'Goodbye. Thank you for the coffee,' and felt ashamed – I couldn't remember the Arabic word for goodbye. I took another peep at the little baby camel as I walked towards the Range Rover where Bob and John were sitting chatting.

We got back to the mess in time to have a wash and a drink before lunch. And what a lunch! Realizing that FOOD was an all important means of keeping the men happy out in the desert away from their families, the company employed the very best chefs. The tomato soup was made with real tomatoes, with a sprig of parsley floating on top of a spoonful of cream. The beef was done to a turn – rare and bloody – just what John liked. Crisp, puffy individual Yorkshire puddings were served with a spicy, rich, brown gravy. There was a choice of five or six vegetables as well as baked and new Jersey potatoes. The mess was full and lively with laughter and chatter.

After John had consumed fruit salad as well as apple pie with cheese, the chef, wearing his tall white hat, appeared at the door triumphantly carrying on a silver tray, an enormous chocolate cake with candles flickering on top. The chef handed me a large knife and while the men stood up and sang Happy Birthday, John blew out the candles and together we cut the cake. David made a little speech and presented John with a model of an Islander made by one of the men. John thanked David and all the boys – and the chef – for the wonderful surprise party. Coffee and chocolates were served in the lounge where we sat in comfortable chairs covered in blue floral linen – Abu Dhabi blue, of course!

After the cool air-conditioned rooms it was a shock to go out into the searing hot sun. Before I climbed into the plane I gave David a big hug. 'Thank you for including me in this party. It's been a great day – a day we'll always remember.' David stood on the sand and waved us goodbye.

We flew over the buildings and John waggled his wings as the plane settled down with a whirr of contentment. The little Islander bounced about in the upward currents of the hot afternoon air. I gazed down dreamily at the desert below with its rich, ochre colours and intricate patterns woven in the dunes. Our five years of amazing experiences in the United Arab Emirates were nearly at an end – for John – over 40 years of flying; for me – a treasure chest of memories – radio, disc-jockey, newspaper reporter, Ikebana, tennis, music, travel – the list was endless. But the most precious memory would be of our life together in this strange land and the many friends we had made during our stay.

We hovered over the airport at Abu Dhabi waiting for a Gulf Air Tristar to land. John taxied to the Islander's stand, away from the busy overseas terminal. The engines were switched off. The passengers shook hands and thanked John as they got out of the aircraft. John sat for a few minutes looking at his instruments as if saying a farewell. He picked up his peaked cap, and clutching his battered brief-case, helped me down the steps.

As we walked slowly away from his beloved 'flying machine', John linked his arm through mine and said: 'What a wonderful send-off – a marvellous party – the surprise of a lifetime! Well, Viv darling, I guess that's it!'

'Yes,' I agreed – with my fingers crossed: 'that's definitely it!' – thinking to myself: I wonder when the next 'standby' will be?

CONCORDE

FLIGHT CERTIFICATE
PRESENTED TO

Vivienne Pascoe

WHO FLEW SUPERSONICALLY
ON CONCORDE FROM

London to New York

ON

G-BOAE   _17d July 1996_

SIR COLIN MARSHALL
CHAIRMAN

CAPTAIN

BRITISH AIRWAYS